Soaring Alone

RANDALL J. BREWER

SOARING ALONE

CONTENTS

INTRODUCTION

Every man dreams of becoming strong, respected, and impactful. But few men realize that the road to becoming that man is often a road few others are willing to walk. The path to true manhood is not crowded. It is not found in the applause of the crowd, the approval of friends, or the comfort of popular opinion. The path to becoming the man God designed you to be is often narrow, difficult, and lonely. It is a road where compromise must be rejected, conviction must be embraced, and faith must become stronger than fear. Many men want greatness, but they do not want the process that produces greatness.

The men who shape history, lead families, influence generations, and fulfill God's purposes rarely travel the easy road. They often find themselves standing where others have walked away, believing when others have doubted, and continuing forward when others have quit. Throughout Scripture, we see this pattern repeatedly. Noah built an ark while the world mocked him. Joseph remained faithful in prison while others forgot him. David faced a giant when an entire army refused to move. Daniel stood firm when an entire nation bowed down. Jesus Himself walked the road to the cross while even His closest followers fled.

Great men of God often walk seasons where they must soar alone. This does not mean they are truly alone. It means they have chosen to rise above compromise, fear, and mediocrity. They have chosen obedience over popularity, conviction over comfort, and purpose over approval. There are moments in every man's life when he must decide, "Will I follow the crowd...or will I follow God? Will I compromise to be accepted...or will I stand firm even if I stand alone? Will I shrink back when the road becomes difficult...or will I rise higher than I ever thought possible?"

The man who chooses God's path may discover something surprising along the way. While the road may feel lonely at times, it is also the place where strength is built, character is refined, courage is formed, and destiny is discovered. This book is written for the man who senses that God is calling him higher. It is for the man who refuses to live a small life. It is for the man who is willing to grow when others settle. It is for the man who understands that greatness is not given - it is forged.

If you are willing to walk the road of discipline, conviction, and faith, you will discover a powerful truth: The man who learns to soar alone with God will eventually rise above the limitations that hold others down. And when he does, his life will become a force that shapes the world around him.

The journey begins now.

| 1 |

"RISE ABOVE THE CROWD"

Every man eventually comes to a crossroads in life where he must decide whether he will move with the crowd or walk with God. The crowd offers comfort, approval, and the safety of blending in, but it rarely leads to greatness or spiritual maturity. The voice of God, however, often calls a man to step away from what is easy and familiar. It invites him onto a path that requires courage, conviction, and faith. Though that road may appear narrow and uncertain, it is the very place where a man begins to discover who he was truly created to be. It is where a man learns to stand firm in his convictions and pursue the calling God has placed upon his life. While the crowd chases comfort and applause, the man who follows God seeks truth, obedience, and eternal impact. In choosing that higher path, he steps into the strength, leadership, and integrity that define true manhood. The decision may separate him from the crowd, but it brings him closer to the destiny God designed for him from the beginning.

The crowd always offers comfort because it asks nothing of a man except that he stay the same. It invites him to blend in and to walk the wide road where expectations are low and accountability is scarce. Among the crowd, a man can avoid the hard questions of purpose, responsibility, and calling. Yet comfort can become a quiet trap. When a man lives only to fit in, he slowly trades his potential for acceptance. The crowd may shield him from criticism, but it also shields him from growth, courage, and the refining work that God desires to do within him. The path of growth often requires stepping away from the noise of the crowd and listening instead for the voice of God. When a man chooses conviction over convenience and calling over popularity, he begins to develop strength, character, and spiritual depth. The crowd may ask little, but the life God calls a man to live asks everything - and in return it produces a man who stands firm, walks with purpose, and leaves a lasting impact.

God never designed a man to drift through life in mediocrity. His voice calls men upward to a higher way of thinking, living, and leading. His call awakens the heart of a man to rise above passivity and fear. It challenges him to stand firm in truth, to walk with integrity, and to pursue what is right even when it is difficult. The voice of God reminds a man that he was created not merely to exist, but to live with strength, honor, and purpose. When a man responds to that call, his life begins to move beyond the ordinary. He becomes a man who influences others by the example he sets and the standards he lives by. God's call elevates his vision, strengthens his resolve, and shapes his character through every challenge he faces. Instead of blending into the crowd, he learns to stand apart as a man who belongs to God. In answering that higher call, a man discovers the life he was truly made for - a life marked by purpose, guided by conviction, and driven by the courage to live according to God's greater design.

Throughout scripture, the men who changed history were those who refused to simply go along with everyone else. Noah built an ark when the world mocked him, trusting the voice of God more than the opinions of men. Abraham left the familiarity of his homeland to follow a promise he could not yet see. David stepped forward to face a giant while seasoned soldiers stood paralyzed by fear. These men were not great because they followed the crowd; they were great because they followed God. Faith often calls a man to walk a road that others do not understand, but obedience to God has always been the birthplace of destiny. Every generation presents the same choice: blend into the crowd or rise in obedience to God's calling. The path of faith may feel lonely at times, but it is the path where courage, character, and purpose are formed. When a man chooses conviction over popularity and obedience over comfort, he steps into the kind of life that leaves a lasting mark.

These men did not follow the crowd - they followed God. While others chose the wide and comfortable road of approval, they chose the narrow path of obedience. Their decisions were driven by a deep conviction that God's voice mattered more than the noise of the crowd. The men who leave a mark on history are the ones who dare to stand when others bow, they believe when others doubt, and they obey when others hesitate. Because they followed God, their lives became living testimonies of courage and faith. Their stories remind us that true greatness is not found in fitting in, but in standing firm for what is right. When a man anchors his life in God's truth, his character becomes steady, his courage grows stronger, and his faith becomes visible to those around him. Long after the voices of the crowd fade away, the legacy of faithful men continues to speak. Their lives become beacons that inspire others to rise, trust God, and walk boldly in the calling He has placed upon them.

Every man hears two voices throughout his life. One voice urges him to blend into the crowd, to take the safe road, to avoid standing out or risking failure. It tells him to lower his standards, soften his convictions, and follow the comfortable patterns that everyone else seems to follow. This voice appeals to fear and convenience, promising acceptance and ease if he simply stays within the boundaries of the ordinary. Yet a man who only listens to this voice slowly loses the fire that God placed within him. He trades purpose for comfort and calling for approval. But there is another voice - the quiet, steady voice of God's calling within the soul. It whispers courage, conviction, and destiny. It says, "Rise. Stand. Become the man I created you to be." This voice invites him to walk a path that may be lonely at times but is filled with meaning and eternal impact. The man who chooses to listen to that voice steps into a life marked not by fitting in, but by faithfully becoming who he was meant to be.

The voice of the crowd usually calls a man toward comfort, approval, and the safety of blending in. It encourages him to follow the path of least resistance, to avoid standing out, and to measure his life by the applause of people. Yet the approval of the crowd is fleeting. What people celebrate today they may criticize tomorrow. When a man builds his life on the opinions of others, he finds himself constantly shifting, adjusting, and compromising just to maintain acceptance. The voice of God, however, calls a man to something far greater - obedience and faith. God does not promise popularity, but He does promise purpose. His call often leads a man away from the noise of the crowd and onto a path of courage, conviction, and trust. While the crowd offers temporary acceptance, obedience to God produces eternal impact. A man who listens to God may stand alone for a season, but his life will echo far beyond the moment, shaping destinies and leaving a legacy that honors heaven.

The road of purpose often separates a man from the crowd. When a man begins to pursue God's calling on his life, he soon realizes that not everyone is willing to walk that path beside him. Some will misunderstand his convictions because they cannot see what God has placed in his heart. Others may criticize him because his commitment exposes their comfort with staying where they are. Yet a man who is truly called by God cannot measure his direction by the approval of people. His compass must be the voice of God, even when that voice leads him onto a road that few are willing to travel. Though the journey may feel lonely at times, it is on these quieter roads that character is forged, faith is strengthened, and purpose becomes unmistakably clear. The man who stays faithful to God's call will discover that obedience is far more valuable than popularity, and that walking with

God - even if it means walking alone - is the path that leads to true fulfillment and lasting impact.

Separation is often the quiet birthplace of destiny. When God begins to shape a man for higher purpose, He frequently leads him away from the distractions of the crowd. Just as the eagle rises above the storms and soars alone in the heights where few birds can fly, a man called by God must sometimes walk a path others do not understand. In those solitary places, character is forged, vision becomes clearer, and the soul learns to depend on God rather than the approval of people. In that sacred distance from the noise, a man begins to hear the voice of God with new clarity. The crowd often speaks loudly, but God speaks deeply. When a man steps away from the pressure to conform, he discovers the courage to follow the calling placed upon his life. What seemed like separation becomes elevation. God does not separate a man to diminish him, but to prepare him to soar in the heights of purpose, strength, and destiny that only those willing to rise above the crowd will ever experience.

Many men struggle with this because they confuse popularity with purpose. The desire for approval is deeply rooted in human nature, and it is easy to measure success by applause, acceptance, and recognition. Yet God's calling rarely operates according to the standards of the crowd. Throughout scripture, the men and women who walked closely with God often found themselves standing apart from popular opinion. Noah built an ark while others mocked him. David faced a giant when others ran away. Jesus Himself was rejected by many while fulfilling the greatest mission in history. Purpose is not validated by the number of people who agree with you; it is confirmed by obedience to God. A man who truly seeks God's calling must be willing to choose faithfulness over popularity. There will be moments when obedience requires him to stand alone, misunderstood or even criticized. He stands firm because the approval that matters most comes from the steady voice of God saying, "Well done."

Popularity depends on pleasing people, and people are constantly changing. What they applaud today they may criticize tomorrow. A man who lives for popularity becomes a prisoner of opinion, always adjusting his words and actions to maintain approval. Yet approval from the crowd is fragile and temporary. The applause fades, the trends shift, and the voices that once praised can quickly disappear. But calling is different. Calling depends on pleasing God, and God does not change. When a man chooses obedience over applause, he steps onto a path that may not always be celebrated by the crowd, but it will always be honored by heaven. Popularity fades quickly but calling leaves a lasting legacy. The men who shaped history and eternity were rarely the most popular in their time, but they were faithful to the voice of God. When a man commits himself to God's calling rather than public approval, he stops chasing momentary praise and begins building something that outlives him.

A man who chases popularity finds his convictions shifting with the crowd and his values bending to whatever gains the most approval in the moment. When acceptance becomes the goal, integrity slowly erodes, because pleasing people requires constant adjustment. The applause of others may feel rewarding for a moment, but it is unstable and fleeting. A man who builds his identity on the approval of people will always feel pressure to compromise, because the crowd's expectations are constantly changing. But a man who lives by calling anchors his life to the unchanging truth of God. His direction is not determined by applause but by obedience. While others may waver with every trend, the man of calling stands firm because his foundation is eternal. He understands that faithfulness to God matters more than popularity with people. When a man chooses calling over approval, his character becomes strong, consistent, and trustworthy because it is rooted in truth rather than opinion.

When a man begins to embrace God's higher standard, the things that once held great importance begin to lose their grip on his heart.

He realizes that the praise of people is temporary, but the approval of God is eternal. Instead of chasing validation from the crowd, he learns to walk quietly in obedience, even when no one is watching. In that place of surrender, his life becomes anchored not in popularity but in purpose, and his decisions are guided more by conviction than by convenience. As this transformation deepens, his focus shifts from seeking comfort to building character. He understands that God is more interested in shaping the man he is becoming than in making his path easy. Trials become opportunities for refinement, discipline becomes a pathway to strength, and obedience becomes a daily act of faith. The man who embraces God's standard learns that true greatness is not measured by ease or applause, but by integrity, perseverance, and a heart that faithfully follows the will of God.

God's standard calls a man to live with integrity when no one is watching. A man who honors God in the unseen places builds a life on a foundation that cannot be shaken. While others may chase convenience or approval, he chooses truth, knowing that the eyes of the Lord see every motive and every choice. In those hidden moments, integrity becomes strength and faithfulness becomes the mark of a man who walks with God. God's standard also calls a man to discipline when others choose laziness and to courage when fear tries to silence him. Discipline forms the backbone of purpose, shaping a man who is steady, dependable, and prepared for the work God places before him. Courage rises when a man decides that obedience to God matters more than the comfort of silence. In that moment, the man who follows God's higher calling becomes a voice of truth, a pillar of strength, and a living example that real manhood is forged through obedience, perseverance, and unwavering trust in God.

Rising above the crowd does not mean believing you are better than others. True elevation in the kingdom of God is not built on pride, comparison, or superiority. Instead, it is born from humility and obedience. A man who rises above the crowd simply chooses a different compass for his life. While many drift wherever comfort, culture, or convenience lead them, he anchors his heart in God's purpose. He understands that life is not merely about fitting in or being accepted by the majority. It is about faithfully answering the call that God has placed on his life, even when that path requires courage, discipline, and separation from the ordinary. When a man recognizes that God created him for more than drifting through life, something powerful begins to awaken within him. He stops living reactively and begins living intentionally. His decisions become guided by conviction rather than popularity. He no longer measures success by applause but by obedience to God's voice.

The world constantly offers the path of least resistance. It promises quick approval, easy applause, and the comfort of blending in with the crowd. Yet these easy roads rarely lead to lives of meaning or lasting impact. God never called men to drift with the current of culture; He calls them to stand firm in truth, even when it is unpopular. The men who make a difference in the world are those who refuse to measure their lives by the approval of people, but instead by their faithfulness to God's calling. History is shaped by men who choose conviction over comfort and faith over fear. They walk the harder road - the road where integrity matters more than acceptance and obedience matters more than applause. This path is not always easy, but it is always meaningful. When a man chooses to live by faith, he becomes a light in a dark world and a voice of courage in a silent crowd. The road of conviction may be narrow, but it leads to a legacy that outlives the man who walked it.

When a man answers God's call, the noise of the world begins to fade, and the voice of purpose grows louder in his heart. What once seemed uncertain becomes clearer as he begins to see life through the lens of God's plan instead of human opinion. His steps become more deliberate, his decisions more thoughtful, and his vision begins to stretch beyond temporary success toward eternal significance. The call of God gives a man direction that the world can never provide. As he walks in that calling, his character is refined and strengthened through obedience, discipline, and faith. Trials no longer feel meaningless, because they become tools that shape him into the man God designed him to be. Courage replaces hesitation, conviction replaces confusion, and purpose replaces wandering. When a man truly responds to God's invitation, his life begins to move with clarity, strength, and divine momentum toward the destiny that Heaven prepared for him.

The call to rise above the crowd is ultimately the call to become the man God designed you to be. It is not a call to pride or superiority, but a call to purpose. God invites a man to live differently - to live intentionally. It is the invitation to live boldly, walk faithfully, and stand firmly for what is right even when it is unpopular. When a man answers that call, he begins to align his life with God's higher standard, allowing courage, conviction, and faith to shape his decisions. When a man chooses this path, his life begins to carry a weight of influence that reaches far beyond himself. His integrity becomes a beacon, his faith becomes an anchor, and his example becomes a guide for others who are searching for direction. The man who rises above the crowd does not simply live for the moment - he lives for eternity. And when he embraces God's calling with humility and courage, he steps into a life that leaves a lasting imprint, a legacy of strength and faith that will echo through generations.

| 2 |

"STRENGTH IN SOLITUDE"

Many men fear solitude because it feels like abandonment. When the noise fades and the crowd disappears, a man can begin to wonder if he has been forgotten. Silence exposes the thoughts we often try to outrun, and isolation can feel like a sign that something has gone wrong. Yet God does not waste these quiet seasons. Throughout scripture, the Lord often withdraws His servants from the crowd so He can shape them in ways that public life never could. What appears to be loneliness is frequently the hidden workshop of God, where character is forged, faith is deepened, and strength is quietly built within the soul. In solitude, distractions fall away and a man learns to depend on God alone. The absence of applause teaches him to seek the approval of heaven rather than the validation of people. Moses was prepared in the wilderness, David in lonely fields, and even Jesus withdrew to desolate places to pray. These moments were not abandonment but divine preparation.

The world teaches that success comes through constant activity, endless noise, and the approval of the crowd. Men are pushed to stay busy, visible, and applauded. Yet God often works in a completely different way. He frequently removes His servants from the spotlight and places them in quiet places where the soul can be shaped. In those hidden seasons, what feels like isolation is often divine preparation. In the silence, faith deepens, humility grows, and a man begins to hear the still, small voice of God more clearly than he ever could in the noise of the world. These quiet seasons are sacred workshops where God forms strength that the public eye cannot see. Character is not forged in crowds but in solitude. When God pulls a man away from the noise, He is not abandoning him - He is developing him. The silence becomes a classroom where wisdom grows, and the hidden place becomes the foundation for future impact. What God builds in the quiet will one day stand strong in the open.

Solitude is not punishment; it is preparation. When God wants to shape a man for greater purpose, He often leads him into seasons where there are fewer voices, fewer applauses, and fewer companions. In those quiet places, distractions fade and the soul becomes more attentive to the voice of God. What may feel like isolation is often the workshop of transformation, where character is refined, motives are purified, and strength is forged. The absence of constant noise allows a man to confront his fears, examine his heart, and develop the inner stability that public life will eventually demand. Many of the men God used most powerfully were first shaped in hidden places. Moses spent years in the wilderness before leading a nation. David learned courage in lonely fields before standing before kings. Even Jesus withdrew to solitary places to pray and prepare for His mission. These seasons of solitude are not signs of abandonment but evidence of divine investment.

In the quiet seasons of life there is no audience to impress and no applause to chase. The silence becomes a mirror that reflects who a man truly is. In that stillness, God often begins a deeper work, revealing attitudes that need correction, wounds that need healing, and strengths that are waiting to be developed. What feels like isolation is often the very place where God begins shaping a man into someone stronger, wiser, and more authentic. Solitude has a way of stripping away pretense and forcing honesty. A man cannot hide behind titles, achievements, or the opinions of others when he stands alone before

God. Instead, he must face the truth about who he is and who he is becoming. In the quiet place, God invites a man to grow, to repent where necessary, and to rebuild his character on a stronger foundation. When a man learns to embrace these silent seasons, he discovers that solitude is not his enemy - it is often the workshop where God forms integrity, courage, and spiritual strength.

Scripture is filled with men who were prepared in isolation. Before Moses ever stood before Pharaoh or led Israel out of Egypt, God first led him into the quiet wilderness. For forty years he walked the lonely hills of Midian tending sheep far removed from the power and prestige of Egypt. In that silent desert, God stripped away pride, impatience, and self-reliance. The wilderness became God's classroom where Moses learned humility, patience, and a deep dependence upon the Lord. Often God works the same way in our lives. Before He entrusts a man with influence, He first shapes his character in seasons of solitude. The quiet places of life - where applause is absent and recognition is scarce - are where God builds strength within the soul. In isolation, a man learns to hear God's voice more clearly and to trust Him more deeply. What feels like loneliness is often divine preparation, because the men God uses greatly are usually the men He has first formed quietly in the wilderness.

David also experienced seasons of solitude. As a young shepherd in the quiet fields of Bethlehem, he spent long hours alone watching over his father's flock. While others may have seen only an isolated boy tending sheep, God saw a heart being shaped in secret. In those lonely fields David learned to depend on the Lord. With no audience but the sheep and the open sky, he sang songs of praise, played his harp, and cultivated a deep relationship with God. What looked like obscurity was actually preparation. The quiet pastures became the place where courage was born, where faith was strengthened, and where David discovered that God was always near even when no one else was around. Those solitary hours prepared David for the battles that would later define his life. Before he ever stood before a giant named Goliath, he had already faced lions and bears with nothing but a sling and a confidence in God's protection. The strength that carried him into public victory was forged in private devotion.

Joseph's years in an Egyptian prison must have seemed like a painful contradiction to the dreams God had given him. Betrayed by his brothers, falsely accused, and forgotten by those he helped, Joseph sat in isolation while the promise of his future appeared distant. The place that looked like a prison had actually been God's classroom. What looked like a delay was actually a divine workshop. In the quiet loneliness of that prison cell, God was strengthening Joseph's character, deepening his humility, and teaching him to depend completely on the Lord rather than on circumstances or recognition. What seemed like a setback was truly a season of refinement. God was preparing Joseph to carry the weight of leadership that awaited him in Egypt. Integrity was forged in the darkness, wisdom matured through patience, and faith grew stronger while no one was watching. When the appointed moment arrived, Joseph stepped out of the prison not as a broken man, but as a prepared leader.

Even Jesus Himself spent time in solitude. Before stepping into the public ministry that would change the world, He withdrew into the wilderness for forty days. In that lonely place, away from crowds and noise, He faced the fiercest temptations of the enemy. Yet the wilderness was not a place of weakness - it was a place of preparation. In the silence and isolation, Jesus stood firm on the Word of God and strengthened His resolve. What appeared to be a lonely season was actually a sacred season where heaven was shaping Him for the mission ahead. In the same way, God often uses seasons of solitude in our lives to deepen our character and sharpen our purpose. When we feel alone, it may be that God is drawing us aside to refine our faith, clarify our calling, and strengthen our spiritual authority. Just as Jesus emerged from the wilderness empowered and ready to fulfill His purpose, those who embrace God in their quiet seasons will also rise with renewed strength, wisdom, and divine direction.

Again and again throughout scripture we see that God prepares His servants away from the spotlight. Before the public victories, before the influence, and before the recognition, there is often a hidden season where character is formed and faith is tested. In these unseen seasons God is not absent - He is actively shaping the heart, strengthening resolve, and teaching His servants to rely on Him rather than applause. These examples remind us that the strength people admire in a person rarely begins in public view. True spiritual strength is forged quietly in prayer, obedience, patience, and perseverance when no one else is watching. The hidden years are not wasted years; they are preparation years. God often develops the deepest faith in places where recognition is absent and the only reward is knowing that you are walking with Him. When the appointed time comes, the strength formed in secret becomes visible, and the servant who was shaped in solitude is ready to stand with courage and purpose.

Silence plays an important role in the shaping of a man's spirit. When a man steps away from the noise, he gives his heart the opportunity to settle and his mind the chance to focus on what truly matters. It is in these quiet moments that God often does His deepest work - refining character, strengthening resolve, and bringing clarity to the path ahead. Silence is the environment where wisdom begins to grow. When the noise fades, God's voice becomes clearer. The whispers of the Spirit are often drowned out by the chaos of everyday life, but in stillness, His guidance rises above every other voice. In silence a man learns to listen, to reflect, and to align his heart with God's purposes. Decisions become wiser, convictions become stronger, and faith becomes steadier. What once seemed confusing begins to make sense because the heart is tuned in to heaven's frequency. A man who learns the discipline of silence will discover that God has been speaking all along - he simply needed the quiet to hear Him.

Many men struggle to hear the voice of God because their lives are crowded with constant noise. Endless activity, entertainment, responsibilities, and the demands of daily life can easily fill every quiet moment. When the mind is always occupied and the heart is always rushing, the gentle whisper of God becomes difficult to recognize. Scripture often shows that God does not shout over the noise of the world; instead, He speaks in stillness. Just as Elijah discovered that the Lord was not in the wind, earthquake, or fire but in a "still small voice," many men today must learn that hearing God requires moments of intentional quiet. When a man slows down, steps away from the constant stimulation, and makes space for reflection and prayer, he begins to tune his heart to the frequency of God's voice. God often reveals direction, wisdom, and conviction when a man is willing to pause long enough to listen. The world urges men to stay busy, but God invites them to be still.

Solitude has a way of slowing the restless pace of the soul. When a man steps away from the noise of constant activity and the endless distractions that fill his days, his heart finally has space to breathe. In those quiet moments, reflection begins. Thoughts settle, prayers deepen, and the mind turns toward God with renewed awareness. Solitude becomes more than just being alone - it becomes a sacred space where a man can examine his life, realign his priorities, and quietly seek the presence of the Lord. It is often in these still and unhurried moments that God speaks most clearly to the heart. His voice is not usually found in the chaos of busyness, but in the gentle whisper that comes when a man is willing to be still and listen. In solitude, clarity replaces confusion, peace replaces anxiety, and direction replaces uncertainty. A man who learns to embrace these quiet seasons discovers that solitude is not emptiness at all - it is where God fills the soul with wisdom, strength, and renewed purpose.

Strength grows in those quiet, unseen moments when a man withdraws from the noise of the world and turns his heart toward God.

In the stillness of prayer and reflection, he begins to hear the gentle whisper of divine wisdom guiding his thoughts and shaping his decisions. These silent conversations with God become a sacred training ground where character is refined, perspective is corrected, and courage is strengthened. When a man learns to seek God's wisdom in private, he builds a foundation that cannot easily be shaken by circumstances, criticism, or adversity. His strength no longer depends on applause or approval because it is rooted in the quiet confidence that comes from walking closely with God. In those private encounters, faith grows deeper, discernment becomes sharper, and the soul is steadied. The man who consistently meets God in secret carries a strength into public life that is calm, anchored, and unmovable.

Solitude also strengthens faith. When no one else is around to affirm or encourage him, a man learns to rely fully on God's presence rather than human approval. In those quiet moments, the heart is stripped of distractions and false supports. A man begins to realize that his identity, his worth, and his strength are not built upon applause, recognition, or validation from others, but upon the steady and unchanging presence of God. What once felt like loneliness becomes sacred ground where faith is refined. In the stillness, he discovers that God has been with him all along, speaking gently to his spirit and strengthening his inner resolve. In solitude his prayers grow deeper, his dependence grows stronger, and his confidence becomes anchored in something eternal rather than temporary. The man who learns to walk with God in solitude no longer needs the approval of the crowd, because he has learned the greater joy of standing secure in the presence of the One who called him.

Hidden seasons are not wasted seasons; they are sacred workshops where the inner man is carefully shaped. In solitude and obscurity, God chisels away pride, refines motives, and strengthens the heart. Character begins to deepen as a man learns patience, humility, and dependence upon the Lord. What is formed in the hidden places becomes the foundation upon which lasting strength is built. During these seasons, spiritual maturity quietly takes root beneath the surface, much like a tree that grows its deepest roots before it ever reaches great heights. A man who allows God to work in these unseen moments develops a steadiness that cannot be shaken by circumstances or criticism. His faith becomes more genuine, his purpose clearer, and his relationship with God more intimate. When the season of preparation is complete, the strength developed in secret will begin to reveal itself openly, proving that the hidden work of God always produces visible fruit in due time.

Solitude with God is never wasted time. In the quiet places where no applause is heard and no recognition is given; God is shaping the inner life of a man. In those private moments strength is quietly formed. Doubts are confronted, character is refined, and faith grows deeper roots. What may feel like isolation is often God's workshop, where He develops resilience, clarity, and spiritual confidence that cannot be produced in the noise of the crowd. Eventually, that hidden season bears visible fruit. A man who has walked closely with God in private will stand firmly when challenges arise in public. His confidence is not built on pride or self-reliance, but on the steady assurance that comes from knowing God personally. When storms come, he does not easily collapse because his foundation was built in the quiet places. The solitude that once seemed lonely becomes the very source of his strength, enabling him to lead, endure, and stand with unwavering faith when it matters most.

Many of the most powerful spiritual transformations happen in the quiet places where no one is watching. In those silent seasons, when a man bows his head in prayer and pours out his heart to God, heaven is paying attention. While the world may overlook those hidden moments, the Lord treasures them, for it is in solitude that character is refined and faith takes deep root. In the quiet seasons of life, God is quietly shaping the heart, deepening faith, and strengthening the soul for the greater purpose that lies ahead. The faith built in silence becomes the foundation for the victories that come later. Just as a seed grows beneath the soil long before it breaks through the surface, the work God does in solitude prepares a man for greater purpose. Heaven records every prayer, every moment of trust, and every act of faithfulness. Though no crowd may witness it, God sees it all and, in His perfect time, the strength formed in secret will reveal itself in power, wisdom, and unwavering faith.

Do not despise the lonely path. Many of the greatest works God accomplishes in a man's life happen in the quiet places where no audience is present and no applause is heard. In seasons of solitude, God strips away distractions, pride, and noise so that a man can hear His voice clearly. What feels like isolation is often divine preparation. In the silence, God shapes character, strengthens conviction, and builds a foundation of faith that cannot be shaken by the storms of life. A man may feel alone in these seasons, but he is never truly abandoned. In fact, solitude often becomes the sacred space where God draws closest. When the world grows quiet, the presence of God becomes louder, clearer, and more personal. It is there that a man discovers that his strength does not come from crowds, recognition, or comfort but from a deep and abiding relationship with the One who called him. The lonely path, though difficult, is often the very road where God forms the strongest, wisest, and most faithful men.

| 3 |

"WHEN THE CROWD WALKS AWAY"

There are seasons in life when the crowd is loud, the encouragement is plentiful, and the support seems endless. In those moments it feels as though the journey will always be surrounded by applause and companionship. The cheers of the crowd may encourage us, but they are not meant to sustain us. Sooner or later every man reaches a point where the noise fades, the excitement settles, and the path becomes quieter and more demanding. In that silence, a deeper question emerges: will you continue walking when the approval disappears? The quiet road reveals who is committed and who was merely present for the excitement. God frequently leads men through lonely stretches so that their strength is drawn from Him rather than from human approval. When the crowd begins to thin and the voices grow quiet, it is not always a sign that you have lost your way. Often it means the journey has become more serious and the calling more personal.

Many people are enthusiastic about the beginning of a journey. They admire the dream, they applaud the ambition, and they enjoy being near the excitement of potential. But when the path becomes steep and the struggle begins, their enthusiasm fades. What once looked inspiring now looks inconvenient. This is a reality every person called to purpose will eventually face. Applause is loud at the starting line, but it grows quiet on the difficult road. Yet God never intended for our strength to come from the crowd. The calling He places on a life is sustained by conviction, faith, and perseverance, not by the temporary approval of others. The wise man learns that the true test of purpose is revealed when the excitement disappears and the work remains. When others step back, it becomes an opportunity to lean more deeply into God's presence and guidance. The narrow path often becomes lonely, but it is also where character is refined and faith grows stronger.

One of the most difficult lessons a man must learn on the path of purpose is that not everyone who walks beside him is meant to stay for the entire journey. In the early stages of life, it is easy to assume that those who begin the road with us will remain until the end. Yet experience teaches us that some people are companions for a season, not partners for a mission. God often allows certain relationships to exist only for a moment in order to teach, refine, or redirect us. When the season changes, those individuals quietly step away. Though it can feel like loss or betrayal, it is often simply the unfolding of God's greater plan, separating temporary company from lifelong calling. A wise man learns not to anchor his purpose to the presence of people, but to the direction of God. When others drift away, he does not abandon the road or question the mission placed in his heart. Instead, he keeps walking with the understanding that some will walk with you for miles, others only for moments - but the calling remains.

The moment when the crowd walks away can feel like betrayal. It can feel confusing and painful. You may begin to question yourself, wondering what you did wrong or why people who once stood beside you suddenly grow distant. Yet many times this moment is not a sign of failure, but a turning point in your spiritual journey. God often allows the crowd to thin out so that your faith is no longer dependent on approval, applause, or companionship. In those quiet seasons God is often doing His deepest work. He is strengthening your character, clarifying your calling, and teaching you to walk by conviction rather than by consensus. The loneliness may sting for a moment, but it also reveals that your purpose was never meant to be carried by the crowd. It was placed within you by God. When others walk away, do not abandon the path. Stand firm and remember that sometimes the strongest faith is forged in the moments when you must keep walking with God - even when you walk alone.

When the road becomes steep and the wind begins to blow, the crowd that once surrounded you may begin to thin. These moments reveal a deeper truth about life and about people. Some relationships are built on comfort, shared excitement, or favorable circumstances, but true loyalty is not measured in sunshine - it is measured in storms. When adversity arrives, the masks fall away and the hearts of people are revealed. This reality, though sometimes painful, is also clarifying. God often allows difficult seasons to separate what is temporary from what is genuine. Anyone can stand beside you when the sun is shining, but loyalty is proven when the storm arrives. Those who remain when the road is hard are the ones whose hearts are anchored in love, faithfulness, and conviction. These moments challenge us to become men of steadfast character - men who do not disappear when life grows difficult, but who remain faithful, dependable, and committed no matter how fierce the storm may be.

Many friendships quietly disappear the moment the journey becomes uncomfortable. When the road becomes steep and success seems uncertain, some people choose the easier path rather than the faithful one. They quietly step aside, distancing themselves from the struggle, leaving you to continue the climb alone. Yet moments like these reveal that not everyone who begins the journey with you is meant to finish it with you. The thinning of the crowd is not always loss - it is often divine refinement. When others drift away, do not mistake solitude for abandonment. The absence of human support can sharpen your dependence on God and strengthen the resolve within your spirit. Keep climbing. Stay faithful to the calling placed on your life. Those who leave were never meant to carry the weight of your destiny, but the One who called you will never walk away. And in time, the very path that felt lonely will become the testimony of your perseverance and your trust in God.

Rejection can cut deeply when it catches the heart unprepared. When people withdraw, criticize, or walk away, it can leave a wound that quietly questions your strength and direction. In those moments, the mind begins to wrestle with doubt, and confidence can feel fragile. The enemy often uses rejection as a whisper of discouragement, suggesting that the road you are on is too hard, too lonely, or perhaps even mistaken. Yet rejection does not define your calling. Many of God's servants walked difficult roads where approval was scarce and misunderstanding was common, but their purpose was not determined by the applause of people. Instead of allowing rejection to shake your faith, let it refine your resolve. The path God sets before a man is not always crowded, and sometimes the truest callings are walked by those willing to stand firm even when others step away. When rejection tries to plant seeds of doubt, answer it with trust in God's guidance. What others abandon, God still sustains.

Rejection does not determine purpose. Many of the men God calls must walk roads that others are unwilling to travel. When applause fades and the crowd thins, it can feel as though something has gone wrong. Yet heaven has never measured obedience by popularity. The prophets often stood alone, misunderstood and uncelebrated, but their words still carried the authority of God. Purpose is anchored in calling, not in approval. The absence of human affirmation does not cancel what God has spoken over your life. A calling is not validated by how many people remain beside you; it is confirmed by your faithfulness to the One who called you. When others step away, it becomes an opportunity to deepen your reliance on God rather than the encouragement of the crowd. True purpose is refined in quiet places where applause is absent and conviction must stand on its own. Stay faithful to the mission. If God assigned the task, its value remains unchanged even when the road must be walked alone.

Scripture reveals that those entrusted with great purpose often walk through seasons of loneliness. Joseph was misunderstood by his brothers, David spent years fleeing in the wilderness before wearing the crown, and even Jesus experienced moments when those closest to Him could not fully stand with Him. The path of calling frequently leads through valleys where applause fades and companionship becomes scarce. The crowd celebrates victories, but it rarely stays for the battles that produce them proving that the struggle that shapes character is usually fought in obscurity. A man of purpose must learn to remain faithful when the cheering stops and the road becomes quiet. In those moments, God reminds His servants that their assignment was never dependent on popular support but on divine calling. Loneliness, when embraced with faith, becomes a sacred workshop where courage is forged, vision is clarified, and a man learns to stand firmly with God even if he must stand alone for a season.

There is a kind of strength that can only be forged in solitude. If a man's strength depended on approval, encouragement, or recognition from others, it will weaken when those voices are gone. But if his strength is rooted in conviction - anchored in truth, purpose, and a calling from God - then solitude does not diminish him. Instead, it refines him. Like steel placed in the fire, a man who stands firm in lonely seasons discovers a deeper resolve that cannot be shaken by public opinion. God often uses solitude as a sacred workshop where character is formed and faith is strengthened. Many of the strongest men in scripture - Moses in the wilderness, David in the caves, Elijah in the desert - were shaped in seasons where the crowd was absent and the path was quiet. Over time, the man who stands firm in solitude emerges stronger, steadier, and more focused, because the strength built in quiet places grows deeper and lasts longer than the praise of any crowd.

Loyalty is one of the rarest treasures in this world. True loyalty grows out of character, integrity, and a heart that understands commitment. Many people will walk beside you when the road is smooth and the atmosphere is comfortable, but loyalty reveals its true nature when the path becomes difficult. In those moments, when circumstances test relationships and pressures cause others to drift away, the faithful few remain. Their presence is steady and dependable. They stand firm because loyalty has become a part of who they are. Spiritually, loyalty reflects a deeper principle found throughout scripture: faithfulness. God Himself honors faithfulness far more than popularity or numbers. Throughout life's journey, you may discover that the circle around you becomes smaller, but within that smaller circle are individuals whose loyalty is genuine and enduring. These are the people who pray for you, stand with you in adversity, and refuse to abandon the assignment God has placed on your life.

When you discover those rare souls who remain when others leave, you begin to understand the true meaning of loyalty. These are the people who stand beside you not only in moments of victory but also in seasons of difficulty, when the road grows lonely and the storms grow fierce. Their presence becomes a quiet reminder that God often works through a faithful few rather than an applauding crowd. Such people are not shaken by changing circumstances because their loyalty is rooted in something deeper than emotion or advantage. They understand that true relationships are forged through trials, patience, and perseverance. Like sturdy anchors in turbulent waters, they remain steady when everything else seems uncertain. When you recognize these rare and faithful souls, treasure them. They are gifts from God - evidence that genuine faithfulness still exists - and their steadfast presence strengthens your journey and reminds you that you were never meant to walk the path entirely alone.

Purpose does not depend on the presence of a crowd. God's calling upon a man's life is not validated by how many people walk beside him, but by the conviction burning within his heart. There are seasons when companions are many and encouragement flows freely, but there are also lonely stretches of the journey when the road grows quiet and familiar faces fade from view. In those moments, a man must remember that his assignment was never given by the crowd - it was given by God. When a man truly understands his calling, he does not abandon the path simply because others have chosen to step off it. A man who knows why he was sent refuses to retreat simply because the road grows narrow. He keeps walking, keeps believing, and keeps building, trusting that obedience matters more than popularity. Even if he must travel part of the journey alone, he moves forward with confidence, knowing that the God who called him is faithful to walk with him every step of the way.

The calling God places on a man's life is refined in solitude. In those silent stretches, when applause is absent and encouragement is scarce, faith is strengthened and conviction is purified. What feels like isolation is often the workshop where God forges endurance, clarity, and unwavering resolve. True purpose proves its authenticity in the difficult seasons. Anyone can carry a vision when the path is crowded and the energy is high, but the man who continues walking when the road grows empty demonstrates a deeper strength. Loneliness does not mean the vision has lost its value; often it means the journey has entered a more sacred phase. God uses these quiet valleys to remind His people that their purpose is sustained not by popularity, convenience, or constant affirmation, but by obedience and faith. When you refuse to abandon the vision in lonely seasons, you step into a maturity of spirit that transforms temporary isolation into a testimony of perseverance.

Standing firm when others leave requires a courage that is not dependent on applause or approval. In those quiet moments, a man must discover where his true anchor lies. If his foundation is popularity, he will waver when the voices disappear. But when his heart is anchored in truth, he can remain steady even when the road becomes lonely. The strength to stand does not come from the size of the crowd but from the depth of one's faith. There is a quiet strength required to keep walking when the noise of companionship has faded into silence. Faith often leads through valleys where affirmation is scarce and encouragement is distant. Yet it is in those silent stretches that character is forged and purpose becomes clear. A man who continues forward, trusting God even when others turn back, demonstrates a courage that cannot be shaken by isolation. When you stand firm in truth while others walk away, you prove that your commitment is not to popularity but to purpose.

Seasons of solitude are not evidence that you have failed or that God has abandoned you. When the noise fades and the crowds thin, God begins a deeper work within. In those quiet places He purifies motives, removes distractions, and teaches us to depend on Him rather than the approval of people. What may feel like isolation is often preparation, where faith is strengthened and character is forged in the hidden places. The lonely path has always been a place where God builds His strongest servants. In these seasons He clarifies purpose, strengthens resolve, and deepens trust. When no applause is heard and few walk beside you, faith learns to stand on its own. The silence becomes a classroom where perseverance grows and conviction becomes unshakable. What appears to be a difficult stretch of road is often the very place where God is preparing you for greater influence, deeper faith, and a stronger walk with Him.

When the crowd walks away, the man who continues forward enters a deeper place of faith. Applause fades, encouragement grows quiet, and the path suddenly feels lonelier than before. Yet it is in that quiet space that something powerful begins to form within him. He realizes that purpose was never meant to be carried by the strength of public approval. God often allows the crowd to thin so that a man learns to walk by conviction rather than by compliments. In those moments, faith becomes personal, courage becomes deliberate, and obedience becomes the compass that guides every step. As he keeps moving forward, his identity becomes anchored not in who stayed, but in the One who never leaves. The absence of the crowd no longer feels like loss; it becomes confirmation that he is learning to follow God's voice above all others. A man who walks this road learns that purpose is sustained by trust in God's calling, and when that trust is firm, even a lonely path leads to powerful destinations.

The crowd often feels powerful when it is present. Their voices are loud, their approval comforting, and their presence reassuring. But the journey of faith was never meant to be governed by the crowd. Crowds are fickle; they gather when the road is easy and disappear when the path grows steep. God has never measured a man's destiny by the number of people walking beside him. Instead, He looks for the heart that refuses to quit when the applause fades. When the noise dies down and the road becomes quiet, the man who continues forward proves that his strength does not come from popularity but from conviction. Faithful men learn that purpose is not validated by the crowd but by obedience to the call of God. In the end, the destination belongs to the one who keeps walking. The man who stands firm when others leave discovers a deeper strength forming within him. The quiet road may feel lonely, but it is often the road where character is forged, faith is strengthened, and vision becomes clear.

| 4 |

"THE COURAGE TO STAND ALONE"

There comes a defining moment in every man's life when the crowd can no longer cover him, when blending in is no longer an option, and the pressure to conform begins to press against his soul. In that moment, the noise of opinions grows louder than the whisper of truth, and the temptation to compromise feels almost overwhelming. Yet it is precisely there, in the heat of that tension, that a man discovers who he truly is. Like Daniel in a foreign land, surrounded by expectations that opposed his faith, a man of God must choose whether he will bow to the culture or stand for what is right. True character is revealed when standing comes with a cost - when it risks rejection, misunderstanding, or isolation. A man who stands in that moment declares that truth matters more than approval, and obedience matters more than comfort. In the end, it is not the crowd that defines a man, but the convictions he refuses to abandon when the pressure is at its greatest.

The pressure to compromise rarely storms into your life with loud defiance - it slips in quietly, appealing to reason and comfort. It speaks in subtle tones, suggesting that bending the truth or lowering your standard is harmless, even necessary. But every small surrender leaves a mark on the soul. What begins as a single exception slowly reshapes the heart, dulling conviction and weakening resolve. The enemy of integrity is not always open rebellion; often, it is the gradual acceptance of less than what God has called you to be. True strength is found in recognizing that compromise, no matter how small, carries a spiritual cost. When you choose truth over convenience and obedience over approval, you reinforce the foundation of your character. God honors the man who stands firm when it would be easier to bend. Refuse the subtle erosion. Guard your heart with vigilance and let your convictions be anchored so deeply in truth that even the softest whisper of compromise cannot move you.

Compromise is dangerous because it disguises itself as relief rather than defeat. It whispers promises of peace, acceptance, and ease, offering a shortcut out of pressure and discomfort. In the moment, it can feel like wisdom - like you've avoided conflict or preserved relationships - but beneath the surface, something sacred begins to erode. Every time a man bends his convictions to fit the expectations of others, he weakens the very foundation of his character. What feels like a small concession today quietly becomes a pattern tomorrow, and over time, that pattern shapes a life that is no longer governed by truth, but by convenience. A man who yields to pressure may gain approval for a moment, but he pays a far greater price within himself - he loses his inner authority. That quiet confidence that comes from standing firm in what is right cannot be replaced by applause or acceptance. True strength is not found in avoiding tension, but in enduring it with integrity.

A man who chooses truth over popularity will quickly discover how lonely that road can feel. You may be misunderstood by those who once stood beside you, overlooked in moments you deserved recognition, or even rejected simply because you refused to bend. Yet conviction was never meant to be convenient - it was meant to be costly, because anything of eternal value always is. God does not measure your life by how well you fit in, but by how faithfully you stand. But hear this clearly: the cost of standing alone is always less than the cost of losing yourself. When you compromise your convictions you forfeit your identity, your peace, and your purpose. When you stand firm, you are never truly alone, because God stands with those who refuse to bow. In the end, it is better to walk a narrow path with integrity than to run with the crowd toward emptiness. Stand your ground, even if you stand alone, because that is where true strength, clarity, and divine favor are found.

Daniel's life reminds us that faith is not proven in comfort, but in resistance. He lived in a culture that constantly pressured him to compromise - pressured to eat differently, think differently, worship differently, and ultimately become someone different. Yet in the middle of that system, Daniel made a quiet but unshakable decision: he would not defile himself. He didn't wait for a crisis to determine his convictions - he had already settled them in his heart. Because of that, when the pressure came, he didn't bend. Daniel shows us that real courage is the ability to stand firm without losing your identity. He didn't blend in to survive; he stood apart to remain faithful, and God honored him for it. When you choose truth over approval, integrity over acceptance, and obedience over comfort, you position yourself for divine favor even in difficult environments. Like Daniel, you were not called to be molded by the culture, but to stand as a witness within it - uncompromising, unwavering, and fully surrendered to God.

Daniel's courage was not born in a moment of crisis - it was cultivated in the quiet, unseen places where character is formed. Long before the lions' den, he made a decision to honor God when it would have been easier to blend in. Refusing the king's food was a line drawn in the sand, a declaration that his identity and allegiance belonged to God alone. Courage is not created under pressure; it is revealed there, having already been built in the hidden places of obedience. When Daniel continued to pray despite the decree, he chose faithfulness over fear, obedience over self-preservation. He did not wait for a dramatic moment to decide who he would be - he had already settled that in his heart. That is why when the public test came, he did not waver. His life reminds us that the victories others see are often the result of disciplines no one applauds. True spiritual strength is forged in consistency with God when no one is watching, and it is that quiet faithfulness that prepares us to face the lions without fear.

Daniel's strength did not come from a favorable environment, but from a settled identity. Long before he stood in Babylon, surrounded by pressure, temptation, and expectations to conform, he had already drawn a line in his heart. He knew who he was, and more importantly, he knew whom he served. That inner conviction became his compass when everything around him tried to pull him in another direction. Because his devotion to God was established in private, he did not have to scramble for courage in public. External pressure only exposes what has already been decided within. When your identity is anchored in God, opinions lose their power, compromise loses its appeal, and fear loses its voice. The world may try to redefine you, but it cannot override what heaven has already established in you. Like Daniel, you must decide now - before the test comes - who you are and whom you serve. Because when your heart is anchored, no storm, no culture, and no opposition can move you.

Courage is not born in applause or affirmed in the presence of a crowd - it is forged in the quiet, hidden places where no one is watching but God. It is in those private moments, when compromise is easiest and accountability feels distant, that a man either strengthens his soul or weakens it. Integrity is built in the unseen, and character is shaped in solitude. The choices made behind closed doors become the foundation for how a man will stand when the pressure is on. When the storm comes - and it always does - it does not create a man's convictions; it exposes them. A man who has disciplined his heart in the secret place will not suddenly collapse under public pressure, because his strength was never dependent on the crowd to begin with. He stands firm not because the moment demands it, but because his life has been built on unshakable truth. Courage, then, is not a reaction - it is a lifestyle. And the man who has learned to stand alone with God will never truly stand alone when it matters most.

A man of faith does not wait until he is in the fire to determine what he believes; he settles it in the quiet place with God. Like Daniel in Babylon, he resolves in his heart what he will stand for, regardless of the cost. Conviction is not formed in moments of crisis - it is revealed there. When your foundation is built through prayer, reflection, and obedience to God's truth, you become immovable when everything around you is shifting. You are no longer reacting to culture; you are anchored beyond it. This kind of life demands alignment with truth over trends. It requires the humility to let God's Word correct, re-fine, and establish your standards, even when it contradicts popu-lar opinion. The world will constantly redefine right and wrong, but truth does not evolve - it stands eternal. When you allow Scripture to shape your thinking, your decisions, and your identity, you develop a strength that is not dependent on approval. You become steady, clear, and unshaken, living not for applause but for obedience.

Conviction is the quiet strength of a soul that has seen truth and re-fuses to let go of it. It is not driven by emotion, approval, or fear, but by clarity that comes from aligning with God's Word and His ways. A man of conviction does not bend with every shifting wind of opin-ion; he stands, not because it is easy, but because there is a settled as-surance that even if the path is difficult, it is right. True conviction carries a quiet confidence that cannot be shaken by pressure or con-sequence. It is rooted in something eternal, formed in the presence of God and refined through obedience. When a man lives by conviction, he no longer needs the applause of others to validate his choices. He walks in integrity when no one is watching and chooses righteous-ness even when it costs him something. This kind of life is not loud, but it is powerful. It becomes a steady light in a world of compromise, proving that strength is not found in force, but in unwavering faithfulness to what is true.

A man without conviction drifts wherever pressure pushes him. Like a reed in the wind, he moves easily but he never stands firmly. This kind of instability erodes identity and weakens purpose, because a man who is governed by opinions will never be grounded in truth. Without conviction, he becomes a reflection of others rather than a man formed by God, and in the process, he loses the strength that comes from knowing who he is and what he stands for. But a man with conviction is anchored deep. His beliefs are not for sale, and his values are not negotiable. Even when he stands alone, he stands secure because his foundation is not built on applause, but on truth. He may face resistance, rejection, or misunderstanding, but he does not bend to it. Like a tree planted by living water, he remains steady in every season. His strength is quiet but unshakable, and his life becomes a testimony that real courage is not found in blending in, but in standing firm when it would be easier to bow.

Living by truth rather than approval is one of the greatest battles a man will fight, because approval feeds the flesh while truth strengthens the spirit. Approval is seductive - it offers immediate reward, a sense of belonging, and the comfort of being liked. But that comfort comes at a cost. When a man begins to measure his decisions by applause instead of conviction, he slowly trades his integrity for acceptance. He starts adjusting his voice to fit the crowd, silencing what he knows is right in order to avoid rejection. Over time, he loses clarity, direction, and ultimately himself. Truth, on the other hand, often stands alone. It requires courage to choose what is right when it is unpopular, to remain steady when others walk away, and to obey God even when no one is clapping. A man who is anchored in truth does not rise and fall with opinions - he stands firm because his foundation is unshakable. He understands that approval is temporary, but truth is eternal.

Truth is not shaped by human preference, nor does it bend to make life easier. It stands unmovable - steady in a world that constantly shifts its standards to accommodate comfort and avoid conviction. There will be moments when standing for truth isolates you, when it costs you acceptance, approval, or even relationships. Yet it is in those very moments that a man proves the depth of his conviction, choosing what is eternal over what is easy. A man who chooses truth over approval walks a narrow but powerful path. He may not always be celebrated by people, but he is honored by heaven. God does not measure a man by applause, but by obedience, integrity, and courage. When you stand firm in truth, you align yourself with something far greater than temporary recognition - you align with the heart of God. And though the crowd may grow silent, heaven takes notice. In the end, it is far better to stand alone in truth than to stand with the masses in compromise.

Jesus Himself embodied a courage that was not swayed by opinion, pressure, or popularity. He spoke truth even when it stirred opposition, confronted darkness without hesitation, and never diluted His message to gain acceptance. His courage was rooted in unwavering conviction and a deep intimacy with the Father. He showed us that real strength is not found in blending in, but in standing firm no matter what the cost may be. He also revealed that true courage is inseparable from obedience. Even when obedience led Him to suffering, rejection, and ultimately the cross, He did not waver. He did not chase applause or approval; He pursued purpose with relentless faithfulness. In a world that constantly pressures us to conform, Jesus calls us to live differently - to value truth over popularity and purpose over comfort. His life is both our example and our empowerment, reminding us that when we stand for what is right, even at great cost, we walk in the same courage that carried Him all the way to victory.

The courage to stand alone is the quiet strength that comes from knowing you are walking in step with God, even when no one else is. When your heart is anchored in God's truth, you are no longer swayed by the opinions of others. You begin to understand that standing alone does not mean being abandoned; it means being accompanied by the presence of the One who called you. Choosing obedience over acceptance is where true spiritual courage is forged. It means saying yes to God when it would be easier to blend in, to compromise, or to stay silent. The lonely path is filled with purpose, clarity, and divine approval. Those who walk this path become living testimonies that faith is not dependent on applause. They understand that pleasing God outweighs pleasing people, and that eternal reward is greater than temporary acceptance. When you are aligned with Him, you gain the strength to stand firm, knowing that even if you stand alone before men, you stand fully supported before God.

There will be moments when standing alone feels heavy - when the silence presses in and the opposition feels louder than the truth you carry. In those seasons, it can seem as though you've been forgotten, as though your stand has cost you more than it's worth. But heaven does its deepest work in hidden places. When no one applauds, when no one affirms, when no one stands beside you - God is strengthening something within you that cannot be shaken. What feels like isolation is often divine preparation. Those are the moments when your roots go deeper, anchoring you in truth rather than opinion, in conviction rather than comfort. It is there that your faith stops being borrowed and becomes your own - tested, proven, and unmovable. Anyone can stand when the crowd agrees, but it takes a man of God to stand when he stands alone. And when the storm passes, you will not be the same - you will be stronger, steadier, and more certain of who you are and whose you are.

You are not truly alone when you stand with God. His presence surrounds you in ways that human affirmation never could. When others misunderstand your convictions or distance themselves from your obedience, God draws nearer. His strength becomes your courage when your own feels insufficient, and His truth anchors you when everything around you pressures you to bend. Standing with Him may cost you comfort, popularity, or acceptance, but it secures something far greater: a life rooted in unshakable purpose and divine alignment. The applause of people is temporary, but the approval of God carries eternal weight. When you choose integrity over compromise and obedience over popularity, heaven takes notice. God honors those who stand firm, even when they stand alone. And in that place of quiet faithfulness, you will discover that you were never truly alone because the One who matters most has been with you all along, strengthening, guiding, and rewarding your unwavering stand.

In the end, the measure of a man is not found in the ease with which he blended into the crowd, but in the courage with which he stood apart when truth demanded it. The world rewards conformity, but heaven honors conviction. There will always be pressure to bend, to compromise, to trade integrity for acceptance but a man of faith anchors his life in something deeper than approval. He stands when it's uncomfortable, speaks when it's unpopular, and remains steady when others drift. His strength is not in fitting in, but in standing firm on the unchanging foundation of God's truth. Applause fades, opinions shift, and recognition is fleeting, but a life rooted in righteousness leaves an eternal impact. A faithful man understands that his audience is ultimately God, not people. So he holds the line in private as well as in public, in weakness as well as in strength. And when the dust settles it is not the cheers of the crowd that will matter - it is the quiet, powerful testimony of a life that refused to compromise.

Stand when it's uncomfortable - when your flesh would rather blend in, stay quiet, or take the easier path. Stand when it's unpopular - when truth costs you approval, when conviction separates you from the crowd, and when obedience to God puts you at odds with the world around you. A man of faith is not shaped by the noise of culture but by the voice of God. Like Daniel in a foreign land, you may find yourself surrounded by pressure to bow, to compromise, to conform but real strength is revealed in the moments where no one applauds your obedience. It is forged in quiet decisions, in unseen faithfulness, in choosing righteousness when it would be easier to choose comfort. Stand when no one else does because that is where your identity is anchored not in people, but in God. When you stand with Him, you stand on unshakable ground. You may feel isolated and misunderstood but you are never alone for God is closest in the moments where you choose Him over everything else.

| 5 |

"THE HIDDEN PLACE"

There is a place where real men are formed, and it is not the spotlight - it is the hidden place. It is in the quiet disciplines, the unseen choices, and the private battles where a man decides who he truly is. When no one is watching, there is no pressure to perform - only the opportunity to become. In those silent moments, integrity is forged, convictions are strengthened, and a man learns to stand without the need for applause. God does His deepest work in the unseen, shaping the heart long before the world ever sees the results. The hidden place is where roots grow deep enough to sustain a life of strength and purpose. It is where a man learns obedience without recognition, faith without validation, and perseverance without reward. A man who is faithful in the quiet will be unshakable in the storm, because his strength was not built on attention, but on truth. True manhood is not proven in front of crowds - it is established in the presence of God, where character is formed, refined, and made unbreakable.

A man's true identity is not forged in the applause of a crowd, but in the quiet, unseen moments where no one is watching and no recognition is given. It is in those private decisions that his character is revealed. The hidden life is where motives are purified, where discipline is tested, and where a man chooses between who he appears to be and who he truly is. What is done in secret becomes the foundation for what is revealed in public. When a man learns to honor God in private, he builds a life that is unshakable in public. Authenticity is not proven by words or image, but by consistent obedience when no one else sees. The quiet victories - resisting temptation, choosing truth, walking in integrity - become the bricks that form a strong and lasting identity. A man who is faithful in the hidden places will not need to perform for the world, because his life will naturally reflect the strength that was forged in secret. In the end, who you are alone with God will always define who you are everywhere else.

It is easy to rise to the occasion when others are watching. Applause has a way of energizing effort, and the presence of people can sharpen our focus and behavior. In those moments, discipline feels natural, faith appears strong, and character seems steady. But God is not measuring the strength you display in public - He is looking at the consistency you maintain in private. The quiet places, the unseen moments, and the hidden decisions reveal who you truly are. What you do when no one is watching is not separate from your character - it is the purest expression of it. When the room is empty and the lights are off, integrity stands alone without support or recognition. True strength is not built in the spotlight; it is forged in secrecy, where obedience is chosen simply because it is right. A man of integrity lives as if God is always present - because He is - and that awareness transforms the unseen places into sacred ground where character is formed, tested, and ultimately proven.

God is not captivated by polished performances or outward displays of spirituality. He is not swayed by eloquent words, visible discipline, or the applause of others. God looks deeper and searches the true condition of the heart. Authenticity is what moves Him. When your devotion is genuine, when your pursuit of Him is sincere, even in the unseen moments, it becomes a fragrance that honors Him far more than any outward performance ever could. What you cultivate in secret is the soil from which your life grows. The quiet prayers, the hidden obedience, the private battles fought with integrity - these are the places where true strength is formed. Long before anything is revealed in public, it is established in the hidden places of the heart. God builds men from the inside out, shaping character where no one else is watching. When your private life is aligned with Him, your public life will carry weight, authority, and authenticity. What is real in the dark will always shine in the light.

Private discipline is the forge where true strength is formed. It is in the early mornings, when the world is still asleep, that a man learns to rise above comfort and choose purpose. It is in the whispered prayers, the time in the Word, and the unseen sacrifices that character is shaped and convictions are deepened. These hidden moments are not wasted; they are sacred investments. While others chase recognition, the disciplined man is being refined, strengthened, and prepared for something greater than applause - he is being prepared for impact. What is done consistently in secret will not remain hidden forever. In due time, it will be revealed in strength, stability, and unwavering resolve. When pressure comes, when storms rise, and when others falter, the man who has trained in private will stand firm in public. His strength will be the result of daily obedience and faithful commitment. A powerful life is the product of disciplined moments that no one else applauded, but heaven fully recorded.

Public victories are never born in the spotlight - they are forged in the quiet, unseen places where a man wrestles with himself before he ever faces the world. In those private battles, character is shaped and convictions are anchored. A man does not suddenly become strong when the pressure rises; he simply reveals the strength he has been building all along. What is practiced in secret will always be displayed in public, for the hidden life is the true foundation of visible power. No man stands firm in the open who has not first learned to stand alone with God, unmoved by distraction and unshaken by compromise. Strength is never accidental - it is intentional, cultivated through countless quiet decisions that seem small but carry eternal weight. Each unseen choice to do what is right, even when it is hard, lays another stone in the structure of a man's life. When the moment of testing comes, he stands because he has already been standing, long before anyone was watching.

Discipline in the hidden places is where a man is truly formed. Long before anyone sees the strength, the influence, or the leadership, there is a private life being shaped in silence. When storms arise, he does not scramble to become strong; he stands firm because strength has already been established within him. Private discipline is not wasted effort - it is the quiet construction of an unshakable life. A man who governs himself in private will not collapse in public because his stability and strength come from a foundation that has been tested and reinforced in the hidden places. He has learned to master his thoughts, guard his heart, and align his actions with truth long before anyone is watching. So when challenges come, he does not bend with the wind of pressure or break under the weight of expectation. He stands steady, rooted, and resilient. His strength is built on disciplined habits and a surrendered life that remains consistent whether in the spotlight or in the shadows.

Integrity is the backbone of true manhood because it anchors a man to something greater than his circumstances, emotions, or public image. It is the quiet, unwavering decision to live by truth when no one is watching and no applause is given. In the hidden places of life, where shortcuts are tempting and compromise feels easier, integrity becomes the defining line between who a man pretends to be and who he truly is. When a man chooses conviction over compromise, he builds a life that can withstand storms and scrutiny alike. Integrity shapes his character, strengthens his decisions, and earns a trust that cannot be manufactured. It is not forged in moments of ease, but in moments of testing when truth demands courage and righteousness requires sacrifice. Though it may go unseen and unrewarded by the world, integrity never goes unnoticed by God. In the end, it produces a strength that is unshakable, a reputation that is lasting, and a legacy that speaks long after the moment has passed.

A man of integrity is not shaped by the shifting winds of his environment; he is rooted in something eternal. When the lights are off and no one is watching, he remains the same man he presents to the world in the daylight. His decisions are not driven by convenience, pressure, or the desire for approval, but by a deep, unshakable conviction of what is right. Because his life is anchored in truth, his consistency becomes his testimony. He does not wear different masks for different crowds, nor does he compromise when it would be easier to blend in. His integrity flows from a deeper source - his relationship with God, who sees all and honors what is done in secret. This unwavering alignment between his inner life and outward actions produces a quiet confidence and authority that cannot be manufactured. A man like this does not need to announce his character; it speaks for itself in every environment, because it was built in the unseen and stands firm in the seen.

Hidden compromise is never truly hidden - it is simply delayed in its exposure. Every quiet justification, every overlooked conviction, every tolerated weakness shapes the direction of his life. What feels insignificant in private gains strength over time, quietly forming patterns that will one day surface. God calls for integrity not just in the spotlight, but in the unseen places, because He knows that destiny is built in the quiet choices no one else witnesses. What is tolerated in private will eventually manifest in public. A man cannot walk in compromise behind closed doors and expect strength when the pressure comes. Collapse is rarely sudden - it is the result of a slow drift away from truth. But the same principle works in reverse: private discipline produces public strength. When a man chooses righteousness in the hidden places, he builds a foundation that cannot be shaken. God honors the man who lives consistently, the man who refuses to compromise even when no one else is watching.

Hidden faithfulness is never wasted - it is seen, recorded, and honored by God. While the world celebrates what is visible, heaven responds to what is consistent in the unseen. The quiet prayers, the private obedience, the unseen sacrifices, and the daily decisions to do what is right when no one is watching are building something far greater than momentary recognition. These hidden moments are where strength is forged, character is refined, and trust in God is proven genuine. What feels unnoticed on earth is often the very thing that moves the heart of God the most. The man who has learned to stand firm in private will not collapse in public. When opportunities come, he will be ready - not because of sudden preparation, but because of a life built steadily behind the scenes. Faithfulness in the hidden places becomes the foundation for influence in the visible ones, and the reward is not just recognition, but a life that reflects the integrity and blessing of God.

There are seasons in life when everything feels still - when prayers seem unanswered, progress appears nonexistent, and recognition never comes. In these moments, it can feel as though you've been forgotten, as if your efforts are falling into silence. But beneath the surface, God is at work in ways you cannot yet see. Just as roots grow deep before a tree rises tall, your character is being strengthened, your faith is being refined, and your foundation is being secured. In these quiet seasons, God is shaping what will sustain you in the visible ones. He is building endurance, integrity, and trust within you - qualities that cannot be rushed or manufactured in the spotlight. The hidden place is where motives are purified and dependence on Him is deepened. Though it may feel slow, nothing about this process is accidental. Stay faithful. Stay consistent. The same God who is working in the unseen will bring fruit in due time, and when He does, it will be rooted in something strong enough to last.

Just as a tree must first establish itself underground before it can rise and withstand the storms, so a man must be developed in hidden places before he is trusted with visible influence. Every moment of unseen obedience, every act of quiet faithfulness, and every choice to remain steadfast when no one is watching is strengthening your character and anchoring your life in truth. What feels like delay is often divine preparation. God is laying foundations within you that can carry the weight of future responsibility, leadership, and impact. If He were to elevate you too soon, without the depth to sustain it, the pressure could break what has not yet been built. But when your roots run deep - when your integrity is solid, your spirit is disciplined, and your faith is unwavering - you become a man who can stand firm no matter how high God raises you. So do not despise the hidden seasons. Embrace them, for in them, God is building a life that will not collapse under the weight of its calling.

The hidden season is not a wasted season; it is sacred ground where God does His deepest work. In the quiet places, away from applause and recognition, He is shaping motives, refining character, and strengthening the inner man. Roots are being driven deeper so that when the weight of responsibility comes, you will not collapse under it. God conceals a man before He reveals him because visibility without depth leads to instability. In the hidden season, He teaches obedience without recognition, faithfulness without reward, and endurance without validation. Do not despise the season where no one sees you, because heaven does. This is where integrity is forged, where your private life aligns with God's truth, and where your strength is built in silence. God develops depth before He grants visibility because He is preparing you to carry influence without losing your soul. Stay faithful in the hidden place - what God is building in you there will sustain everything He does through you later.

Public trust is simply the overflow of private faithfulness. The unseen moments are the proving grounds where a man either becomes trustworthy or disqualifies himself. What a man consistently does in private will eventually surface in public, because character cannot be hidden forever. God uses these hidden seasons as a test of readiness, shaping a man long before He ever elevates him. Faithfulness in the small, unnoticed things - choosing honesty, maintaining discipline, honoring God when no one else knows - these are the very acts that prepare a man for greater responsibility. Scripture shows that promotion does not come from striving, but from stewardship. When a man proves he can be trusted with little, God entrusts him with much. The weight of greater influence requires the strength of proven character, and that strength is built in secret. A man who masters his private world positions himself for public impact, because God promotes those who have already passed the test no one else could see.

Do not despise the hidden place - embrace it as sacred ground where God does His deepest work. The world celebrates what is seen, applauds what is loud, and rewards what is immediate, but heaven often moves in quiet places, away from the spotlight. It is in the hidden place that distractions lose their grip and your vision becomes clear. There, without the pressure to perform or impress, your heart is refined, your motives are purified, and your character is strengthened. What feels like isolation is often divine preparation. Lean into the hidden place, for it is there that a man learns to truly hear the voice of God. When the noise of the world fades, His whisper becomes unmistakable. In that stillness, direction is given, identity is confirmed, and purpose is awakened. The hidden place is not where you are forgotten - it is where you are formed. And when God brings you out of it, you will not step forward empty, but equipped with clarity, conviction, and a strength that was forged in silence with Him.

True strength is not forged in moments of applause, but in the quiet, unseen choices made day after day. Long before there is any outward evidence of growth, God is shaping something deep within - refining motives, strengthening resolve, and anchoring the heart in truth. What feels small and insignificant in the moment is often the very thing heaven is using to prepare you for something greater. Daily obedience, quiet consistency, and unwavering commitment form the rhythm of a life that honors God. It is in the repetition of righteous habits that character is solidified and integrity becomes second nature. The man who shows up, prays, works, and stands firm when it's hardest is the man who will stand strongest when it matters most. Do not despise the routine or grow weary in the process, for God does His greatest work in the hidden places. Stay faithful in the ordinary, and you will become extraordinary - not by the world's standards, but by heaven's. Strength is not built in a day; it is built daily.

In the quiet moments where no applause is given and no recognition is earned, God is shaping the core of a man. It is there, in unseen decisions and private disciplines, that strength is built layer by layer. Integrity is not developed in public display but in personal surrender. When a man chooses truth when no one is watching, when he remains faithful in obscurity, he is laying a foundation that cannot be shaken. When life begins to test what has been built, the difference becomes clear. The winds will come, the pressure will rise, and the storms will reveal what is real. But the man who was forged in secret will not collapse under the weight - he will stand. Strong, steady, and unmovable, not because of outward appearance, but because of inward strength. What was built in silence will speak in strength. What was developed in private will endure in public. And in the end, it is not the man who was seen the most who stands the longest, but the one who was shaped the deepest when no one else was looking.

| 6 |

"THE WILDERNESS SEASONS"

There are seasons in a man's life when the noise fades, the crowd disappears, and the path ahead becomes unclear. These wilderness moments can feel unsettling, even isolating, but they are not signs of abandonment - they are invitations into deeper intimacy with God. In the quiet, distractions are stripped away, and a man is confronted with what truly lives inside him. It is here that faith is no longer theoretical, but tested and proven. What once depended on applause must now stand on conviction. What once leaned on visibility must now be rooted in trust. The wilderness silences the world so that a man can finally hear the voice of God with clarity and power. These seasons are not designed to break a man, but to build him. In the dryness, God develops endurance. In the uncertainty, He strengthens trust. In the hidden place, He shapes character that can carry future responsibility. What feels like delay is often divine preparation for something greater than a man can currently handle.

The wilderness is not a place of abandonment - it is a place of divine construction. In that quiet and often uncomfortable place, a man begins to see himself clearly, not through the lens of others, but through the truth of who he is before God. What feels like isolation is often an invitation to be reshaped, refined, and rooted in something eternal. In the wilderness, identity is no longer sustained by what a man does, but by who he is becoming. It is here that purpose is forged, not in the spotlight, but in surrender. The distractions fall away, and what remains is raw, honest, and real - a heart laid bare before God. And in that sacred space, God is shaping your character, strengthening your spirit, and preparing you for the purpose only He can fulfill through you. He replaces insecurity with confidence, confusion with clarity, and striving with calling. The wilderness may not be comfortable, but it is essential, for it is where a man learns that he was never defined by the crowd but always destined for purpose.

God sends men into wilderness seasons not to punish them, but to prepare them. In those quiet, uncomfortable places where distractions are stripped away, God begins a deeper work - shaping character, strengthening faith, and refining motives. While we often ask for elevation, influence, and open doors, God understands that promotion without preparation can destroy a man. So He allows seasons of isolation where a man must learn to depend fully on Him. It is there that pride is broken, identity is clarified, and strength is forged in the hidden places. Every moment of waiting, every closed door, and every silent stretch is working together for your development. When a man embraces the process instead of resisting it, he emerges not weaker, but stronger - anchored in God rather than circumstance. The wilderness is not where you are forgotten; it is where you are formed, equipped, and made ready for the assignment only a prepared man can carry.

In the wilderness, a man is stripped of every false support he once leaned on. Comfort is gone, distractions are silenced, and the noise of the world fades into stillness. Hunger teaches dependence, waiting builds endurance, and silence sharpens spiritual hearing. What once felt like lack becomes divine training. In that place, a man discovers that God is not just present in abundance - He is faithful in absence, steady in stillness, and powerful in what seems like nothing. These wilderness lessons carve strength into the soul that comfort could never produce. Success may elevate a man publicly, but the wilderness transforms him privately. It humbles pride, refines motives, and anchors identity in God alone. When a man emerges from that season, he carries a depth, a clarity, and a resilience that cannot be shaken. He no longer fears the quiet or the unknown, because he has met God there. And what was once a barren place becomes the very ground where unshakable faith was forged.

The spiritual desert has a way of stripping away everything that once made a man feel strong, revealing what lies beneath the surface. In seasons of comfort, weaknesses can remain hidden behind routine, success, or outward appearances. But when God leads a man into the desert, the silence, the pressure, and the isolation expose what is truly in his heart. It is there that shallow faith is uncovered, impure motives are brought into the light, and self-reliance is revealed for what it is - insufficient. What once seemed like strength is tested, and what cannot endure begins to break. Though the process is uncomfortable, even painful, it is a necessary step in true transformation. God does not reveal weakness to shame, but to refine. He exposes the cracks so they can be repaired, the impurities so they can be purified, and the misplaced trust so it can be redirected back to Him. In the desert, a man learns to depend fully on God, not as an idea, but as his source of strength, provision, and identity.

In the wilderness, a man is stripped of every distraction that once competed for his attention. In the stillness, a man discovers that God has been speaking all along - he simply could not hear Him over the noise. The wilderness becomes a divine classroom where listening replaces striving, and intimacy replaces performance. In that place, direction is no longer guided by what the eyes can see, but by what the heart learns to trust. The familiar markers are gone, and each step forward becomes an act of faith, not because the path is visible, but because the One who leads is faithful. The wilderness teaches a man to walk by trust, not by sight, to move when God says move, and to wait when God says wait. It is there that his spiritual senses sharpen, his faith deepens, and his confidence shifts from his own understanding to God's perfect wisdom. What feels like isolation is actually divine alignment, preparing him to walk with clarity, conviction, and unshakable trust.

The road in the wilderness is rarely straight. It bends through valleys of uncertainty, climbs hills of resistance, and winds through seasons that seem to defy logic. In those moments, a man can feel disoriented, questioning whether he has missed God or taken a wrong turn. But every twist is shaping something in you. What feels like chaos to you is a carefully designed path where God is building endurance, character, and unshakable faith. God is never confused by the road you are on. He sees the end from the beginning, and every step has already been accounted for in His divine plan. What feels uncertain to you is perfectly ordered by Him. The winding path is not a sign that you are lost - it is evidence that you are being led. Stay faithful in the bends. Keep walking through the unknown. Because on the other side of the wilderness, you will not just arrive at a destination - you will emerge as the man God intended you to become, refined, strengthened, and fully prepared for what lies ahead.

Trust becomes the currency of the wilderness because everything else is stripped away. In seasons where clarity is gone, a man is forced to lean fully on God. The wilderness exposes the limits of human strength and reveals the necessity of divine guidance. When the path disappears and the future is hidden, trust becomes the only way forward. It is in these barren places that a man learns that God is not just present in the promise, but faithful in the process. When a man cannot see what lies ahead, he must rely on the One who does. Faith is no longer an idea he talks about - it becomes the breath he lives by. Each step forward is an act of surrender, each decision a declaration that God's wisdom is greater than his own. In the wilderness, faith matures from theory into survival. It becomes daily, intentional, and unwavering. And through that process, God shapes a man who no longer depends on what he sees, but on who He knows - preparing him for a future that requires unshakable trust.

In these seasons, God slows a man down not to frustrate him, but to form him. What once felt like urgency is revealed to be immaturity, and what he called delay is actually divine development. The man who used to rush ahead, driven by impulse or ambition, begins to understand that God is not in a hurry and neither should he be. In the waiting, his character is refined, his motives are purified, and his dependence on God deepens. He learns that patience is an active trust that God is working even when nothing seems to be moving. Through this process, he comes to see that timing is just as sacred as obedience. It is not enough to do the right thing - he must do it at the right time. Moving too soon can open doors God never intended him to walk through, while waiting on God positions him for favor, clarity, and strength. In patience he gains direction. And when the moment finally comes to move, he steps forward not with reckless haste, but with confidence, knowing that he is aligned with God's perfect timing.

The wilderness is where endurance is forged in the quiet, unseen places of the soul. It is where comfort is stripped away and faith is stretched beyond what feels sustainable. In the wilderness, you learn that endurance is not about feeling strong, but about choosing to keep walking when everything in you wants to stop. It is in these moments that your roots grow deeper, your faith becomes steadier, and your dependence on God becomes unshakable. Resilience is not built by escaping hardship, but by walking through it hand in hand with God. Every difficult step, every weary moment, every silent cry is shaping something within you that comfort never could. The wilderness teaches you to trust God when you cannot trace Him, to believe when you cannot see, and to stand when you feel like falling. What feels like a season of depletion is actually a season of divine construction. God is building endurance in you that will carry you into greater purpose, greater strength, and greater impact.

Provision in the wilderness rarely looks like what a man expects. It does not come in overflowing barns or visible security, but in quiet, consistent supply - just enough for today. In those barren seasons, God strips away dependence on comfort and replaces it with reliance on Him. What feels like lack is often divine training. The wilderness teaches a man to recognize that God's hand is still present, even when resources seem scarce. Every small provision becomes a reminder that he is seen, sustained, and never abandoned. God's goal is not to overwhelm a man with abundance, but to anchor him in trust. Daily bread requires daily faith. It calls a man to wake up each day believing that what God provided yesterday, He will provide again today. In this rhythm, strength is built, character is refined, and faith becomes steady. The wilderness reveals a powerful truth: when a man learns to trust God for enough, he will never fear not having more.

The desert strips away the noise, the comforts, and the illusions a man often leans on without realizing it. In that barren place, the heart can no longer hide behind convenience or routine - it must confront what it truly trusts. Whether it is pride, control, approval, or material security, the desert has a way of bringing every hidden dependency into the light. What once felt strong is tested, and what was shallow begins to crumble. In that sacred place of refining, idols begin to fall and true devotion is forged. When everything else is removed, a man is invited to lean fully on God as his only source. It is here that faith becomes real, not theoretical - where trust is no longer spoken, but lived. The desert becomes a proving ground where dependence on God replaces dependence on self. And from that place, a deeper strength is born - one rooted not in circumstance, but in unwavering trust. What emerges from the desert is not the same man who entered, but one who has been purified, anchored, and fully devoted.

There is a refining fire in the wilderness, and it is not sent to destroy you - it is sent to transform you. The wilderness exposes what success and strength can often conceal - pride, self-reliance, and false confidence. Yet this is not loss - it is purification. The fire burns not to consume you, but to cleanse you, removing everything that cannot stand in the presence of God's purpose for your life. What emerges from that fire is a different man - one who no longer leans on his own understanding but walks in humble dependence on God. His strength is no longer rooted in ego, but in surrender. His confidence is no longer loud and self-made, but quiet and unshakable because it is anchored in truth. The wilderness does not leave him weaker; it leaves him refined - stronger in spirit, clearer in vision, and purer in heart. He becomes a man God can trust, not because he has everything figured out, but because he has been emptied of himself and filled with something far greater.

In the quiet, barren places where distractions fade and certainty disappears, a deeper work begins. What a man loses in comfort, he gains in character - resilience is forged, discipline is sharpened, and endurance is built. The wilderness exposes what is fragile and refines what is lasting. It is not a punishment, but a divine process where God shapes a man into someone stronger, wiser, and more grounded than before. In the wilderness, a man comes face to face with his limitations and learns to lean fully on God. Plans no longer go as expected, and outcomes cannot be forced, but it is here that a man learns to walk by faith and not by sight, to listen more closely, and to depend more deeply. The wilderness teaches him that God is not absent in the silence, but powerfully present in the process. And when he emerges, he does not come out empty - he comes out transformed, carrying within him a strength and trust that could only be gained in the wilderness.

God never wastes a wilderness season. What feels like delay is often divine development, where God is shaping strength in silence and forging character in obscurity. Every unanswered question is an invitation to trust deeper, to walk by faith when sight is limited. In the wilderness, God strips away distractions, pride, and self-reliance so that what remains is a man fully dependent on Him. It is in these barren places that roots grow deeper, conviction becomes unshakable, and identity is no longer defined by circumstances but by calling. God is working behind the scenes, aligning your heart, refining your motives, and equipping you for greater responsibility. What feels like silence is often sacred instruction. When the season shifts - and it will - you will step forward not as the man you were, but as the man you were being prepared to become. The wilderness is not your end; it is your proving ground, and on the other side of it lies purpose, strength, and a calling that could not have been fulfilled any other way.

Preparation often unfolds in the quiet places where no applause is heard and no audience is watching. While the world celebrates visibility, heaven values integrity formed in secrecy. A man may feel overlooked, but he is not forgotten; he is being developed. Just as roots grow unseen beneath the surface before a tree ever rises tall, so God establishes a firm foundation in the private moments of surrender, discipline, and obedience. In that lonely stretch, distractions are stripped away, and dependence on God becomes essential. It is there that endurance is forged, identity is clarified, and trust is deepened. What God builds in obscurity becomes the strength that sustains a man in visibility. When the time comes for him to step into greater responsibility, he will not be shaken, because his foundation was not built on applause, but on truth. The hidden work always precedes the public assignment, and those who embrace the wilderness will be ready when their moment arrives.

When a season comes to an end, it leaves behind more than memories - it leaves transformation. The man who walks out of that chapter is no longer who he once was. The trials he endured have stripped away pride, fear, and self-reliance, replacing them with humility, endurance, and a deeper dependence on God. What once confused him has now clarified him. What once weakened him has now strengthened him. In the quiet battles and unseen struggles, God was refining his character, sharpening his discernment, and anchoring his faith in something unshakable. He may not have understood it while he was in it, but looking back, he can now see that every moment had purpose. Now he stands on the other side with a stronger resolve and a clearer vision. His faith is no longer shallow or situational - it is rooted, tested, and proven. The season did not break him; it built him. And now, he moves forward not as who he was, but as who God has called him to become.

If you find yourself in a wilderness season, do not resist it - embrace it. In the quiet places where distractions are stripped away, God strengthens your character and teaches you to depend on Him in ways comfort never could. The wilderness is where faith is no longer theory but necessity, where trust is built not on what you see, but on who He is. Every moment in that dry place is shaping you for something greater than you can currently understand. Do not mistake the wilderness for abandonment - it is alignment. God is positioning you, preparing you, and equipping you for the assignment ahead. Just as warriors are trained before the battle and leaders are forged before they are revealed, so are you being formed in this season. The wilderness is not your end - it is your becoming. Stay faithful, stay obedient, and stay expectant, because the same God who led you into this season will lead you out of it, stronger, wiser, and ready to walk boldly into the purpose He has prepared for your life.

| 7 |

"THE BATTLE FOR YOUR MIND"

The fiercest battles a man will ever face are often the ones no one else can see - the silent wars fought in the hidden chambers of his mind. It is there that thoughts either rise up in truth or fall into deception, where fear wrestles with faith, and doubt challenges destiny. The enemy knows that if he can control a man's thoughts, he can weaken his resolve, distort his identity, and delay his purpose. But when a man anchors his mind in truth - when he disciplines his thoughts and aligns them with what God says - he begins to win battles that shape his future long before the world ever sees the result. What is conquered internally will eventually manifest externally. A man who learns to guard his mind, renew his thoughts, and stand firm in truth becomes unshakable, regardless of what surrounds him. He understands that the battlefield within is not a place of defeat, but a proving ground where God refines him, equips him, and prepares him for greater victories ahead.

The mind is a battlefield, and loneliness often becomes the terrain where that battle intensifies. When a man walks a solitary path, the silence can either strengthen him or slowly begin to erode his confidence. In those quiet moments, thoughts grow louder, doubts whisper, fears exaggerate, and past failures attempt to rewrite his identity. Yet, this same silence can become sacred ground if he learns to master it. It is here that a man must choose what voice he will agree with.

Will he entertain the lies that tell him he is forgotten, incapable, or alone? Or will he anchor himself in truth - that God is near, that his life has purpose, and that this season is not punishment but preparation? The battle is not against loneliness itself, but against the thoughts that try to define him within it. A man who wins in his mind will not be defeated in his life. Loneliness, when surrendered to God, becomes a forge rather than a prison. It sharpens discernment, builds resilience, and deepens dependence on the Lord.

Loneliness has a voice. It tells you that you've been overlooked, that others have moved ahead while you remain stuck, that somehow you are less than what you were meant to be. These thoughts do not arrive loudly - they creep in quietly, repeating themselves until they begin to feel familiar. But these whispers are not truth; they are distortions designed to pull you away from your identity, your purpose, and your worth. If left unchecked, those whispers will grow louder, shaping your perspective and influencing your decisions. That is why you must confront them with truth. Speak over your life what God has already declared - that you are chosen, seen, and deeply loved. Refuse to let isolation redefine your identity. Even in seasons where you feel alone, God is working in the unseen, strengthening your character and preparing your path. Loneliness may try to convince you that you are not enough, but the truth is this: in Christ, you are more than enough, and your story is still unfolding exactly as it should.

In the quiet places where no voices affirm you and no crowds applaud you, your true foundation is uncovered. It is there that your beliefs are no longer theoretical but tested. What you say you trust in is weighed against what you actually cling to when all comfort is stripped away. Loneliness becomes a mirror, reflecting the condition of your faith, your thought life, and your identity. It exposes whether your strength is rooted in God or in the approval, presence, and validation of others. But this place is not meant to break you - it is meant to build you. In loneliness, God invites you into a deeper, more authentic relationship with Him, one that is not sustained by emotion or environment, but by truth. It is here that your faith is refined, your mind renewed, and your confidence anchored in Him alone. When you learn to stand firm in the silence, you emerge stronger, clearer, and unshakable. What once felt like isolation becomes transformation, and the battlefield of loneliness becomes the birthplace of unwavering belief.

In these moments, discouragement often whispers lies that feel louder than truth. It tries to convince you that your labor is in vain, that nothing is changing, and that what you are building carries no weight. But what discouragement cannot see is what God is doing beneath the surface. Just as roots grow deep before fruit appears, your unseen faithfulness is strengthening you in ways that will soon become evident. Every quiet act of obedience, every time you choose to keep going when it would be easier to quit, is laying a foundation that cannot be shaken. Do not allow discouragement to drain what God has placed within you. The same God who called you is the One who sustains you, and He does not abandon the work He begins. This season is not a sign of failure; it is a proving ground where endurance is being built and character is being refined. Stay steady, stay rooted, and refuse to give discouragement the final word because what God has spoken over your life will stand.

Doubt often slips in quietly after discouragement has worn your strength down. When your spirit is tired and your expectations feel unmet, doubt begins to whisper questions that seem reasonable but are rooted in fear, "Did God really call you? Are you truly capable?" What began as a moment of discouragement can quickly turn into a crisis of identity if doubt is allowed to take root. Doubt disguises itself as reflection, but its goal is to erode your confidence in God and in who He has called you to be. But doubt does not have to win. Return to what God has spoken, not what your emotions are saying in the moment. Your calling is not invalidated by a difficult season, and your identity is not determined by temporary setbacks.

God's promises are not fragile - they are established, unchanging, and faithful even when you feel weak. Refuse to entertain what contradicts truth and instead anchor your mind in what is eternal. In doing so, you silence the voice of doubt and strengthen the voice of faith within you.

Not every thought that crosses your mind carries truth or authority. Some thoughts are born out of fear, shaped by past wounds, or whispered by the enemy in an attempt to distort your identity and weaken your faith. Just because a thought is loud does not mean it is right. The battlefield of your life is often within your mind, where lies disguise themselves as truth and emotions try to take the place of discernment. But you are not called to believe everything you think - you are called to examine it. When a thought tells you that you are not enough, that you will never change, or that God has forgotten you, you must pause and measure it against the truth of God's Word. Learn to recognize these thoughts for what they are - intruders, not residents. You have authority through Christ to reject what does not align with truth and to replace it with what is pure, powerful, and life-giving. Take every thought captive and bring it into obedience, refusing to let fear or lies take root in your heart.

A man who wins the battle of his mind does not blindly accept whatever thought enters his mind, because he knows that thoughts can be influenced by fear, past wounds, lies, or the enemy's deception. Instead, he becomes a gatekeeper - examining each thought carefully, questioning its origin, and asking whether it aligns with truth. He knows that victory is found in choosing which thoughts to believe and which ones to cast down. This is why he refuses to be ruled by impulse or emotion, choosing instead to filter his thinking through the lens of God's Word. In doing so, he takes authority over his inner world rather than being controlled by it. This man measures every thought against truth - what God says, not what fear whispers. When doubt arises, he confronts it with faith. When discouragement speaks, he answers with hope. When lies try to take root, he uproots them with truth. This is the discipline of a renewed mind - a daily, intentional practice of rejecting what is false and embracing what is life-giving.

The renewal of your mind is not a one-time moment of inspiration - it is a daily, intentional discipline. Just as your body weakens without consistent nourishment, your mind becomes vulnerable when it is not continually fed with truth. If you are not actively renewing your mind through God's Word, through prayer, and through intentional reflection, you will drift toward discouragement, fear, and confusion. Renewal is a choice to reject lies, to confront negative thinking, and to replace it with what is true, pure, and life-giving. When you commit to this daily discipline, your thinking becomes clearer, your perspective becomes stronger, and your spirit becomes steadier. You begin to see yourself and your circumstances through the lens of faith rather than fear. This consistent renewal reshapes not only your thoughts but your entire life. The battles you once struggled with lose their power because your mind is no longer a battlefield of confusion - it becomes a place of clarity, strength, and alignment with God's truth.

Truth is your weapon. It is sharp, unchanging, and powerful. In a world filled with noise, deception, and fear, truth cuts through the confusion and exposes what is real. When you anchor yourself in God's Word, fear begins to lose its grip, and the shadows that once seemed overwhelming are brought into the light. As you consistently fill your mind with God's truth, something begins to shift within you. Your perspective changes. You no longer see yourself through the lens of failure or limitation, but through the promises and identity God has spoken over you. Your situation may not immediately change, but your understanding of it does - you begin to see purpose where there was pain, opportunity where there was opposition, and hope where there was heaviness. Truth restores clarity. It realigns your thinking with heaven's perspective and empowers you to walk forward with confidence, knowing that what God has said is greater than anything you feel or face.

Not every thought that enters your mind was sent to guide you. Some arrive as distractions, doubts, or quiet whispers of fear. You are not responsible for their arrival, but you are responsible for what you entertain. Just as a gatekeeper stands watch over a city, you must stand watch over your mind. When a thought comes that contradicts truth, identity, or purpose, you have the authority to reject it. You do not have to give it a seat at your table. Instead, you can choose thoughts that align with faith and the promises of God. The battle is not in the arrival of the thought - it is in the agreement with it. What you allow to remain will begin to take root, and what takes root will eventually bear fruit in your life. Your mind is like soil - whatever you plant and nurture will grow. So uproot what is harmful, and cultivate what is life-giving. Fill your mind with what is pure, strong, and hopeful. Over time, your thoughts will shape your beliefs, your beliefs will shape your actions, and your actions will shape the man you become.

Guarding your thoughts is a deliberate act of spiritual discipline. Every day, your mind becomes a battlefield where truth and deception compete for influence. You cannot afford to let every thought settle in unchecked. Instead, you must stand watch over your mind with vigilance and awareness, recognizing that what you consistently entertain will shape who you become. The thoughts you allow to take root will either strengthen your faith or weaken your resolve. To guard your mind is to take responsibility for the direction of your inner life, choosing to align your thinking with truth rather than emotion, fear, or false narratives. This kind of guarding requires courage - the courage to confront lies, reject negativity, and cast down anything that contradicts what God has spoken over you. When you guard your thoughts with courage, you create space for peace, clarity, and strength to grow. In doing so, you position yourself to walk in alignment with God's will, no longer controlled by every passing thought.

Many men do not fall in a single moment of weakness - they fall slowly, quietly, in the hidden battlefield of the mind. Long before defeat shows up in their actions, it has already taken root in their thoughts. Negativity whispers lies that erode confidence. Comparison steals identity and replaces it with insecurity. Fear magnifies obstacles until they feel insurmountable. When these thoughts go unchallenged, they become patterns of thinking that shape decisions, reactions, and ultimately destiny. A man who allows his mind to drift without discipline will find himself living a life directed by doubt instead of purpose. But the victory is just as real, and it begins in the same place. When a man takes authority over his thoughts, he begins to reclaim authority over his life. He learns to embrace his God-given identity and to confront fear with faith. The mind must be renewed daily for what a man consistently thinks, he will eventually become. Win the war in your mind, and you will begin to win the battles in your life.

You are not at the mercy of every thought that enters your mind. God has entrusted you with the ability to govern what you dwell on, what you believe, and what you allow to take root in your heart. When you align your thinking with God's truth, you begin to see clearly, stand firmly, and move forward with confidence, knowing that your mind is no longer a battlefield you are losing - but one you are learning to win. Choosing truth is declaring that God's Word has the final say, not your feelings, not your past, and not your circumstances. When fear tries to rise, you answer it with faith. When confusion clouds your direction, you return to purpose. This is how transformation happens - one thought at a time. As you take control of your mind, peace will replace anxiety, confidence will replace insecurity, and direction will replace wandering. As you consistently choose what is true, right, and life-giving, you will walk in the freedom and victory that God has already made available to you.

In your loneliest moments, when silence feels heavy and the path ahead seems empty, you must remind yourself that what feels like isolation is often divine preparation. It is here, away from the applause and affirmation of others, that your roots grow deeper. Loneliness may feel like loss, but in God's hands, it becomes a sacred space where identity is clarified, purpose is sharpened, and dependence on Him is solidified. God often does His deepest work in the quiet places because that is where your heart is most attentive. When there are no crowds to impress and no voices to influence you, His voice becomes clearer. In those still moments, He speaks life, direction, and truth into your spirit. You are not being overlooked - you are being prepared for something greater than you can currently see. Trust the process. Embrace the stillness. For when the season of quiet is complete, you will emerge stronger, wiser, and ready to walk boldly in the calling God has been shaping within you all along.

Discouragement feeds on silence, but it loses its power when confronted with the promises of God. Speak what is true, even when you don't feel it. Remind your soul that God is faithful, that He has not abandoned you, and that what He began in you, He will finish. Truth is not based on your emotions - it is anchored in God's unchanging Word. So when your heart feels heavy and your thoughts grow dark, let truth become your weapon. Declare it. Meditate on it. Let it reshape the atmosphere of your mind. When doubt begins to speak, answer it with conviction. Do not entertain every thought that passes through your mind, for not every voice deserves your attention. Your spirit was never designed to live in fear, confusion, or defeat. You were created to walk in clarity, confidence, and faith. Guard your mind with diligence, and refuse to drift into places of worry, insecurity, or despair. Instead, anchor your thoughts in what is pure, strong, and life-giving.

The man who masters his mind becomes unshakable because he has learned where true strength is found. While others are tossed by fear, anger, and uncertainty, he stands firm, rooted in what God has spoken rather than what he feels. He understands that thoughts are seeds, and what he allows to take root will shape his life. So he guards his mind with diligence, rejecting lies and renewing his thinking with truth. This kind of man is not emotionless, but he is disciplined. He feels deeply, yet he is not controlled by what he feels. His purpose leads, and his emotions follow. When doubt whispers, he answers with truth. When pressure rises, he leans into purpose. His life becomes a reflection of inner order, where clarity replaces confusion and peace overcomes chaos. Anchored in truth and guided by purpose, he walks with authority, resilience, and unwavering focus becoming a man who cannot be easily shaken because he has already conquered the battlefield within.

Win the battle within, and you will change the course of your life. The greatest victories are in the quiet, unseen places of your heart and mind. When you allow God to renew your thinking, lies lose their power and clarity begins to break through like light at dawn. You start to see not as your circumstances dictate, but as God has declared. Your identity becomes anchored, your purpose becomes steady, and your perspective shifts from limitation to possibility. As your mind is renewed, your strength is restored by the power of a transformed inner life. No longer are you driven by fear of failure. Instead, you move forward with a confidence rooted in faith, trusting that God is guiding your steps and shaping your journey. The path ahead may still require courage, but it is no longer clouded by uncertainty or controlled by anxiety. When faith takes the lead, your decisions align with purpose, your steps carry conviction, and your life begins to reflect the victory that was first secured within.

| 8 |

"STRENGTH THROUGH DISCIPLINE"

Discipline is the backbone of masculine leadership. It is the hidden strength that forms a man in the unseen places. It is built in the early mornings when no one is watching, in the quiet decisions to stay consistent when motivation fades, and in the choice to honor God even when it is inconvenient. While charisma may draw people in and talent may create opportunity, it is discipline that refines character, aligns a man with purpose, and establishes a foundation that cannot be shaken. A disciplined man becomes a pillar others can rely on because his life is not driven by emotion but anchored in conviction. He understands that every small act of consistency is shaping his future, and every act of self-control is strengthening his authority. Over time, discipline produces clarity, endurance, and quiet confidence. When storms come, it is not the gifted or the loud who endure, but the disciplined. For it is discipline that sustains growth and enables a man to lead with strength, integrity, and unwavering faith.

A disciplined man does not wait for motivation - he moves by commitment. He understands that motivation is unreliable, rising and falling with circumstances, emotions, and comfort. But commitment is rooted in purpose, and purpose is anchored in something far greater than how he feels in the moment. His strength is not found in bursts of inspiration, but in the quiet, consistent decisions to do what is right. When emotions fluctuate, discipline becomes his compass. It keeps him aligned with truth when feelings try to lead him astray. A disciplined man chooses obedience over impulse, purpose over pleasure, and growth over comfort. He builds his life on steady habits, daily surrender, and unwavering focus. In doing so, he reflects a deeper spiritual truth: that faithfulness is proven not in moments of passion, but in a lifetime of consistency. And through that discipline, he becomes a man who is not easily shaken - a man grounded, reliable, and ready for whatever God calls him to do.

Masculine leadership is revealed in the unseen moments, in the daily decisions that no one applauds. A man who leads well understands that leadership begins within, forged in the discipline of his own thoughts, habits, and choices. When he chooses to rise despite fatigue, to act despite doubt, and to remain faithful in the small things, he builds a foundation that cannot be shaken. His strength is not in overpowering others, but in mastering himself. This kind of leadership carries weight because it is consistent. It shows up day after day, long after emotions fade and excuses present themselves. It is a commitment to finish what was started, to honor responsibility, and to walk in integrity whether anyone notices or not. A man who leads himself well becomes a man others can trust to lead them. His life speaks louder than his words. And in that steady, unwavering pursuit of what is right, he reflects the kind of leadership that transforms not just his own life but the lives of those who follow his example.

Discipline is formed in the quiet, unseen decisions that shape a man's character day by day. It is forged in the early mornings when no one is watching, in the choice to rise when it would be easier to stay still, and in the steady commitment to do what is right rather than what is convenient. These small, consistent acts become the framework of strength within him. They train his mind, sharpen his resolve, and align his life with purpose. A disciplined man does not drift - he directs his steps with intention, understanding that every choice, no matter how small, is laying a foundation for who he is becoming. Discipline becomes the steel within his spirit, enabling him to stand firm when pressure comes and remain steady when others waver. He learns that compromise weakens, but conviction strengthens; that comfort may feel good in the moment, but growth produces lasting power. Over time, these repeated decisions form a life marked by integrity, resilience, and purpose.

Daily habits are the quiet training ground where discipline is forged and character is revealed. What a man repeatedly does when no one is watching are the very actions that shape the trajectory of his life. Discipline is not built in a single act of strength, but in the steady rhythm of obedience to what is right. A man who honors God in the ordinary moments - rising with purpose, stewarding his time wisely, feeding his mind with truth, and choosing integrity over convenience - is laying bricks that will one day become an unshakable foundation. A disciplined man understands that every habit carries weight. He guards his time because it is a gift, his thoughts because they guide his direction, and his actions because they define his legacy. He refuses to live carelessly, knowing that small compromises lead to great collapse, but small acts of faithfulness lead to lasting strength. What he practices daily, he becomes permanently: a man of strength, consistency, and unwavering purpose in the hands of God.

A man who desires to lead cannot drift through his days - he must rise with intention. Waking up with purpose sets the tone for everything that follows. When he feeds his mind with truth, he sharpens his discernment and anchors his thoughts in what is right, not what is easy. When he strengthens his body, he honors the vessel God has given him and builds the endurance required to carry responsibility. And when he seeks God daily, he aligns his spirit with divine wisdom, drawing strength that goes far beyond his own ability. These are sacred disciplines that form the backbone of a man's life. Without these foundations, leadership becomes fragile and inconsistent. But with them, a man becomes steady, focused, and resilient. Every intentional morning becomes a declaration that he will not live passively, he will not lead carelessly, and he will not neglect the calling on his life. Instead, he builds daily - mind, body, and spirit - becoming the kind of man others can trust, follow, and depend on.

There is power in routine, though it rarely feels glamorous in the moment. The world celebrates spontaneity and dramatic breakthroughs, but the disciplined man understands that true transformation is usually quiet, consistent, and unseen. He rises when he doesn't feel like it, prays when no one is watching, works when others are waiting for motivation, and shows up day after day with unwavering commitment. In those repeated, ordinary moments, something extraordinary is taking place - his character is being forged, his spirit strengthened, and his foundation solidified. What feels like monotony is actually mastery in motion. Greatness is not built in flashes of intensity but in faithful repetition over time. Just as a river carves through rock not by force but by persistence, so a man becomes strong through steady obedience and disciplined habits. Every small act of faithfulness compounds and every day he stays the course; he steps closer to the man he is called to become.

Discipline is the training ground where a man learns to rule himself before he ever attempts to lead anything else. Without discipline a man will be pulled by every impulse, weakened by every craving, and scattered by every temporary desire that promises satisfaction but delivers emptiness. He becomes reactive instead of intentional, living at the mercy of his feelings rather than anchored in purpose. But discipline interrupts that cycle. It sharpens his mind, strengthens his resolve, and aligns his actions with the man God has called him to be. Through discipline, his choices become deliberate, his reactions measured, and his path directed instead of random. This is where true strength is formed - not in bursts of motivation, but in consistent obedience and self-control. Over time, discipline shapes not only his habits, but his character, and ultimately his destiny. A disciplined man does not just hope for a better future - he builds it, one faithful decision at a time.

This is why discipline separates winners from quitters. The disciplined man understands that growth is rarely found in ease, and that God often shapes strength in seasons of pressure. The winner presses forward, not because it feels good, but because it is right. He has trained his mind to obey purpose over emotion, conviction over convenience. In those unseen moments he is being forged into a man who can be trusted with more. The quitter, on the other hand, allows discomfort to dictate direction. When things get hard, he pulls back, seeking relief instead of refinement. The difference between the two is not always talent, gifting, or opportunity - it is endurance. It is the willingness to stay, to fight, to remain steadfast when everything inside says "stop." Discipline anchors a man when feelings fluctuate, and endurance carries him through the fire. And in the end, it is not the one who started with the most ability who stands victorious, but the one who refused to give up when it mattered most.

Many men begin their journey with passion, vision, and bold declarations, but somewhere along the path, the fire fades. It is not because the calling was wrong or the opportunity was insufficient - it is because discipline was absent. Discipline is the unseen strength that sustains a man when motivation runs dry. The beginning is fueled by excitement, but the middle s where true character is forged. This is where discipline becomes the difference between those who drift away and those who press on. A man who finishes well shows up daily, not because he feels like it, but because he has committed to becoming who God called him to be. Discipline teaches him to remain steady when others quit, focused when others get distracted, and faithful when results are delayed. In the end, finishing well is about a lifetime of disciplined obedience. It is the man who endures, who stays the course, and who refuses to give up, that ultimately fulfills his purpose and leaves a lasting legacy.

A disciplined man does not negotiate with excuses because he understands their true nature. He sees that excuses are not harmless thoughts - they are subtle invitations to surrender, cloaked in comfort and convenience. Where others justify delay, he chooses obedience. Where others rationalize weakness, he rises in strength. He does not wait for the perfect moment, the right feeling, or ideal conditions. Instead, he acts in alignment with purpose, knowing that discipline is not built in ease but in resistance. Each time he rejects an excuse, he strengthens his character, sharpens his resolve, and reinforces the man God is calling him to become. Rather than retreating when things grow difficult, he leans in with responsibility and conviction. He understands that growth demands confrontation - confrontation with laziness, fear, doubt, and every internal voice that whispers "not today." Through action, he silences those voices. Through consistency, he builds a life that reflects integrity and strength.

Strength through discipline is about coming into alignment with who God has called you to be. Discipline becomes the bridge between vision and reality, shaping daily decisions so they reflect a higher calling. When a man aligns his habits with truth, he begins to walk with clarity and intention. He no longer drifts through life reacting to circumstances; instead, he moves forward with direction, anchored in conviction. This kind of discipline becomes especially powerful when the noise of the world tries to pull him off course. When challenges mount and the weight feels heavy, discipline keeps him steady and grounded. It trains his spirit to remain faithful in the unseen moments, where true strength is forged. Over time, this alignment produces a man who is dependable, focused, and unwavering - a man whose life reflects consistency, not chaos. And in that consistency, he becomes a living testimony that strength is not found in bursts of effort, but in a life faithfully aligned day after day.

Building a disciplined life is never formed by accident or sustained by emotion alone. It is built through deliberate choices, repeated daily, even when motivation fades. A man must first decide what truly matters - his relationship with God, his character, his calling, and his responsibilities - and then align his time, habits, and energy accordingly. When a man orders his life around eternal priorities rather than temporary desires, he begins to walk in clarity, strength, and direction. This kind of discipline demands unwavering commitment. It requires saying no to distractions, no to comfort that weakens resolve, and yes to the routines that build strength over time. A disciplined man does not drift; he directs his life with intention. And over time, that structure becomes a foundation that cannot easily be shaken. What begins as effort becomes identity, and what is practiced daily becomes who he is. In this way, discipline is not just something a man does - it is something he becomes.

There will be days when every step forward feels like resistance, and the progress you hoped for seems distant and unseen. In those moments, the temptation is to ease up, to wait for motivation to return, or to question whether the effort is even worth it. But discipline was never meant to feel easy; it was meant to shape you. What feels like slow progress is actually steady transformation. Do not despise these heavy days, for they are building a strength that cannot be shaken. Discipline in the hard moments develops resilience, sharpens your character, and anchors your life in purpose rather than emotion. It teaches you to keep moving when feelings fade and to remain faithful when results are delayed. Over time, what once felt like effort becomes part of who you are - a man grounded, steady, and prepared for greater responsibility. Stay the course. What you are building in discipline today is preparing you for the calling you will walk in tomorrow.

God honors discipline because it reveals a heart that is surrendered to His process. A disciplined man is not driven by impulse, but by purpose. He chooses consistency over comfort, obedience over ease, and growth over complacency. Discipline becomes the evidence that a man is willing to be molded, corrected, and strengthened according to God's design. Just as a skilled craftsman patiently refines his work with careful intention, God uses discipline to chisel away weakness and build strength within a man. Every act of self-control, every moment of perseverance, and every commitment to stay the course becomes part of the refining process. Through discipline, a man becomes steady in storms, trustworthy in responsibility, and firm in conviction. What begins as effort becomes identity, and what is practiced in private is revealed in power. In this way, discipline is not restriction - it is transformation in the hands of God.

A disciplined life may feel like a narrow road at first, but it is the very path that leads to true freedom. Discipline trains the heart to choose what is right over what is easy, and in doing so, it aligns a man with God's order rather than the world's confusion. Where there is discipline, there is direction. Where there is direction, there is peace. A man who submits himself to disciplined living is liberated from the very things that once controlled him. Over time, discipline sharpens focus, strengthens character, and builds a foundation that can withstand pressure and adversity. Instead of being driven by emotion or circumstance, a disciplined man is anchored in conviction and guided by intention. His life begins to produce fruit that endures. What once felt like sacrifice becomes strength, and what once required effort becomes identity. In the end, discipline does not take from a man - it gives him back control, purpose, and the freedom to become all that God has called him to be.

The man who embraces discipline becomes unshakable because his life is anchored in truth, not feelings. He does not rise and fall with circumstances, nor is he driven by impulse or convenience. It trains his mind to choose what is right over what is easy, and in doing so, it forms a foundation rooted in principles that do not bend with the winds of adversity. When storms come - and they will - this man does not collapse under pressure. He stands firm, not because the storm is weak, but because his preparation is strong. The trials that shake others only serve to reveal the unshakable strength he has forged within through faith, discipline, and perseverance. His endurance is not accidental; it is cultivated. Through discipline, he has learned to trust God, remain steady, and move forward even when the path is difficult. And in standing firm, he becomes a testimony: that a life built on discipline, guided by faith, and grounded in truth cannot easily be shaken.

Strength through discipline is forged in the quiet, unseen decisions made day after day. In the early mornings, in the hidden battles, and in the moments when no one is watching, he is becoming stronger. God honors this kind of pursuit, because discipline reflects a heart that is surrendered, focused, and willing to be shaped. It is in this daily refining that a man is prepared for greater responsibility and divine assignment. Over time, discipline produces clarity, stability, and unwavering character. The man who commits himself to this path becomes dependable in chaos, steady under pressure, and faithful in his calling. Others begin to recognize in him something rare: integrity that doesn't bend and conviction that doesn't break. He becomes a leader not by title, but by example - a warrior not by force, but by self-mastery. And as he continues to choose discipline each day, he grows into a man that others can trust, follow, and respect, reflecting the strength and order of the God he serves.

| 9 |

"THE LONELINESS OF LEADERSHIP"

Leadership is often admired from a distance where the spotlight highlights strength and confidence. From afar, it appears as influence, recognition, and impact. But up close, leadership carries a weight that few truly understand. It demands decisions that not everyone will agree with, convictions that not everyone will support, and sacrifices that often go unseen. There are moments when a leader must stand firm even when others walk away and remain steady when misunderstood. True leadership is not just about standing in front of people; it is about standing apart when necessary. It is the willingness to walk a path others may not choose, to carry burdens others may not see, and to remain faithful when the journey feels lonely. Yet, the isolation is not without purpose. It is in those solitary places that a leader learns to depend fully on God rather than the approval of others. When God entrusts a man with influence, He first teaches him how to stand alone with unwavering strength, humility, and clarity of purpose.

There is a sacred loneliness that walks hand in hand with responsibility - a quiet, unseen weight that rests on the shoulders of those called to lead, provide, and decide. When no one else fully understands the burden you carry, God does. In those moments when the path is unclear and the voices of others fall silent, His voice becomes clearer. The loneliness is not a sign of abandonment, but an invitation to draw nearer, to listen deeper, and to trust Him more fully than ever before. For it is often in solitude that the most important decisions are made - decisions that shape lives, direct futures, and carry consequences far beyond the moment. Though others may benefit from the outcome, they may never feel the weight of the process. Yet God sees every thought, every struggle, and every step taken in obedience. If you remain faithful in that lonely place, He will strengthen you, guide you, and sustain you. The burden may be yours to carry, but you were never meant to carry it alone.

Throughout scripture, those God used most powerfully were first led into seasons of separation - Abraham leaving his homeland, Moses in the wilderness, David in the fields, and even Jesus withdrawing to lonely places. These moments were sacred spaces where identity was formed, dependence on God was deepened, and clarity of calling was refined. When God separates a leader, He is not isolating them for loss but positioning them for alignment. This separation can feel like loneliness, but it is actually preparation. In the quiet places where applause fades and familiar voices grow distant, God does His deepest work. He strips away distraction, builds resilience, and anchors the leader's heart in Him alone. What feels like distance is often divine development. And in time, what was forged in isolation begins to produce impact in public. The leader emerges not seeking validation from people but carrying authority from God - ready to step into the assignment they were set apart to fulfill.

The path of leadership is not crowded because it demands a price that many admire but few are willing to pay. Influence may look appealing from a distance, but up close it requires sacrifice, discipline, and a willingness to stand alone when necessary. There are moments when the applause fades and when the weight of responsibility presses in with quiet intensity. In those seasons, a true leader is not sustained by recognition, but by conviction. It is in the hidden places that character is refined, motives are purified, and strength is forged. The higher the calling, the narrower the road becomes because greater purpose requires greater surrender. Not everyone will understand your decisions, nor are they meant to walk with you at every level. What feels like loneliness is often God setting you apart for an assignment that requires focus, courage, and unwavering obedience. Stay the course, even when it feels solitary, for the narrow road is sacred ground where God walks closely with those He has called.

There are moments in a leader's life when the voices around him grow loud. Advice may be abundant and opinions well-meaning, but clarity is not found in the crowd. It is found in stillness before God. A true leader must step away from the noise and lean into the presence of the One who sees what others cannot see. For it is God who knows the end from the beginning, who discerns the hidden motives, and who directs the path that others may not yet understand. In those sacred spaces, leadership becomes deeply personal and profoundly spiritual. It is there that a man wrestles not with people, but with purpose. It is there that obedience is forged, even when affirmation is absent. To lead well, you must be willing to stand alone with God before you ever stand strong before men. For when your direction is rooted in divine clarity, you can walk forward with confidence even if you are misunderstood. The crowd may question, but God confirms. And when God confirms, that is enough.

True leadership is revealed in the moments when the path forward is not clear. Difficult decisions are the proving ground of a leader's character. These are not the easy choices between right and wrong, but the agonizing decisions between what feels good and what is required. A true leader does not chase approval or applause but seeks alignment with purpose and conviction. Even when the necessary path is lonely, costly, or misunderstood, they choose it because they understand that leadership is not about pleasing people - it is about stewarding responsibility with integrity before God. A leader must be willing to carry the burden of being misunderstood, knowing that temporary discomfort can produce lasting impact. When guided by wisdom and anchored in faith, these difficult decisions become defining moments shaping not only the leader but also those who follow. For in the end, true leadership is not measured by popularity, but by faithfulness to do what must be done.

A leader must sometimes walk a road that few understand - the narrow path where conviction outweighs comfort. It is the path marked by difficult decisions, unpopular stands, and moments where silence from others feels louder than support. Yet this is often where true leadership is forged. When a man chooses obedience over approval, he aligns himself not with shifting opinions, but with eternal truth. The voices of critics may rise, and misunderstanding may follow, but the leader who is anchored in God does not drift with the winds of public opinion. He stands firm, knowing that faithfulness is more valuable than favor. There will be seasons when doing what is right costs you relationships, reputation, or recognition. In those moments, the temptation to compromise will whisper loudly. But a leader who fears God more than man will not bend. He understands that approval from people is fleeting, but obedience to God carries eternal weight. Even when the path is lonely, it is never empty for God walks it with him.

Misunderstanding is a frequent companion of leadership because true leadership is forged in places others cannot see. People witness the decisions, but they are not present in the long nights of prayer, the wrestling of conscience, or the weight of responsibility carried in silence. They evaluate the outcome without understanding the process, forming opinions without bearing the burden. Yet this is where a leader must remain anchored - not in the approval of others, but in the conviction that comes from God. When you are misunderstood, it does not mean you are wrong; it often means you are walking a path that others have not been called to walk. A faithful leader learns to endure misinterpretation without losing clarity or compassion. Jesus Himself was misunderstood, questioned, and even rejected, yet He never abandoned His assignment. In the same way, you must lead with integrity, even when your motives are doubted and your decisions are criticized.

There will be seasons when your path is misunderstood, when your obedience to God looks strange to those who cannot see what He has shown you. People may question your motives, your decisions, and even your heart but their perspective is limited to what is visible, while your calling is rooted in what is eternal. If you build your identity on the approval of others, you will constantly shift with their opinions. But if you are anchored in your calling, you will stand firm even when the winds of doubt and criticism rise against you. God did not call you to be understood by everyone - He called you to be faithful to Him. Jesus Himself was misunderstood, criticized, and falsely judged, yet He never wavered from His purpose. You must carry that same resolve. Stay steady. Stay obedient. When your heart is aligned with God, you do not need to defend your calling to every voice - you simply need to walk it out with integrity. In time, what is genuine will bear fruit, and what God has ordained will stand.

Leadership requires a strength that is quiet but unshakable. It is the kind of strength that remains anchored in purpose and guided by truth. When pressure builds and uncertainty clouds the path ahead, a true leader does not abandon their post or compromise their values. They become still enough to discern, strong enough to endure, and disciplined enough to move forward with wisdom rather than impulse. This steady strength is forged through prayer, perseverance, and a deep trust that God is at work even when clarity feels distant. In those moments when the way forward is unclear, leadership becomes less about having all the answers and more about choosing faith over fear, patience over panic, and resolve over retreat. A steady leader becomes a refuge for others - a calm presence in chaos, a voice of assurance in uncertainty. As they remain grounded, trusting God through every unknown, they not only navigate the storm - they become the example others look to when the winds begin to rise.

There are responsibilities leaders carry that cannot be fully explained to those who have never stood in that place. A true leader often walks with this invisible burden, making decisions in discernment, prayer and faith, even when clarity is incomplete. They must move forward not because everything is certain, but because they are called. In these moments, leadership becomes less about position and more about trusting that God, who gave the vision, will also supply the strength to carry it. Yet within that weight is also a sacred privilege. God does not entrust such responsibility lightly; He places it on those He is shaping, strengthening, and refining. God walks with them sustaining what He has assigned. The pressure that feels overwhelming is often the very tool He uses to deepen dependence and sharpen obedience. When leaders feel the strain of responsibility, they must remember that in the hands of God, the burden becomes a platform for purpose, and the weight becomes a witness of His trust.

There are moments in leadership when the world around you is quiet, yet your mind is anything but. While others rest, you find yourself awake, carrying decisions that no one else can see and few would fully understand. This is the unseen cost of leadership - the private weight of responsibility that doesn't make announcements or seek applause. In those late hours, it can feel isolating, even overwhelming. Yet it is often in these hidden moments that God does His deepest work in you. He refines your discernment, strengthens your resolve, and draws you closer to His voice. What feels like pressure is shaping you into a vessel capable of carrying greater purpose. Do not mistake these quiet burdens as a sign that something is wrong; they are often evidence that something is right. The same God who called you is present in the stillness, guiding your thoughts and anchoring your heart. Instead of resisting these moments, lean into them, pray through them, and listen carefully within them.

God often draws His leaders into quiet places, not to isolate them, but to reveal Himself more clearly. It is in the silence that His voice becomes unmistakable. What feels like loneliness is often divine invitation - a sacred space where distractions fade and intimacy with Him deepens. In those hidden moments, He reminds you that your calling was never sustained by people, but by His presence. In the solitude, God does more than comfort - He strengthens. He builds resilience in your spirit, clarity in your mind, and conviction in your purpose. While others may not see the weight you carry, God not only sees it - He helps you bear it. The quiet becomes a training ground where faith is refined and dependence on Him grows stronger. So do not fear the lonely seasons. Embrace them. For it is there, in the unseen and often uncelebrated moments, that God shapes leaders who can stand firm, lead boldly, and walk faithfully knowing they were never alone to begin with.

It is in the quiet, unseen places that God does His deepest work in a man. When no one is watching, when there is no applause, and when the outcome feels uncertain, character is being shaped with precision. It is there in those hidden moments that integrity is proven, faith is stretched, and trust in God is strengthened. What is developed in private will eventually be revealed in public, but only if it is first forged in truth, humility, and obedience behind the scenes. Leadership is not born in the spotlight; it is cultivated in the shadows where faith must stand on its own. Before God entrusts a man with influence, He develops him in obscurity. In those moments of testing, when doubt whispers and pressure rises, a deeper dependence on God is formed. Trust is no longer theoretical - it becomes personal and unshakable. And when the time comes to step forward, the strength to lead does not come from recognition, but from a foundation built in the unseen, where God alone was enough.

The loneliness of leadership is not a punishment - it is a sacred preparation. In the quiet places where applause fades and affirmation is scarce, God begins to reshape the heart of a leader. He removes the need for constant validation and replaces it with a deeper hunger for His presence. What feels like isolation is often a calling into intimacy where motives are purified, character is strengthened, and identity is rooted not in people, but in Him. In these moments, God is teaching you to stand firm even when no one is clapping, and to lead from conviction rather than comfort. Dependence on the approval of others will always limit the depth of your calling, but dependence on God will sustain it. When a leader learns to draw strength from Him alone, they become unshakable, no longer driven by praise or discouraged by misunderstanding. The loneliness becomes a training ground where trust is forged and faith is refined. God uses it to prepare you to lead with courage and an unwavering reliance on Him.

When you are misunderstood, it can feel like your voice has been lost in the noise of other people's opinions. Yet in that very tension, God draws you closer not to defend yourself, but to refine you. In those moments, you learn that being known by God is far greater than being validated by man. When you are isolated, the distractions fade, the voices quiet, and suddenly there is room to hear Him more clearly. When you are alone, you begin to rediscover the true source of your strength. What once felt like emptiness becomes an encounter. What once felt like weakness becomes empowerment. In solitude, God rebuilds your confidence not in people, but in His presence within you. You realize that you were never truly alone. Strength that comes from God is not shaken by opinions, absence, or silence - it is steady, rooted, and unbreakable. So do not resist these seasons. Embrace them. For in misunderstanding, isolation, and solitude, God is not abandoning you - He is establishing you.

Do not fear the loneliness that comes with your calling, for it is not a sign of abandonment but a mark of distinction. When God sets a man apart, He often draws him away from the noise, the crowds, and the constant affirmation of others so that his identity is rooted in Him alone. Loneliness becomes the sacred space where clarity is formed, where conviction is strengthened, and where purpose is refined. What feels like isolation is often God removing distractions so you can hear His voice more clearly and carry His assignment more faithfully. Embrace the solitude because it is evidence that you are carrying something weighty and significant. Not everyone can walk the path you've been chosen for, and not everyone is meant to understand it. The loneliness you feel today is shaping the strength you will need tomorrow. Stand firm in it, lean into God through it, and recognize it for what it truly is: a sign that your life carries purpose, and your calling is worth the cost.

When your heart is anchored in His will, you are no longer dependent on human approval to move forward. His wisdom becomes your counsel, His peace your confirmation, and His presence your strength. When the crowd fades and the noise quiets, you are not lacking - you are positioned. For the one who walks in step with God carries within them everything necessary to lead with purpose, conviction, and authority. So walk boldly, even when the road is quiet and the journey feels solitary. Do not mistake isolation for abandonment; often, it is divine refinement. God will sometimes remove the noise so you can hear Him more clearly, stripping away distractions to strengthen your dependence on Him alone. There is a sacred confidence that comes from knowing you are aligned with heaven, even when misunderstood on earth. Stand firm and lead without fear because when God goes before you and walks beside you, you are never truly alone, and you are never without what you need.

| 10 |

"FAITH THAT STANDS ALONE"

There comes a defining moment in every man's journey when the noise of the crowd fades and the comfort of affirmation disappears. In that quiet, often uncomfortable place, faith is no longer supported by applause or strengthened by agreement - it is tested in its purest form. This is where true faith is revealed. Not a borrowed belief, not a faith sustained by others, but a deep, unshakable trust in God that stands on its own. Like Abraham, who believed God when there was no evidence and no visible path forward, a man of faith learns to anchor himself in the promises of God rather than the opinions of people. It is in these solitary seasons that strength is forged and conviction is solidified. When no one else sees what you see or believes what you believe, you are invited to walk closer with God than ever before. Your faith becomes less about validation and more about obedience. You keep moving, not because others are cheering you on, but because God has spoken.

True faith is not built on consensus; it is built on conviction. It is anchored in the unchanging character of God, not the changing opinions of man. When your faith is rooted in Him, it stands firm even in silence, even in opposition, even in seasons where no one else sees what you see. It does not need applause to endure, because it has already been secured by the One who spoke the promise. There will be moments when what God has placed in your heart is misunderstood, unsupported, or even rejected by others. In those moments, you must decide whose voice carries the greatest authority in your life. Faith matures when it learns to stand alone, when it chooses obedience over approval, and when it clings to God's word above every competing voice. Trust Him when it is lonely. Trust Him when it is unclear. Trust Him when it costs you something. For the faith that survives isolation is the faith that will carry you into fulfillment, because it is not sustained by agreement - it is sustained by God Himself.

God will often call you into places where validation is absent, where the voices that once affirmed you grow quiet, and the applause you once heard is replaced by silence or even doubt. In these moments, it can feel unsettling, even isolating, but this is not abandonment, it is divine intention. God is stripping away the need for human approval so that your faith is no longer sustained by people but anchored in Him alone. When validation disappears, clarity is refined. When applause fades, purpose is purified. What feels like loss is often the beginning of a deeper, more authentic walk with God. Do not mistake the absence of affirmation for the absence of God. He is closer in the quiet than He ever was in the noise. In these hidden seasons, He is building a strength within you that cannot be shaken by opinions or circumstances. He is teaching you to move when He speaks, not when others agree; to stand firm when no one understands; to trust His voice above every other.

Holding on to God's promises when you stand alone requires more than belief - it requires spiritual endurance. It is the quiet strength to return again and again to what God has spoken, even when everything around you seems to contradict it. In those lonely moments, you must become your own encourager, rehearsing His promises in your heart until they drown out the noise of doubt. Faith is not sustained by what you see; it is sustained by what God has said. When no one else affirms you, when no evidence appears, and when the silence feels heavy, you anchor yourself in His Word and choose to believe that what He promised is still true. This kind of endurance refuses to let circumstances rewrite the truth. It stands firm when emotions fluctuate and when outcomes delay. It declares that God's voice is final, not your situation. The one who learns to hold fast in isolation develops an unshakable faith - one that is not dependent on applause, agreement, or visible progress.

Abraham is the embodiment of unwavering faith that stands firm when there is no visible evidence to support what God has spoken. When God promised that he would become the father of many nations, everything in the natural world contradicted that word. His body was aged, Sarah's womb was barren, and year after year passed with no sign of fulfillment. Yet Abraham chose to believe not what he could see, but what God had said. He anchored his hope in the character of God, trusting that the One who made the promise was faithful to perform it. This is the essence of real faith - to trust God beyond logic, beyond circumstance, and beyond the limits of human understanding. Abraham's journey teaches us that faith is not built on evidence but on obedience and trust. When nothing around you confirms what God has spoken, that is when your faith is being refined. Hold on. Refuse to let go of the promise. For just as God was faithful to Abraham, He will be faithful to you.

Abraham stood in a place where logic could not support him. His body said one thing, time said another, and reality seemed to contradict the promise. And in that moment, Abraham made a decision that defines true faith: he chose belief over logic. He chose to trust what God said more than what he could see. This is the essence of radical faith - not denying reality but refusing to let reality have the final word. Faith steps beyond human reasoning and anchors itself in the unchanging character of God. There will be moments when what God has promised you will not make sense, when circumstances will challenge your confidence, and when logic will urge you to let go. But radical faith calls you to stand firm anyway - to trust God's word when it feels unreasonable, to believe when there is no evidence, and to hold on when others would walk away. Choose God's word above all else and you will step into a dimension of faith where the impossible becomes possible.

Scripture tells us that Abraham "did not waver through unbelief regarding the promise of God but was strengthened in his faith." This kind of faith is not blind to circumstances - it sees them clearly yet chooses to elevate God's word above them. Abraham looked at his age, his body, and the impossibility surrounding him, but he refused to let what he saw determine what he believed. True faith does not deny reality; it simply refuses to let reality have the final say. It anchors itself in the unchanging character of God, trusting that what He has spoken is greater than what is seen, felt, or understood. This is the kind of faith you are called to walk in - a faith that stands firm when evidence seems contrary, a faith that grows stronger under pressure instead of collapsing beneath it. When doubt whispers and circumstances shout, faith responds by clinging tighter to God's promise. It declares that God is faithful, even when the outcome has not yet appeared.

When no one else believes, your faith must become deeply personal. It is in those quiet, unseen moments that your relationship with God is refined and strengthened. There comes a point where you must stand alone, anchored not in what others say, but in what God has spoken to your heart. This is where faith matures from something you've heard about into something you truly know. In that place, your confidence is no longer dependent on agreement, validation, or visible results. It is rooted in trust - steady, unwavering trust in the character and promises of God. Like Abraham, who believed even when the evidence said otherwise, you are called to hold fast to what God has declared, even when no one else understands. This kind of faith does not need to shout to be seen, for its quiet trust in God carries a strength that moves mountains and endures every storm. It endures and when your faith becomes personal, it becomes unshakable and that is the kind of faith that moves mountains and fulfills destiny.

There will be seasons in your life when the vision God has placed inside you is clearer to you than it is to anyone else. Even those who love you most may not understand what you're pursuing or why you refuse to let go of it. They may question your direction, doubt your calling, or try to pull you back into what feels safe and familiar. But you must remember this: God does not reveal everything to everyone. What He shows you is entrusted to you. Just because others cannot see it does not mean it isn't real. Faith often requires you to walk forward without validation, trusting that what God spoke in private is still true in public. Do not allow the limitations of others' understanding to shrink the magnitude of God's vision in your heart. Stay anchored in what He has spoken. Protect the promise, even when it feels lonely to carry it. Like Abraham, who believed before he saw, you are called to move forward based on God's word - not people's opinions. In time, what God has shown you will speak for itself.

Faith is not anchored in what your eyes can confirm - it is anchored in the unchanging character of God. What you see may shift, delay, or even contradict what you hoped for, but God does not change. His word is not subject to circumstances, and His promises are not weakened by time. True faith rises above the evidence and declares, "If God said it, it is already established," even when the physical reality has yet to catch up. Faith is not wishful thinking; it is confident trust in a faithful God who cannot lie and will not fail. So stand firm, even when the results are not yet visible. Refuse to measure God's faithfulness by what you can currently see. Instead, measure your situation against His word. There is power in believing before the breakthrough, in trusting before the manifestation, and in holding steady when nothing around you seems to be changing. What God has spoken is already in motion. Your role is not to figure it out but to believe, to remain unshaken until what was spoken becomes what is seen.

Trusting God beyond visible evidence is one of the clearest marks of spiritual maturity. It is easy to believe when doors are open, when provision is obvious, and when outcomes align with expectations, but real faith is forged in the moments when nothing adds up. It is in the silence, the waiting, and the uncertainty that your trust is truly tested. In those seasons, God is not asking for your understanding; He is asking for your obedience. To stand when nothing makes sense is to build your life on the unshakable truth that God is always working, even when you cannot see it. When you choose faith over fear, you begin to realize that delays are not denials, and that unseen work is often the most important work God is doing. So keep walking, even in the dark. Keep believing, even when the evidence is absent. Because the same God who called you forward is faithful to lead you through, and what He is building in you is far greater than what you are waiting to see.

You will be tempted to abandon the vision when progress feels painfully slow, as if nothing is moving and your efforts are unseen. In those moments, remember that God often works beneath the surface long before anything becomes visible. Seeds grow in silence before they break through the soil. What feels like stagnation is often God strengthening your roots so that when the time of elevation comes, you will stand firm and unshaken. You will be tempted to compromise when opposition rises and to quit when loneliness settles in like a heavy weight. But pressure does not mean you are off course - it often confirms you are walking in purpose. Stand your ground. Guard the vision God placed in your heart. Even if no one else believes, heaven does. You are never truly alone. God walks with you in the quiet, strengthens you in the struggle, and honors those who refuse to surrender. Stay faithful. Stay focused. Stay committed. The breakthrough will come to those who endure.

The man of faith does not measure God's faithfulness by what he can see - he anchors his trust in who God is. When doors seem closed and progress feels delayed, he does not retreat in frustration or abandon the promise in disappointment. Instead, he stands firm, knowing that heaven's timeline is not bound by human urgency. His confidence is not rooted in visible movement but in the unchanging character of God, who is always working with purpose, precision, and perfect timing. So he waits with expectation, with endurance, and with unwavering belief. He refuses to walk away because he knows that delay is not denial - it is refinement, alignment, and positioning. Beneath the surface, God is arranging what cannot yet be seen, connecting what has not yet come together, and preparing what is not yet ready to be revealed. The man of faith holds his ground, knowing that at the appointed time, what God has promised will come forth. And when it does, it will be worth every moment of the wait.

Refusing to abandon the vision God has placed in your heart is spiritual warfare. Every time doubt whispers, every time circumstances contradict what God has spoken, and every time others question what you carry, your decision to stand firm becomes a bold declaration of faith. It says, "God, I trust You more than what I see, more than what I feel, and more than what anyone else says." Faith is not proven when the path is clear; it is proven when the road is uncertain and you still refuse to turn back. When you refuse to let go of the vision, you align yourself with heaven's authority and resist the enemy's attempts to wear you down. The battle is often internal but your persistence becomes your weapon. You are declaring that what God started, He will finish, and that His word over your life is greater than any obstacle before you. Hold the vision. Guard it. Nurture it in prayer and obedience. Because in doing so, you are not only preserving your future - you are advancing the very will of God in your life.

There is a sacred strength that can only be forged in the quiet places where no applause is heard and no crowd is present. When you stand alone with Him, your faith is refined like gold in the fire. It is tested, stretched, and made pure. In that stillness, you begin to discover that your confidence is not built on what others say or do, but on who God is. His voice becomes clearer, His promises more real, and His presence more sustaining than any external affirmation. In those solitary moments, your faith takes on a deeper root - one that cannot be shaken by doubt, delay, or opposition. You learn to trust God because you have encountered Him personally. What once needed reinforcement from the outside now stands firm on divine truth within you. This is the kind of faith that endures storms, resists fear, and holds steady when everything else falls away. Solitude is not your weakness - it is your proving ground. For when a man learns to stand alone with God, he discovers he is never truly alone at all.

There comes a moment in the journey of faith when what God has spoken in secret is revealed in the open. The promise that once lived only in your heart begins to take shape before your eyes. Those who questioned your path, who doubted your conviction, and who could not see what God showed you will now stand as witnesses to His faithfulness. Not because you proved them wrong, but because God proved Himself true. Faith held in the dark will always shine in the light. Every lonely step, every silent battle, every moment you chose to believe when there was no evidence will speak louder than words. The impossible will become undeniable, not by human effort, but by the power of a God who honors those who trust Him completely. Let it remind you that faith is never wasted, even when it is unseen. For in due time, what God has ordained will rise, and when it does, it will declare to all who witness it: unwavering faith always leads to undeniable fulfillment.

So hold on. Even if you are the only one who believes, you are never truly standing alone because faith anchors you to a God who is greater than the voices around you. When everything around you says it cannot happen, remember that His promises were never dependent on popular opinion or visible evidence. Faith is not proven in agreement - it is proven in endurance. It is the quiet, unshaken confidence that what God has spoken will come to pass, even if you must stand in that belief by yourself for a season. Even if the evidence says otherwise, refuse to let your conviction be shaken. There will be moments when circumstances contradict the promise, but this is where true faith is forged. Hold on not because it is easy, but because it is necessary. Hold on because God is faithful. The same God who planted the vision in your heart will bring it to fulfillment in His time. Stay rooted, stay steady, and trust that what looks impossible today is already being shaped by His hand for tomorrow.

If God has spoken it, it is already set in motion. His Word does not return empty, nor does it depend on human agreement to come to pass. What He declares is backed by His authority, sustained by His power, and fulfilled in His perfect timing. So stand firm even when the ground feels uncertain beneath your feet. Believe boldly even when doubt whispers louder than truth. Your confidence is not rooted in what you see, but in who He is. You must walk forward, even if you must walk alone. There will be moments when others do not understand, when support fades, and when the path grows quiet, but God's presence has not left you. Every step you take in faith is a declaration that you trust Him more than your fears, more than opinions, and more than circumstances. Do not shrink back. Do not second-guess what God has already confirmed in your spirit. Keep moving. Keep trusting. Because the same God who spoke the promise is walking with you every step of the way and He will bring it to completion.

"THE POWER OF PRIVATE PRAYER"

There is a sacred workshop of God that few truly understand - a place hidden from applause, untouched by recognition, and free from distraction. It is there, in the quiet, that true strength is forged. When a man enters into stillness with God, he begins to encounter a deeper reality. In that place, motives are refined, character is shaped, and identity is secured. The quiet is not a void to be feared - it is a sanctuary where God speaks, corrects, strengthens, and trans-forms. What is developed in private will always sustain what is re-vealed in public. A man who neglects the hidden place may appear strong for a moment, but he will lack the depth to endure. Yet the man who consistently meets God in the stillness carries within him a well of strength that does not run dry. He is not dependent on crowds, af-firmation, or circumstances, because his foundation was formed in communion with God. In the quiet, he learns to hear God's voice, to trust His leading, and to draw from His presence.

Many men spend their lives striving to be seen, measuring their worth by applause, titles, and recognition. Yet God offers something far greater than visibility - He offers intimacy. He does not begin with your platform; He begins with your heart. Long before He entrusts you with influence, He invites you into relationship. In the quiet place, away from the noise and the need to impress, a man discovers who he truly is before God. It is there that identity is formed, not in the spotlight but in surrender. The world may reward performance, but God honors men who choose to sit with Him, listen to Him, and walk with Him daily. Before a man can lead others with strength and clarity, he must first learn to follow with humility and obedience. The voice that carries weight in public is the one that has been refined in private. In silence, God shapes your character, aligns your desires, and strengthens your spirit. It is in those unseen moments that courage is built, wisdom is gained, and conviction is deepened.

Walking with God begins with a deep, internal hunger that is not driven by duty or routine but by a genuine longing to know Him more. When a man truly desires God, his pursuit becomes intentional. He no longer approaches God casually or occasionally, but consistently and passionately. This hunger reshapes his priorities, redirecting his focus from the noise of the world to the voice of the One who created him. In that pursuit, time with God becomes the foundation upon which everything else is built. A man who longs for God will make space for Him, even when life is full and demanding. He guards that time fiercely, recognizing it as sacred ground where strength is renewed, wisdom is given, and identity is clarified. In those quiet moments, away from distraction, he is shaped, corrected, and strengthened. The man who chooses to dwell in the presence of God will carry a quiet strength, a steady confidence, and a life marked by the unmistakable evidence that he has been with God.

This relationship with God is not formed in a single powerful moment, but in the steady rhythm of daily pursuit. It is built in the quiet places - when no one is watching, when there is no applause, when it's just you and Him. Just as any meaningful relationship grows through time, attention, and intentional connection, so your walk with God deepens through consistent surrender, prayer, and listening. It is in these unseen moments that trust is established, faith is strengthened, and your heart becomes aligned with His. Consistency in the quiet is where spiritual depth is formed. It is where God shapes your character, refines your motives, and anchors your soul. The man who meets God daily, even in silence, becomes a man of strength, clarity, and unwavering conviction. While others may chase visible results, you are being built from the inside out. And over time, what is cultivated in secret will produce a life that carries authority, peace, and the unmistakable presence of God.

Private prayer is the unseen battlefield where victories are secured long before they ever manifest in the visible world. It is in those quiet, hidden moments with God that the weight of life is lifted off the shoulders, clarity replaces confusion, and courage begins to rise within the heart. When a man kneels in prayer, he is not retreating - he is advancing in the spirit. God meets him there, speaking direction into his uncertainty and pouring strength into his weakness. What looks like silence to the outside world is actually sacred conversation, where heaven equips him for everything he will face. In solitude, he finds companionship. In stillness, he finds power. Prayer becomes his refuge in storms and his anchor in uncertainty. It shapes his character, sharpens his discernment, and fortifies his spirit. While others rely on their own strength, the praying man draws from an endless source and that is why he stands firm when others fall. His strength is not just in what he can do, but in who he walks with.

There is power in speaking to God honestly with a heart that is open and real. God does not measure your prayers by how impressive they sound, but by how sincere they are. When you drop the mask and come before Him as you truly are, something shifts within you. Walls begin to fall, burdens begin to lift, and your spirit finds rest in His presence. When you speak to God as a son, not a stranger, intimacy begins to grow. You stop performing and start connecting. Your prayers become conversations, your silence becomes communion, and your relationship becomes personal. In that place of authenticity, you begin to recognize His voice more clearly and feel His nearness more deeply. You are no longer reaching out to a distant God but walking with a loving Father. And as that intimacy grows, so does your strength, your confidence, and your peace because you are no longer carrying life alone, but living it in close fellowship with the One who knows you best and loves you most.

In the quiet, God speaks - not always through thunder or dramatic displays, but through the gentle whisper that reaches the heart willing to listen. Too often, life is filled with noise that drown out the subtle voice of the Spirit. When a man intentionally steps away from the noise and creates space for silence, he positions himself to hear what cannot be heard in the rush. It is in these sacred moments of quiet that God reveals direction, brings conviction, and reminds us of who we are and whose we are. Stillness is a deliberate pause to align with heaven. In the quiet, clarity begins to form where confusion once lived. Decisions become sharper, purpose becomes clearer, and peace replaces striving. A man who learns to be still before God will walk with greater confidence before men, because he is no longer led by pressure but by presence. Make room for the quiet for it is there, in the stillness, that God shapes your heart, sharpens your vision, and speaks the words that will guide your life.

Many avoid the quiet because it strips away the noise that keeps them distracted from what is truly within. In the silence, there are no masks to hide behind, no crowds to impress, no movement to escape into - only the honest condition of the heart laid bare before God. When a man dares to be still, he begins to hear what he has long ignored - the gentle correction, the quiet conviction, and the steady voice of God calling him higher. What feels uncomfortable at first is actually sacred ground, because it is here that truth is revealed and the process of transformation begins. God does His deepest work in these moments of solitude, when distractions fade and intimacy is restored. In the quiet, He reshapes desires, renews strength, and aligns the heart with His purpose. The quiet is not emptiness - it is fullness waiting to be discovered. And those who embrace it will find that what once felt like isolation becomes the birthplace of clarity, strength, and a deeper walk with God.

A man who walks with God carries a strength the world cannot explain and cannot take away. It is not loud, boastful, or dependent on recognition - it is quiet, steady, and deeply rooted. Trials may come, storms may rise, and opposition may press in, but his spirit does not collapse under the weight. Why? Because his confidence flows from an unbroken connection with the One who is unchanging. In that connection, he finds peace in chaos, clarity in confusion, and courage in moments that would cause others to retreat. His stability is the result of time spent with God in the unseen places where character is formed, faith is strengthened, and identity is secured. When pressure comes, it does not destroy him; it reveals what he is rooted in. And because he is rooted in God, he bends but does not break, he feels but does not fold, and he endures without losing himself. His life becomes a testimony that a man anchored in God cannot be shaken by the winds of this world.

Spiritual intimacy sharpens your ability to discern the voice of God above all the noise of the world. You start to recognize the difference between your own thoughts and His leading, between emotional impulses and divine direction. His voice carries a distinct peace, a steady authority, and a loving conviction that draws you closer rather than pushes you away. As this discernment grows, so does your sensitivity to His correction and guidance. You no longer resist conviction; you welcome it, knowing it is evidence of His care and involvement in your life. The more you listen, the more you understand His ways, and the more naturally you walk in alignment with His will. What once required struggle now flows from relationship. You are no longer guessing - you are walking with God, attentive and aware. And in that closeness, your life becomes anchored in clarity, direction, and a deep assurance that you are being led by the One who sees all things.

There is a profound difference between knowing about God and truly knowing Him. One is gathered through study, sermons, and second-hand understanding - it informs the mind but does not always transform the heart. The other is forged in quiet moments, in prayer, in surrender, and in walking daily with Him. It is the difference between reading about fire and feeling its warmth. A man can recite truths about God and still feel distant, but when he knows God personally, those truths become alive within him. His faith is no longer borrowed - it is built. His confidence is no longer rooted in knowledge alone, but in relationship, experience, and trust. A man who truly knows God carries something that cannot be manufactured or imitated. There is a steady peace in him that is not shaken by circumstances, a wisdom that flows beyond his own understanding, and an authority that comes from alignment with heaven. He does not strive to prove himself, because he is already anchored in who he is before God.

Time with God has a way of quietly but powerfully reshaping who you are. The more you sit with Him, the more His truth replaces the lies you've believed about yourself. You start to understand that your past does not disqualify you; it becomes part of the story God is redeeming. What once felt like shame is transformed into testimony, and what once held you back becomes the very ground from which God lifts you forward. As your relationship with Him deepens, your identity is no longer rooted in circumstances but in calling. You begin to see yourself the way He sees you - chosen with purpose, equipped with strength, and capable through His Spirit. You walk differently, not because everything around you has changed, but because something within you has. Confidence replaces insecurity, clarity replaces confusion, and hope replaces fear. When you know who you are in God, you stop striving to prove your worth and start living from it.

In the quiet places where no one is watching and no applause is heard; God does His deepest work within you. It is there that pride loses its grip, because there is no audience to impress. In the stillness, distractions fade and truth rises to the surface. You begin to see yourself clearly - not as you pretend to be, but as you truly are. And in that sacred honesty, God meets you with both conviction and grace, chiseling away what does not belong and strengthening what will endure. Do not despise the quiet seasons for God is not merely arranging circumstances for your future; He is forming the man you must become to carry it. In the hidden place, He builds integrity, resilience, and dependence on Him alone. Your weaknesses are not ignored - they are refined into strength through surrender. What feels like stillness is actually transformation. And when you emerge, you will not just step into a new season - you will step into it as a man who has been shaped, anchored, and prepared by God Himself.

The strength you gain in private is the strength that will carry you in public. Long before the spotlight ever finds you, God is shaping you in the unseen places through quiet prayers, honest surrender, and moments when no one is watching but Him. It is in those hidden hours that your roots grow deep. When the storms of life inevitably rise, you will not be shaken, because your stability was built on a personal relationship with God. Never underestimate the power of quiet moments with God. Those still, sacred spaces are where resilience is forged, where your spirit is strengthened, and where your identity is secured. While others may chase visible success, you are being prepared in ways that cannot be seen but will one day be undeniable. When pressure comes, you will stand firm not because life is easy, but because you have been with God in the quiet. And that hidden strength will rise up within you, steady, unshaken, and ready for whatever lies ahead.

Walking with God produces a kind of peace that the world cannot manufacture or take away. It is not rooted in perfect circumstances or the absence of trouble, but in the steady, unshakable presence of God Himself. Storms may still rise, battles may still come, and uncertainty may still surround you - but deep within, there is a quiet assurance that you are not alone. This peace anchors your soul, reminding you that the One who walks beside you is sovereign, faithful, and fully in control. When your heart is aligned with Him, fear loses its grip, and anxiety gives way to trust. Even in the unknown, you remain calm - not because you have all the answers, but because you know the One who does. His presence steadies your steps and guards your mind, allowing you to move through uncertainty with confidence instead of panic. This is the peace that carries you through the darkest valleys and the most confusing seasons simply because you walk with Him.

A man who truly knows God is not driven by the need for applause or the approval of others, because his identity is anchored in something far greater than human opinion. He understands that his worth is not determined by popularity, success, or recognition, but by the unchanging truth of who God says he is. This kind of man is not easily shaken by criticism or inflated by praise - he is steady, grounded, and at peace. His confidence is quiet but unmovable, flowing from a deep inner assurance that he belongs to God. Because of this, he can walk boldly even when the path is lonely. He does not fear isolation, because he is never truly alone. While others seek the crowd for validation, he seeks the presence of God for direction. In the silence, he grows stronger; in the hidden places, his character is refined. His steps are ordered by the voice of God. And so he moves forward with courage and clarity, knowing that a life aligned with God will always lead him exactly where he is meant to be.

The quiet place is not an obligation you drag yourself into - it is a refuge your soul longs for. It is where the noise fades, the pressure lifts, and the presence of God becomes unmistakably real. In that sacred stillness, you are not performing, striving, or proving anything; you are simply being with Him. When you are alone with God your spirit is renewed, your thoughts are realigned, and your heart is restored. In the quiet place, you encounter the One who sustains you. You do not go there to escape reality - you go there to be strengthened for it. The quiet place becomes the source you depend on, the well you draw from daily. It is where clarity replaces confusion, peace overcomes anxiety, and truth silences every lie. A man who learns to return there consistently becomes steady, grounded, and spiritually alive. He is not easily shaken, because he is continually anchored in God's presence. The quiet place is no longer optional - it is essential, the place where you are rebuilt again and again.

In the end, the greatest strength a man can possess is measured by the depth of his relationship with God. Spiritual strength is forged in the quiet moments where no one is watching but God alone. It is built through prayer, shaped by surrender, and sustained by trust. A man who knows God personally carries a steady confidence that cannot be shaken by circumstances, because his foundation is not in this world, but in the One who created it. When storms come, he does not collapse because he has learned to stand in the presence of God before he ever had to stand in the pressures of life. This is the strength that sets a man apart - the strength to remain steady when others panic, to remain humble when others boast, and to remain faithful when others fall away. It is not loud or boastful, but it is undeniable. For when a man walks closely with God, he does not just visit strength - he becomes a vessel of it, reflecting the power, wisdom, and presence of God everywhere he goes.

Step away from the noise that constantly demands your attention but never feeds your soul. The world is loud, urgent, and relentless, but God often speaks in the quiet places where distractions fade and truth becomes clear. When a man intentionally creates space to seek Him, he positions himself to hear what truly matters. In that stillness, your identity is strengthened, your burdens are lifted, and your spirit is aligned with something greater than your circumstances. Quiet time with God is not wasted time - it is the place where strength is renewed and vision is restored. Because the man who walks with God in the quiet will never walk without purpose, power, or direction. Even when the path ahead seems uncertain, he carries an inner clarity that cannot be shaken. In the secret place, his character is deepened, his courage refined, and his faith made unshakable. And when he steps back into the world, he walks with authority, grounded in the presence of the One who has already gone before him.

| 12 |

"REFINED THROUGH FIRE"

The refining fire is rarely a place we would willingly enter, yet it is often where God does His deepest work. When comfort is removed and the familiar is stripped away, we are left face to face with what truly lives within us. In that sacred tension, God is not punishing- He is purifying. He allows the heat not to destroy your identity, but to reveal it. The fears, the pride, the hidden dependencies - these rise to the surface, not to shame you, but to free you. What cannot survive the fire was never meant to sustain you. And what remains, though tested, is strengthened, clarified, and anchored in Him. God refines those He is preparing, shaping you into someone who can carry greater weight, deeper purpose, and lasting impact. And when you emerge, you do not come out as ashes, but as something stronger, purer, and more resilient. The fire does not have the final word - God does. And what He is forming in you will endure long after the flames have passed.

Trials have a way of revealing what comfort quietly conceals. In seasons of ease, it is possible to move through life on the strength of habit rather than the depth of conviction. Routine can mask fragility, and success can give the illusion of strength. But when pressure rises - when the unexpected shakes your foundation - what is truly within you comes to the surface. Faith that is genuine stands firm, while areas built on assumption or convenience begin to crack. This is not exposure meant to shame you, but revelation designed to awaken you. The refining fire is an invitation to grow deeper, not a verdict of failure. Where your faith feels thin, God is calling you into greater trust. Where fear rises, He is offering courage. Where doubt lingers, He is building conviction. Every trial carries within it the opportunity to strengthen your foundation and purify your heart. If you lean into the process, allowing God to shape you in the fire, you will emerge stronger, clearer, and more anchored than before.

Just as gold is placed in the fire to burn away what does not belong, so your life is sometimes led through seasons of heat and pressure. In those moments, what rises to the surface reveals what has been hidden within: pride that resists surrender, fear that questions His faithfulness, and self-reliance that competes with trust in Him. Though the process may feel uncomfortable, even painful, it is not meant to destroy you - it is meant to refine you. God is not removing your strength; He is purifying it, shaping your heart until it reflects His character more clearly. What emerges from the fire is not a diminished version of who you were, but a transformed one - stronger because it is rooted in Him, steadier because it has been tested, and purer because it has been surrendered. Trials strip away the temporary so that the eternal can take its place. When the fire has done its work, you will carry a faith that is unshaken, a character that is refined, and a life that bears the unmistakable mark of God's hand.

In the fire, God does more than test your strength - He transforms your desires. What once drove you begins to lose its grip as the heat of His refining presence exposes what is temporary and self-centered. In that sacred tension, your questions begin to change. No longer consumed with "What do I want?" your spirit starts to cry out, "What does God desire?" This is the turning point of true maturity, where ambition bows to surrender and personal gain is replaced by divine purpose. The fire burns away hidden motives and brings clarity to what truly matters, reshaping your heart until it beats in rhythm with

His will. As the refining continues, your focus shifts from what is fleeting to what is eternal. You begin to see beyond immediate rewards and start living for lasting impact. God uses the fire to align your priorities with heaven's agenda, teaching you to value obedience over recognition and faithfulness over applause. What once seemed important fades in comparison to the weight of eternal significance.

Suffering, though it cuts deep, is never without purpose in the hands of God. It strips away the illusion of self-sufficiency and brings you face to face with your need for Him. In seasons of comfort, faith can remain something you agree with but have never truly leaned on. But when the weight becomes too heavy and your strength runs out, you are driven to a deeper place of surrender. It is there, in that raw and vulnerable space, that you discover God is present, sustaining, and faithful. In that place of dependence, your faith is forged into something real and unshakable. You no longer rely on what you can control, but on who God is. The trials that once threatened to break you become the very tools that establish you. Your confidence shifts from your own ability to His unchanging nature. And when the storm passes, you emerge not just having survived, but transformed - anchored, steady, and strengthened. What you once believed in theory now stands firm in your spirit, tested by fire and proven true.

Faith that has never been tested remains unproven. It may appear strong on the surface, but until it is challenged, its depth is unknown. Trials reveal what comfort often conceals. When the heat is turned up and circumstances press in, faith becomes a lifeline. What you once said you believed is now something you stand on, cling to, and live by. The fire strips away shallow confidence and replaces it with something rooted, steady, and unshakable. The beauty of tested faith is not found in the fire itself, but in what emerges from it. Endurance is forged where comfort once ruled, and hope matures into a quiet, resilient strength. When you come through the fire, you carry a deeper authority, a stronger trust, and a faith that has weight. It is no longer fragile or easily swayed, because it has been proven in the hardest places. What once flickered now burns steadily, illuminating the path not only for yourself, but for others who are walking through their own refining season.

The refining fire does more than test you - it trains you. In the heat of trials, perseverance is forged deep within your spirit, not as a fleeting emotion, but as a steady resolve anchored in God. When everything around you begins to shake, when circumstances feel uncertain and pressure mounts, you discover a strength you did not know you possessed. This endurance is not born from comfort, but from conviction. It is the quiet confidence that God is at work in the fire, shaping you, strengthening you, and preparing you to stand firm when others fall away. As the flames rise, you learn to hold your ground not because the storm has lost its power, but because your foundation has gained strength. Rooted in truth and built on faith, you become unshakable. What once would have caused you to retreat now becomes the very ground where you stand with boldness. The refining fire teaches you that perseverance is not passive - it is active trust, steady faith, and unwavering commitment.

Adversity is not an interruption to God's plan - it is often the very instrument He uses to fulfill it. The weight of trials presses beyond surface-level faith and exposes what is truly within a man. In the fire, pride is stripped away, self-reliance is broken, and a deeper dependence on God is formed. What comfort can never teach, hardship engraves into the soul. It is in these difficult seasons that God develops leaders who are anchored in humility, shaped by surrender, and strengthened by trust. The pain is not wasted - it is purposeful, forging a depth of character that cannot be manufactured any other way. Those who emerge from adversity carry more than survival - they carry wisdom, compassion, and spiritual authority. They understand the struggles of others because they have walked through valleys themselves. Their leadership is no longer theoretical; it is tested, proven, and refined. The fire teaches them how to stand firm, how to listen with empathy, and how to lead with grace under pressure.

A man who has been through the fire carries something that cannot be taught in comfort - it is forged in the unseen places of struggle, pain, and surrender. The fire strips away illusion, pride, and self-reliance, leaving behind a man who knows God in a deeper way. There is a weight to his words because they have been tested, a calm in his spirit because he has learned to trust, and a discernment in his decisions because he has walked through the refining process. He no longer chases validation or fears opposition, because the fire has already settled those battles within him. Such a man is not easily shaken, not because life has become easier, but because he has become stronger. He has learned that God is faithful in the flames, present in the pressure, and powerful in the process. His purpose is no longer vague - it is clear and unmovable. And when he stands, he stands with quiet authority, not striving to prove himself, but simply living as one who has been refined, strengthened, and prepared.

Leadership that is forged in adversity carries a weight that cannot be imitated or manufactured. It is shaped in moments where comfort is stripped away and true motives are exposed. In those seasons, a man learns that leadership is not about being seen, but about being faithful. It is not sustained by applause, but by obedience. Trials have a way of silencing ego and sharpening conviction, teaching a leader to stand firm when others fall back. What emerges is not a personality-driven influence, but a steady, grounded authority rooted in integrity. The refining fire burns away the need for recognition and replaces it with a deep commitment to serve others, regardless of the cost. In that fire, selfish ambition gives way to selfless responsibility. This kind of leadership does not demand loyalty, yet it inspires it. Because when a man has been refined by adversity, he no longer leads to be noticed - he leads because he has been prepared, and because others can trust the strength that was forged in the fire.

In the midst of the fire, when the pressure feels unbearable, the enemy whispers that you have been abandoned. But that is a lie. The very place that feels the most desolate is often where God is most present. Just as He stood with the three Hebrew men in the fiery furnace, He stands with you now - unseen perhaps, but unmistakably active. He is not a distant observer of your pain; He is an ever-present help, walking beside you, strengthening your spirit, and sustaining your soul when your own strength runs dry. Do not mistake the intensity of the fire for the absence of God. In those moments when you feel alone, He is drawing closer, not stepping away. His presence becomes your shield, His peace your anchor, and His voice your guide through the chaos. You are not alone in the flames - you are accompanied by the One who controls the fire itself. And when you come out on the other side, you will not smell like smoke but carry the mark of having walked through the fire with God.

The fire may feel overwhelming, pressing in on every side, but it is not without purpose or restraint. God is not careless with your life - He is intentional. Every trial, every moment of pressure, is measured by His wisdom and guided by His hand. Just as a refiner carefully controls the flame to purify precious metal, God allows only what is necessary to shape your character and strengthen your faith. What feels like too much is never beyond His control. He sees the end from the beginning, and He knows exactly how to refine you without allowing you to be consumed. In the midst of the heat, you are not abandoned - you are protected. The same God who allows the fire stands with you in it, guarding your soul and preserving your purpose. He is not trying to break you; He is building you. Trust the process, even when it is painful, because the Refiner's hands are steady and His intentions are good. When the fire has done its work, you will emerge stronger, purer, and prepared for what lies ahead.

What you lose in the fire was never meant to remain. God allows the flames of testing to expose what cannot endure the weight of your calling. Though the process is uncomfortable, even painful, it is deeply intentional. God is removing what would hinder you from becoming who you were created to be. What falls away in the fire is a clearing of space for something stronger, purer, and more aligned with His will. In the refining, God is strengthening your character, anchoring your faith, and increasing your capacity to carry what is ahead. Just as gold is purified by intense heat, your life is being shaped to reflect something of greater value and endurance. The things that survive the fire - your faith, your trust in God, your obedience - are the very things that will sustain you in the next season. Do not grieve what was burned away; instead, embrace what is being built within you. For when the fire has done its work, you will emerge refined and ready to step fully into the purpose God has prepared for you.

Emerging from the fire, you are not the same person who entered it. The weakness that once defined your response has been replaced with strength rooted in Him. The confusion that clouded your vision has been cleared by the wisdom forged in hardship. And the fear that once held you captive has given way to a peace that can only come from walking through the flames and discovering that He was with you the entire time. What you thought would destroy you has instead revealed who you are becoming. The fire always leaves a mark, but for the one who trusts God, it is a mark of transformation. It is evidence that you endured and came out stronger, wiser, and more anchored than before. Your character has been strengthened and your faith made unshakable. You now carry within you a testimony that cannot be taught, only lived. So do not hide the marks - carry them boldly. They are proof that you walked through the fire and did not burn; you were transformed and positioned for something greater.

The scars you carry are living testimonies of God's faithfulness in your life. Each one tells a story of a moment when you could have been overcome, but instead, God sustained you. They remind you that even in your darkest seasons, He never abandoned you. What once caused pain has now become proof of His presence, His mercy, and His power to bring you through. When you look back, you don't just see wounds - you see evidence that God was writing a greater story all along. Do not hide your scars or be ashamed of them, for they are symbols of survival, growth, and transformation. They declare that what tried to break you did not succeed, because God was with you in the fire. Your scars now carry purpose - they encourage others, strengthen your faith, and remind you that you are still standing by His grace. What you have been through has refined you, not ruined you. And in the hands of God, even your deepest wounds become powerful witnesses of His redeeming love.

When you have been refined, you carry a testimony that breathes life into others. The fire you endured was not meant to destroy you, but to shape you, strengthen you, and reveal the depth of God's work within you. What once felt like breaking has now become building. And in that transformation, you become a steady voice for those still in the flames. Your life begins to speak in ways words alone cannot, declaring that God is faithful, that endurance is possible, and that the fire has an end. Your scars become signals of hope, and your perseverance becomes a guiding light for those who feel overwhelmed by their own trials. When others see that you made it through, they begin to believe that they can too. Your strength becomes their encouragement, your faith becomes their courage, and your journey becomes a roadmap through their wilderness. God never wastes the refining - He uses it to multiply strength, to ignite faith, and to turn your survival into someone else's breakthrough.

Do not resist the refining process when it comes - lean into it with faith, knowing that God is actively at work within you. The fire you face is not sent to destroy you, but to purify you - to burn away what cannot remain and reveal what God has placed within you from the beginning. In the heat of trials, your character is strengthened, your faith is deepened, and your dependence on Him becomes unshakable.

What you endure today is preparing you for what you are called to carry tomorrow. The fire is forging resilience, sharpening discernment, and building the kind of strength that cannot be developed in comfort. God is shaping you into someone capable of greater responsibility and a higher purpose, someone who can be trusted with more because you have been tested in the fire. So stand firm and do not shrink back. Embrace the process, even when it is difficult, because on the other side of refinement is clarity, strength, and a life that reflects the power and glory of God.

The refining fire is not sent to destroy you, but to shape you into the man God has called you to be. What feels like hardship is often the very tool heaven uses to strip away what is weak, impure, and temporary. In the fire, your faith is tested, your character is strengthened, and your dependence on God becomes deeper than ever before. Though the flames may be intense, they are burning away fear, pride, and compromise so that something far greater can emerge. What remains is not a broken man, but a forged one - steady, resilient, and anchored in truth. Stand firm when the heat rises. On the other side of the fire is a version of you that could not exist without the trial - a man marked by strength, refined by faith, and prepared for greater purpose. So endure the fire with confidence, knowing that every moment in the flame is producing something eternal. You will not come out diminished - you will rise stronger, sharper, and ready to step fully into your calling.

| 13 |

"THE DISCIPLINE OF ENDURANCE"

Endurance is not built in the spotlight - it is formed in the silence where no applause is heard and no recognition is given. It is in the long, unseen seasons where progress feels slow and the results seem invisible that true strength is developed. God often does His deepest work not in the breakthroughs, but in the waiting where character is tested, motives are purified, and resolve is strengthened. What feels like stagnation is often sacred shaping. A man proves who he truly is not when everything is going his way, but when he continues to stand firm when nothing seems to move. Endurance reveals authenticity. It separates those who are driven by momentary emotion from those anchored in purpose and conviction. In the quiet grind of perseverance, a man is becoming unshakable, dependable, and mature. Every step taken in faith, every moment of quiet obedience, is building a foundation that will one day carry weight, influence, and lasting impact.

Many men begin their journey with fire in their hearts and strength in their stride, but time has a way of revealing what passion alone cannot sustain. The truth is, starting strong requires inspiration but finishing well requires transformation. Endurance is forged in the quiet places, in the unseen battles, in the days when nothing seems to move and no one is watching. It is in those moments that a man proves whether he is driven by emotion or anchored in purpose. When others grow weary and step back, the enduring man leans in. He remembers his calling, not as a fleeting feeling, but as a divine assignment. He understands that greatness is not built in bursts of intensity, but in steady, faithful obedience over time. Endurance is the mark of a man who has learned to trust God beyond what he can see. When progress feels invisible and results seem delayed, he does not abandon the path - he deepens his resolve. He presses forward, not because it is easy, but because it is necessary.

This kind of perseverance separates those who merely respond to a moment from those who commit to a mission. The man who endures becomes unshakable, not because he avoids hardship, but because he has walked through it and remained. And in the end, it is not the one who started with the loudest voice who leaves the greatest impact but the one who stayed, who endured, and who finished what God called him to do. Do not despise the hidden place, for it is there that God does His deepest work. In the quiet, He teaches you to trust without evidence, to remain faithful without applause, and to persevere without immediate reward. These seasons build a strength that cannot be shaken and a faith that cannot be easily broken. When the time of revealing comes, you will stand not just with blessing, but with the capacity to sustain it. So keep going. Stay rooted. Stay faithful. The season may feel long, but it is not wasted - God is working, even now, beneath the surface.

Perseverance in long seasons requires a transformation of how you see time, progress, and purpose. Too often, we measure growth by what we can immediately see, but God works in ways that are deeper than surface results. In the waiting, in the repetition, in the unseen moments He is forming strength within you that cannot be rushed. Roots grow long before fruit appears. Faithfulness in the process is never wasted, even when it feels unnoticed. What seems like delay is often divine development, shaping your character, refining your patience, and preparing you for what you are not yet ready to carry. When you shift your perspective to value the process, you begin to trust that every step matters. Every act of obedience, every quiet moment of discipline, every decision to keep going when nothing seems to change - these are the building blocks of lasting growth. God is not only concerned with where you are going, but who you are becoming along the way.

Endurance is the quiet work of God in a man's life, forming depth where surface strength once lived. Anyone can rise in a moment of excitement, but it takes endurance to remain when the emotions fade and the pressure increases. It is in the long seasons - when prayers seem unanswered, when progress feels slow, and when no one is watching - that true greatness is forged. God is not in a hurry, because He is not just building success - He is building substance. Endurance teaches you to stand when it would be easier to quit, to trust when you cannot see, and to keep moving forward when everything in you wants relief. This is where shallow roots are replaced with deep ones, and where a man becomes unshakable. What is built slowly carries a strength that cannot be easily broken. The world celebrates quick wins, but heaven honors lasting faithfulness. When you endure, you develop the character to sustain the very blessings you once prayed for.

When pressure lingers, it strips away the surface and reveals what is truly within a man. It is easy to appear strong when circumstances are favorable, but prolonged difficulty exposes the foundation of the heart. Under the weight of endurance, excuses lose their power, and hidden fears come into the light. In these moments, a man is faced with a choice - retreat into comfort or rise into growth. Endurance is not just about surviving hardship - it is about becoming strong through it. When a man refuses to quit, even when the pressure does not lift, his resolve deepens and his character is forged. He learns discipline when he wants to give up, courage when fear whispers, and faith when answers seem distant. These long seasons shape him into someone who can carry greater responsibility and walk in greater purpose. What once felt like a burden becomes the very thing that built his strength. And when he emerges, he is steadier, stronger, and prepared for the calling that awaits him.

There is a race set before every man, uniquely marked out by the hand of God. It is not a sprint driven by bursts of emotion, but a marathon shaped by faith, obedience, and daily consistency. The path will stretch you and at times leave you weary but it is in the endurance that strength is formed and character is refined. You are not competing with other runners, nor are you measured by their pace or progress. Your calling is not to outrun another man, but to remain faithful to the lane God has assigned you, step by step, mile by mile. Stay your course, even when the road feels long and the results seem slow. Faithfulness in the unseen seasons builds a foundation that cannot be shaken. Obedience in the small things prepares you for greater assignments ahead. Do not be distracted by comparison or discouraged by delay for God is working in your persistence. Keep running with purpose, fixing your eyes on Him, and trusting that every step taken in faith is leading you exactly where you are meant to be.

Running your race requires patience - not the kind that sits still and waits for life to change, but the kind that rises daily with quiet determination and refuses to quit. It is an active persistence, a steady commitment to keep moving forward even when the path feels long and the results seem invisible. True patience is built when no one is watching, when encouragement is scarce, and when progress feels painfully slow. Yet it is in those very moments that strength is formed, character is refined, and faith is proven genuine. Every small step matters more than you realize. God is not measuring your speed - He is honoring your consistency. The race is not won by those who rush ahead for a moment, but by those who endure with unwavering resolve. So rise each day with purpose. Keep walking and keep building.

For in due time, what was once slow and steady will become strong and unshakable, and you will look back and see that every faithful step carried you exactly where you were meant to be.

Patience is the quiet strength that refuses to be driven by impulse, fear, or frustration. A man who walks in patience is not standing still; he is moving forward with discipline, choosing endurance over escape. While others rush ahead and burn out, he remains steady, rooted, and unshaken. Patience keeps his hands steady, his heart guarded, and his vision clear. It allows him to stay committed when progress feels slow and to keep building when results are not yet visible. To walk in patience is to trust God at a deeper level. Even when doors seem closed and answers seem distant, patience anchors your soul in confidence that God is still working behind the scenes. The process is shaping you, strengthening you, and preparing you for what is ahead. Do not rush what God is refining. Do not abandon what He has assigned. Stay the course, remain faithful, and trust that in the right moment, what has been forming in silence will be revealed in power.

Endurance is not forged in moments of ease, but in the quiet, repeated decisions to keep going. Every time you show up again, every time you choose discipline over comfort, you are strengthening something deeper than your circumstances - you are strengthening your spirit. God often does His greatest work in repetition, shaping your character through consistency, teaching you faithfulness in the ordinary, and building a resilience that cannot be shaken by temporary hardship. True strength is steady, rooted, and unwavering. It is the man who continues to do what is right when it is difficult, when it costs something, and when it seems to go unnoticed. This is the kind of endurance that produces lasting greatness. It is here, in the daily grind of obedience and perseverance, that God forms a foundation within you that can carry weight, withstand storms, and finish strong. Do not despise the repetition - embrace it. For in every faithful step, you are becoming the man God has called you to be.

There will be moments when the journey presses hard against your soul - when progress feels slow, resistance feels strong, and the temptation to quit whispers louder than your calling. In those moments, you must not measure your strength by how you feel, but by the purpose God placed within you. Feelings are temporary, but purpose is eternal. When the weight feels too heavy and the road too long, go back to the beginning - back to the fire God lit in your heart, back to the assignment He entrusted to you. What God initiates, He also equips you to endure. Purpose is the fuel that keeps a man moving when everything in him wants to stop. It reminds you that your struggle is not meaningless and your pain is not wasted. Every step forward is shaping you into the man God designed you to become. When quitting feels close, anchor yourself in purpose. Let it push you beyond the moment because those who remember why they started are the ones who find the strength to finish.

Finishing what you start is a quiet but powerful declaration of integrity. It reveals a heart that does not waver when the excitement fades or when the path becomes difficult. Commitment is proven not in beginnings, but in endurance. Discipline carries a man through the moments when motivation disappears, and honor compels him to remain faithful to what he said he would do. When a man finishes what he starts, he is not only building trust with others - he is strengthening something deep within himself. Each completed task reinforces his identity as a man of resolve, a man who does not quit when things get hard. This internal trust becomes a foundation for greater responsibility, greater purpose, and greater impact. God can entrust more to the man who proves faithful in the small things and diligent in the long journey. Finishing is not just about the task - it is about who you are becoming in the process. And over time, that consistency shapes a life marked by strength, credibility, and lasting influence.

Too many dreams do not die at the beginning, where vision is fresh, or at the end, where victory is near - they die in the middle, where the excitement has faded and the outcome is still uncertain. It is in this unseen stretch that many turn back, not because the dream was too great, but because the endurance required felt too heavy. Yet this is the very place where God does His deepest work, strengthening your spirit, refining your character, and teaching you to walk not by sight, but by faith. Do not despise the middle. It is not a sign that you are failing - it is proof that you are progressing. The same place where many surrender is the place where champions are forged. Endurance is what separates those who start from those who finish. Keep going when it's hard. Press forward when nothing seems to be changing. For if you refuse to quit in the middle, you will discover that what once felt like a breaking point was actually your building place - and on the other side of it, victory is waiting.

God is not only the Author of your beginning - He is the Finisher of your faith. He does not start what He does not intend to complete. The same God who placed the vision in your heart is actively working through every season, every delay, and every challenge to bring it to fulfillment. What feels like waiting is often preparation. What feels like pressure is often refinement. He is strengthening your character, deepening your faith, and aligning your spirit so that when the promise is fulfilled, you have the capacity to sustain it. God is not rushing the process, because He is more concerned with who you are becoming than simply what you receive. You are being shaped into someone who can carry the weight of what He has promised. That is why God develops endurance in you. He builds stability within you so that you do not crumble when the weight increases. Trust the process because when God completes what He started in you, it will be lasting, steady, and able to stand through every season that follows.

Endurance is not just about surviving the moment - it is about becoming someone stronger through it. God uses those long, stretching seasons to build a quiet confidence deep in your spirit - a confidence not rooted in pride, but in proof. You have walked through difficulty before, and you did not break. That realization becomes a foundation you can stand on when the next challenge comes. With every step you refuse to surrender, strength is being formed in you - steady, resilient, and unshakable. What once felt impossible begins to feel familiar, and what once intimidated you begins to lose its power. Endurance teaches you that you are capable of more because God is working through you, strengthening you from the inside out. So keep moving forward, even if the progress feels slow. Every step matters. Every moment of perseverance is shaping a stronger, more confident version of you - one who knows that quitting is no longer an option.

The discipline of endurance is not something a man is born with - it is something he builds, one decision at a time. Endurance is developed in the daily choice to remain faithful, to stay steady when emotions fluctuate, and to remain committed when circumstances resist you. God uses these moments not to break you, but to shape you. Each act of perseverance strengthens your spirit, deepens your character, and aligns your heart with His purpose. What feels like repetition is actually preparation. Do not despise the process of endurance, because it is producing something far greater than comfort - it is producing maturity, strength, and unwavering faith. The man who endures is the man who finishes. He is not swayed by temporary setbacks or discouraged by long seasons of waiting, because he understands that God is working beneath the surface. Stay the course. Keep showing up. Keep believing. The reward is not just in what you achieve, but in who you become through the journey.

Stay the course even when the road stretches longer than you expected, and the silence around you grows heavy. There are seasons where progress feels invisible, where prayers seem to echo without response, and where the weight of obedience feels greater than the reward. But it is in these very moments that something sacred is taking place beneath the surface. What feels like stillness is often divine construction. What feels like delay is often preparation. You are not stuck - you are being built. Even when it's lonely, even when it's hard, even when it seems like nothing is changing - stay faithful. Roots grow deeper before fruit appears. Foundations are laid long before anything rises above the ground. One day, what you've been faithfully building in obscurity will stand strong in the open, and you will realize that none of it was wasted. So hold your ground. Keep walking. Keep trusting. What you are building is deeper than what you can see - and stronger than anything that tries to stop you.

Greatness is not measured in the excitement of beginnings, but in the faithfulness of completion. Many start with passion, vision, and energy, but the true test of a man is revealed in the long, quiet middle where challenges arise, motivation fades, and the road grows difficult. It is here that endurance is forged. It is here that character is built. When you feel weary, when progress seems slow, and when quitting feels easier than continuing, remember that your strength is not found in your own ability, but in your willingness to remain steadfast. There is purpose in the process. In the end, it is not the one who starts fast, but the one who finishes faithfully that receives the reward. Refuse to be counted among those who quit. Rise each day with a renewed resolve to move forward, no matter how small the step. Trust that God is working in every moment, shaping you, strengthening you, and preparing you for what lies ahead. Finish strong because you were created to carry your assignment to the very end.

| 14 |

"THE DANGER OF ISOLATION"

There is a difference between solitude and isolation, and wisdom is found in knowing when one has crossed into the other. Solitude strengthens a man - it is where he hears God clearly, refines his thoughts, and renews his spirit. But isolation drains him. It cuts him off from the sharpening influence of others, from accountability, and from the encouragement that keeps his fire burning. What begins as self-reliance can quietly become self-deception, convincing a man he does not need counsel, correction, or connection. Yet scripture reminds us that iron sharpens iron, and no man was designed to stand alone. When a man isolates himself, he becomes vulnerable - not always outwardly, but inwardly, where discouragement, bitterness, and distorted thinking can take root. God never intended for His people to walk this journey alone. Even the strongest men in scripture walked in community, leaned on others, and remained connected to the presence of God.

Strength is not proven by how well a man can stand alone, but by how faithfully he stays connected - to truth, to brotherhood, and to God. A man may tell himself he doesn't need anyone, that standing alone proves his strength. But God never designed him to fight life's battles in isolation. Isolation slips in through disappointment, through wounds left unhealed, through expectations that were never met. And before long, the man who once stood strong finds himself cut off from the very relationships that could bring healing, wisdom, and renewal. True strength is found in connection - first with God, and then with others He has placed in your life. When a man opens his heart, he makes room for accountability, encouragement, and growth. Scripture reminds us that iron sharpens iron, and no man sharpens himself alone. Let God heal the places that caused you to withdraw and allow others to walk beside you. Because a man who stands with God and with others is far stronger than a man who stands alone.

Solitude is a sacred choice, not an escape. It is the intentional stepping away from the noise of life in order to draw nearer to the voice of God. In solitude, clarity is restored, burdens are lifted, and strength is renewed. Jesus modeled this rhythm perfectly, withdrawing from the crowds not out of weakness, but out of wisdom. He understood that when a man chooses solitude, he is not running from life - he is being prepared for it. Isolation, however, is a very different path. It is not intentional connection with God, but often a slow drift away from Him and from others. Isolation feeds discouragement, distorts perspective, and leaves a man vulnerable to lies and bitterness. Where solitude strengthens, isolation weakens. That is why it is critical to guard your heart and remain rooted in both God's presence and godly relationships. Step away when you need to be refreshed but never disconnect to the point where you are alone without truth, without accountability, and without light.

Isolation, however, is not the quiet strengthening of the soul that solitude provides - it is a slow drifting away. It is born out of wounds left unhealed, disappointments left unresolved, and pride that refuses to be vulnerable. A man in isolation may convince himself he is protecting his peace, when in reality he is walling himself off from the very life God intends for him. Without the sharpening influence of godly relationships, his heart becomes susceptible to bitterness, and his mind begins to echo lies that would have been corrected in the presence of truth. God never designed a man to thrive in isolation. From the very beginning, He declared that it was not good for man to be alone. Isolation cuts off encouragement, distorts identity, and weakens resolve. But connection restores what isolation steals. When a man humbles himself, reaches out, and re-engages with God's people, he steps back into alignment with divine design. Healing begins, clarity returns, and strength is renewed.

A man in healthy solitude steps away with intention, not escape. He withdraws to seek God, to realign his heart, and to sharpen his purpose. In that quiet place, his thoughts become clearer, his spirit steadier, and his direction more defined. Like Jesus who often withdrew to pray, solitude becomes a place of renewal, not retreat. But isolation is different. Isolation is not guided by purpose - it is driven by pain, disappointment, or bitterness. Instead of drawing closer to God, a man begins to drift. What he calls "needing space" may actually be a slow disconnection from truth, from accountability, and from the strength found in godly relationships. This distinction is critical, because the enemy often disguises isolation as independence. A man may convince himself he just needs time alone, when in reality he is pulling away from the very people and principles that would keep him grounded. Healthy solitude strengthens your walk; isolation weakens it. One builds you up, the other slowly tears you down.

Isolation becomes especially dangerous when wounds go unhealed. When a man is hurt, his instinct is often to retreat - to build walls, to guard his heart, to avoid the risk of being wounded again. At first, it feels wise, even strong. But over time, that guarded silence hardens into distance, and distance into loneliness. The very walls meant to protect him begin to suffocate him. Wounds left in the dark do not fade - they deepen. True strength is not found in shutting people out, but in allowing God to bring healing through honesty, community, and grace. Those walls that keep pain out also keep restoration out, blocking the very relationships God uses to restore and strengthen a man's soul. Healing requires courage - the courage to open up again, to forgive, to trust wisely, and to let others in. It is in safe, godly connection that wounds begin to close and hearts are made whole. When a man brings his pain into the light, he doesn't become weaker - he becomes free.

Bitterness thrives in isolation because it feeds on unchallenged thoughts and unhealed wounds. When a man withdraws and continually replays offenses in his mind, he begins to interpret those moments through pain rather than truth. Without God's perspective, what happened to him becomes larger than what God is doing in him. The wound is rehearsed again and again until it takes root deep within the heart. What was once a moment of hurt slowly transforms into a mindset, and that mindset hardens into a stronghold. In that place, the enemy whispers lies that feel like truth, convincing him that he has been wronged beyond repair and must guard himself at all costs. Bitterness distorts vision, turning allies into adversaries and pushing away the very people God has placed for healing and support. A bitter heart cannot see clearly, cannot love freely, and cannot grow fully. That is why God calls men out of isolation and into connection with Him and with others who walk in truth.

Healing begins when a man brings his pain into the light, submits it to God, and chooses forgiveness over resentment. Freedom is found not in holding on, but in letting go. When he releases the offense, what once enslaved him becomes the very ground where God grows strength, wisdom, and peace. Guarding against bitterness is essential to a man who desires to walk in strength, clarity, and purpose. A bitter man may still function outwardly, but inwardly he is constrained, unable to lead with wisdom or love with freedom. But God never intended for a man to live bound by the wounds of his past. Healing begins when bitterness is confronted and released, not ignored or excused. It requires humility to admit the hurt, courage to forgive, and faith to trust that God is both just and able to restore what was lost.

When a man lays down bitterness, he reclaims his freedom. His vision clears, his heart softens, and his capacity to lead and love is renewed. He no longer operates from pain, but from purpose.

God never designed man to carry life alone. From the beginning, His declaration was clear, "It is not good for man to be alone." This truth reaches far beyond companionship; it speaks to the very structure of a man's strength. We were formed for connection, for brotherhood, for accountability that refines and relationships that reinforce. A man may appear strong in isolation, but true strength is forged in the presence of others who challenge him, encourage him, and stand with him. God places men in our lives not as a crutch, but as a sharpening force - voices that call us higher when we are tempted to settle lower. Iron sharpens iron, but iron cannot sharpen itself. In the same way, a man cannot fully grow, mature, or stay aligned with God on his own. When men unite in purpose, faith, and accountability, they become stronger together than they could ever be apart. Isolation weakens, but connection fortifies and, in that unity, a man finds not only strength, but the fullness of God's design for his life.

Healthy relationships are a God-designed necessity. Every man needs voices in his life that are grounded in truth - men who are committed to his growth. These are the ones who will challenge him when he drifts, correct him when he is wrong, and encourage him when he is weary. Iron sharpens iron, and without that sharpening, a man can slowly become dull without even realizing it. True strength is not found in standing alone, but in being humble enough to be known, corrected, and strengthened by others walking the same path. When a man rejects accountability, blind spots begin to multiply, and struggles take root in secrecy. What goes unchecked eventually grows, and what grows in the dark will one day surface in the light. But when a man surrounds himself with godly relationships, he places himself in an environment where truth has permission to speak and growth has room to flourish. These relationships become a safeguard keeping him aligned, grounded, and moving forward in purpose.

Maintaining meaningful relationships is intentional, and often sacrificial. It requires stepping beyond comfort and choosing connection when isolation feels easier. There are moments when withdrawing seems safer, when silence feels stronger, and when pride convinces you that you are better off handling things alone. But God did not design you to walk alone. He uses relationships to sharpen you, support you, and sustain you. Every time you choose to reach out instead of retreat, you are resisting the pull of isolation and stepping into the life-giving design of community. True connection demands courage. It requires laying down pride and embracing vulnerability, even when it feels uncomfortable or unnatural. Healing flows through shared burdens. Strength is multiplied when it is connected. When you choose connection over comfort, you align yourself with God's intention for your life, and you position yourself to be both strengthened by others and a source of strength to them.

There will be moments when isolation feels easier - that it is safer to withdraw than to risk being hurt again. In those moments, retreat can feel like protection, but it often becomes a prison. God never designed you to heal in hiding. The very pain that tempts you to pull away is often the place where God desires to meet you through others. He works through encouragement, accountability, and the presence of people who remind you of truth when your perspective has been shaken. What feels like self-preservation can quietly become separation from the very source of strength God has provided. What you withdraw from may be exactly what God wants to use to restore you. The conversation you avoid, the fellowship you resist, the hand you hesitate to reach for - these may carry the healing you need. Restoration often comes through reconnection. When you choose to step back in, even when it feels uncomfortable, you make room for God to rebuild what was broken.

Isolation magnifies pain, but connection multiplies grace. So resist the urge to disappear for in the presence of others God often restores courage, renews hope, and reminds you that you were never meant to walk this journey alone. Staying connected to God's people is a safeguard for your soul because isolation distorts your vision, but community restores it. In fellowship, strength is multiplied, burdens are shared, and hope is rekindled. God never designed you to fight every battle alone; He placed you within a body so that when one grows weak, another can help lift him up. In shared faith, you are constantly reminded that your struggle is not unique. Others have walked through valleys, faced doubt, endured hardship and yet they found victory through Christ. Their testimonies ignite the strength you need to keep going and become fuel for your perseverance. The enemy thrives in isolation, but breakthrough often comes in unity. Stay planted among God's people and you will find that you are never truly alone.

The enemy thrives in isolation because isolation distorts reality. In the silence, lies grow louder and begin to sound like truth. A man cut off from godly voices will often start believing that he is alone, that he is failing, that he cannot overcome. Without accountability and encouragement, his thoughts go unchallenged, his burdens feel heavier than they truly are, and his strength begins to erode. What once was a passing struggle can become a consuming weight when it is carried in secret. Isolation is the enemy's breeding ground because it removes the very relationships God designed to sharpen, support, and strengthen a man. But everything changes in the light of community. When a man steps out of isolation and into honest, godly connection, the enemy loses his advantage. Truth begins to replace deception, encouragement lifts what felt unbearable, and clarity breaks through confusion. In the presence of others who walk with God, lies are exposed, burdens are shared, and hope is restored.

Connection is one of God's greatest gifts to a man, because it pulls him out of isolation and places him in an environment where growth becomes unavoidable. When you walk alongside other men who are pursuing God with sincerity, accountability naturally takes root. You are no longer hidden - you are seen, challenged, and called higher. In that kind of brotherhood, encouragement flows freely. When one is weary, another speaks strength. When one stumbles, another helps him rise. A man becomes stronger not by withdrawing, but by locking arms with others who refuse to settle. You begin to rise to a higher standard because you are surrounded by men who are doing the same. Together, you build resilience, deepen your walk with God, and grow into the man you were created to be. Standing alone may feel strong for a moment, but standing together produces lasting transformation. In unity, there is strength. In brotherhood, there is sharpening. And in that connection, there is life.

Not every relationship that enters your life is sent to build you. Some will drain you, distract you, or slowly pull you away from the man God is calling you to become. Discernment is essential. A wise man surrounds himself with men who are anchored in truth, who pursue growth with intention, and who are unafraid to challenge compromise when they see it creeping in. These are the men who sharpen you, who call you higher, and who refuse to let you settle for a lesser version of yourself. True brotherhood is forged in accountability, honesty, and a shared pursuit of purpose. The right men will remind you of who you are when you forget, stand with you in battle, and push you forward when you feel like stepping back. When you choose your circle wisely, you are not just choosing friends - you are choosing the environment that will either fuel your destiny or fight against it. Choose men who make you stronger, not softer, and who lead you closer to God, not further away.

Isolation begins as a slow drift, a quiet pulling away from people, from accountability, and even from God. What feels like a need for space can gradually become a dangerous separation if left unchecked. That is why you must recognize it for what it is: a warning sign. Your spirit was never designed to thrive in disconnection. When you sense that drift, don't ignore it or justify it - confront it. Pause, examine your heart, and choose to move in the opposite direction. Take the step. Make the call. Start the conversation. Re-engage with the people God has placed in your life. Growth does not happen in isolation, it happens in connection, in sharpening, in shared faith and encouragement. When you step back into community, you position yourself again under the flow of God's support, wisdom, and grace. What once felt heavy begins to lift, and what felt distant becomes alive again. You were never meant to walk this path alone so step back in and let strength be restored.

The journey of faith was always meant to be shared with people who sharpen you, support you, and stand with you in both victory and struggle. When you try to carry everything on your own, you step outside of God's design and into unnecessary burden. True strength is not found in isolation, but in humility, in the willingness to receive encouragement, correction, and help from those God has placed in your life. There is a powerful grace that flows through godly relationships. The right people can remind you of truth when you feel weary, lift your arms when you grow tired, and walk beside you when the road gets difficult. God often answers prayers through people, sends direction through people, and provides strength through people. When you embrace the relationships He has given you, you position yourself to experience His provision in a deeper way. You were never meant to do life alone so walk boldly, not just with God, but with the people He has strategically placed around you.

Choose connection over isolation, for God never designed you to walk this journey alone. Isolation may feel safe in moments of pain, but it slowly erodes the soul, whispering lies that you are better off alone. Connection, on the other hand, is where healing begins. It is in honest conversations, in shared burdens, and in standing shoulder to shoulder with others that God restores what has been broken. When you choose connection, you step out of the shadows and into the light where grace, accountability, and encouragement can do their perfect work. Brotherhood reminds you that you are not the only one fighting battles, that you are part of a greater body, a family bound together by faith. As you open your heart again, as you trust God enough to let others in, you will discover something powerful: the strength you were searching for is found in unity, in shared faith, and in the presence of God moving through His people. Together, you are strengthened, sharpened, and sustained exactly as He intended.

| 15 |

"THE POWER OF INNER STRENGTH"

There is a strength that is not built in the gym, applauded on stages, or validated by the world's standards. It is formed in the quiet places - through surrender, obedience, and trust in God when no one is watching. This inner strength is born in the moments of testing, when a man chooses faith over fear, patience over panic, and truth over compromise. It is the strength that held David in the wilderness before he ever wore a crown, and the strength that anchored Jesus in the desert before His ministry began. This is the strength that carries a man through storms without breaking him. It steadies his heart when uncertainty rises and gives him peace when answers are nowhere to be found. Inner strength is not about controlling circumstances - it is about being controlled by the Spirit of God within you. It is the quiet confidence that says, "Even here, God is with me." And from that place, a man becomes unshakable - not because life is easy, but because his foundation is secure.

Inner strength is not handed to you at birth - it is forged in the unseen places of your life. It is built in the quiet moments when no one applauds, in the hidden battles where no one understands the weight you carry, and in the daily decisions to stand firm when it would be easier to fold. Every act of obedience, every moment of perseverance, and every choice to trust Him is adding strength within you that the world cannot take away. And when the pressure comes - when life tests you and quitting feels justified - it is that cultivated strength that rises up and carries you through. Inner strength grows each time you choose endurance over escape, faith over fear, and purpose over comfort. It is not the absence of struggle that defines you, but your refusal to surrender in the midst of it. As you continue to press forward, even when it's hard, you will discover that God has been building something powerful within you all along - a strength rooted not in your own ability, but in His sustaining grace.

The world measures strength by what can be displayed outwardly but God measures strength by something unseen by human eyes. True strength is forged in the quiet places of endurance, in the moments when no one is watching, and in the decision to keep trusting when everything around you feels uncertain. It is the strength to remain steady when life presses hard, to hold onto faith when answers are delayed, and to stand rooted in truth when everything else feels like it's shifting. This kind of strength unshakable. It is the quiet resolve that refuses to give up, the faith that anchors your soul in the middle of the storm, and the trust that declares God is still faithful no matter what you face. When circumstances try to push you down, true strength rises from within because it is not your strength alone, but His strength working through you. And when you stand unwavering and grounded in Him, you become a living testimony that real power is in the unbreakable spirit formed through faith.

There will be seasons when the ground beneath your feet feels unstable, when what once seemed certain begins to shift and unravel. Relationships may change and carefully laid plans may fall apart in ways you never expected. In those moments, the temptation is to grasp for control or place your hope in what can be seen. But anything built solely on external stability is vulnerable to collapse. When your strength depends on people or circumstances, it will rise and fall with them. Yet God never intended for your foundation to be so fragile. He calls you to a deeper strength - one that is not shaken by what happens around you, because it is rooted in Him. When your strength comes from being anchored in God, you discover a resilience that cannot be broken by life's storms. His presence becomes your stability, His truth your anchor, and His Spirit your source of endurance. Even when everything around you feels uncertain, there is a steady confidence rising within you that says, "I will not be moved."

Spiritual resilience is the backbone of inner strength. Life will knock you down, sometimes unexpectedly and sometimes repeatedly, but resilience is what whispers, "Get back up." It is the deep-rooted confidence that God is still with you in the valley, still working through the struggle, and still strengthening you through the fire. True resilience is not the absence of pain, but the refusal to let pain have the final word. To walk in spiritual resilience is to rise again and again with unwavering faith, knowing that every setback is an opportunity for growth and every trial is shaping something greater within you. It is the courage to press forward when progress feels slow, the discipline to keep believing when doubt creeps in, and the strength to trust God even when the outcome is unclear. You may bend, but you will not break. You may be wounded, but you are not defeated. With God as your foundation, you become unmovable - anchored, strengthened, and prepared to overcome whatever stands before you.

Resilience is not formed in comfort - it is forged in resistance. Just as muscles grow under tension, so the spirit of a man is strengthened through the pressures he endures. Every hardship carries within it the potential to refine your character, sharpen your endurance, and anchor your faith more deeply in God. What feels like opposition is often God's training ground, where He is developing perseverance, maturity, and unshakable trust within you. Do not despise the pressure. What feels heavy today is building strength for tomorrow. God is not trying to break you - He is building you. In the middle of the struggle, your faith is being stretched, your perspective is being transformed, and your spirit is being fortified. Stand firm, knowing that every challenge you overcome is adding weight to your testimony and depth to your walk with Him. What you are going through is not just resistance - it is preparation for the strength you will carry into your calling.

The storms of life are not sent to break you - they are sent to uncover you. When the winds rise and the rain falls, everything superficial is stripped away, and what remains is the truth of your foundation. It is easy to feel strong when life is calm, when circumstances are favorable, and when there is no resistance. But storms have a way of revealing what comfort can conceal. They expose where your trust truly lies - whether in your own strength, in temporary things, or in the unshakable presence of God. What feels like pressure is often revelation. God is not trying to destroy you; He is showing you who you are becoming and where you are anchored. If your foundation is weak, the storm will shake you - but even that shaking is an invitation, not a condemnation. It is a call to rebuild on something eternal. And when your life is rooted in God, the storm does not weaken you - it refines you. What once would have broken you now builds endurance, faith, and spiritual authority within you.

Inner strength is not something you stumble upon in moments of crisis - it is something that is formed in the quiet places where identity is settled. When a man does not know who he is, every storm feels personal, every setback feels defining, and every opinion feels like truth. He becomes like a wave tossed by the wind, shaped by circumstances instead of grounded in purpose. But when you anchor your identity in God, you begin to see yourself not through the lens of failure, fear, or insecurity, but through the unchanging truth of who God says you are chosen, called, equipped, and loved. That identity becomes a foundation that cannot be shaken by external pressure. When your identity is rooted in God, circumstances lose their power to define you. You stand firm because your foundation is secure. Inner strength flows from knowing who you belong to and what has been placed within you. And from that confidence, you walk with boldness, endure with resilience, and lead with clarity.

You are not defined by the moments you wish you could erase. Your past may have shaped parts of your journey, but it does not have the authority to name your future. The voices of others do not carry the weight of truth over your life. God alone is the author of your identity, and His voice speaks something far greater: you are chosen, set apart, and deeply loved. What He has spoken over you cannot be undone by what you have been through. When you anchor your identity in Him, shame loses its grip, insecurity loses its voice, and purpose begins to rise within you. You are designed for something meaningful that reaches beyond your own life. God has placed strength within you, not just to endure, but to overcome and to walk boldly in the path He has prepared. Stand firm in this truth and, as you step forward in faith, you will discover that who God says you are is more powerful than anything you have ever believed about yourself.

When your identity is secure in God, your strength no longer rises and falls with circumstances. You are no longer defined by opinions, past failures, or fleeting emotions. Doubt loses its voice, fear loses its grip, and insecurity no longer dictates your steps. Instead, you stand firm in who God says you are - chosen, called, equipped, and deeply loved. It is the strength of a man who knows where he stands and therefore cannot be easily moved. From that place of security, you become unshakable. Storms may come, pressure may rise, and opposition may surround you, but your foundation remains intact. You are not striving to prove yourself - you are living from a place of assurance. Your decisions grow clearer, your courage grows stronger, and your faith becomes resilient. When identity is rooted in God, stability follows. And when stability is established, strength becomes consistent. You no longer live reactively - you live intentionally, grounded in a truth that cannot be broken and a foundation that will never fail.

Becoming unshakable does not mean you will never feel pressure - it means pressure no longer has the power to define you. Life will bring moments that test your resolve, shake your confidence, and challenge your faith, but an unshakable spirit is rooted deeper than circumstance. It is anchored in God, not in comfort. When fear rises, it does not take control because faith has been cultivated to rise higher. This is the strength that comes from knowing who you are in God - steady, grounded, and secure even when everything around you feels uncertain. An unshakable life is the quiet confidence that God is still in control, even when the path ahead is unclear. When uncertainty surrounds you, peace remains within you because your trust is not in outcomes, but in His promises. You stand firm, not because you are strong on your own, but because you are strengthened by His Spirit. And in that place, you become immovable - unshaken by fear, unbroken by pressure, and unwavering in faith.

An unshakable man is not defined by a life free of hardship, but by a spirit that refuses to surrender in the midst of it. Storms may come, pressures may rise, and moments of weakness may visit him, yet he does not allow those moments to define his identity. Like a tree planted deep by living waters, he may bend under the force of the wind, but his roots hold firm. He does not quit when it gets hard - he stands, he endures, and he presses forward. His strength is not drawn from his own ability, but from the sustaining power of God within him. It is in surrender to God that he finds true resilience, and in faith that he discovers unbreakable endurance. He knows that he is not fighting alone, and that truth gives him courage to rise again and again. Though tested, he is not defeated; though shaken, he is not moved. For the man who is anchored in God becomes immovable in spirit - unshakable not because life is easy, but because his foundation is eternal.

There is a quiet but undeniable power in a man who has learned to govern what lies within him. When his thoughts are disciplined by truth rather than driven by fear, when his emotions are steadied by faith instead of tossed by circumstance, and when his spirit is rooted deeply in God, he becomes unmovable. He is no longer a prisoner to impulse, insecurity, or doubt. Instead, he walks with clarity, purpose, and conviction. His strength is cultivated in the hidden place, where character is formed and identity is secured in the presence of God. Storms may come, pressure may rise, and opposition may surround him, but he remains steady because his inner world is aligned with eternal truth. And when a man reaches this place, he becomes more than strong - he becomes influential. His life speaks. His presence carries weight. And through him, God's power is revealed, not in chaos, but in calm strength, unwavering faith, and a spirit that refuses to be moved.

Guard your inner life with intentional vigilance, for it is the wellspring from which your strength flows. Every thought you entertain, every word you dwell on, and every influence you permit into your heart is shaping the man you are becoming. If your mind is filled with fear, doubt, and deception, your strength will quietly erode. But when you choose to fill your spirit with truth - God's promises, His Word, and His voice - you begin to build an unshakable foundation. Be deliberate about what you feed your soul. Starve the lies that whisper inadequacy, defeat, and despair, and instead nourish your spirit with truth that declares who you are in God. What grows within you will eventually reveal itself in how you stand, how you speak, and how you endure. A man anchored in truth stands firm when pressure comes so guard your heart fiercely, not out of fear, but out of purpose because the strength you are building within today will determine the legacy you walk in tomorrow.

Silence is often where God does His deepest work within you. In a world filled with noise, pressure, and constant distraction, it is in the quiet moments that your soul finally has room to breathe. When you step away from the chaos and sit in stillness before Him, you begin to hear what truly matters. Your identity is reaffirmed, your burdens are lifted, and your perspective is realigned with truth. In that sacred silence, God renews your mind, restores your peace, and reminds you that your strength does not come from striving - but from abiding in Him. It is in these hidden moments that your spirit is fortified for the battles ahead. Long before strength is visible on the outside, it is built in the unseen places - through prayer, reflection, and quiet trust. When you emerge from those moments with Him, you carry a strength that cannot be shaken by circumstance. You walk with clarity, confidence, and peace, not because life is easy, but because you have been anchored in the presence of the One who sustains you.

Do not neglect the hidden place, for it is there that true strength is formed. In the quiet moments of prayer, God is shaping your character and fortifying your spirit. Private surrender is not weakness - it is the birthplace of power. It is where pride is broken, where identity is anchored, and where your dependence on God becomes unshakable. Long before any public victory is won, the battle is first surrendered in the hidden place. What is built in secret will sustain you in the open. When the pressures rise and the spotlight intensifies, you will not draw from hype or emotion - you will draw from depth. The discipline, the intimacy, and the obedience forged behind closed doors become the foundation that holds you steady when everything else is shaking. Those who endure are not those who perform well in public, but those who have learned to bow low in private. Guard your hidden place, for it is there that God prepares you, strengthens you, and equips you for every battle you are called to face.

Inner strength is often misunderstood as self-sufficiency - the ability to stand alone, to endure without help, to rely solely on one's own power. But true spiritual strength is not found in independence from God; it is discovered in complete dependence on Him. The strongest man is not the one who needs nothing, but the one who recognizes his need for God in everything. When you surrender your will, your fears, and your limitations to Him, you tap into a strength that is not your own. The more you rely on Him, the stronger you become - not because your circumstances change, but because His power begins to flow through you. When you trust Him fully, you are no longer striving to hold everything together; you are being carried by the One who holds all things together. In that dependence, fear loses its grip and you rise with a quiet, unbreakable strength that cannot be shaken by storms. This is the power of a life rooted in God - strength that endures, faith that stands firm, and a spirit that cannot be defeated.

In the end, the power of inner strength is not found in human willpower alone, but in the quiet, unyielding presence of God within you. Storms may rise, pressures may mount, and opposition may come from every direction, yet you remain standing - not because you are untouched by adversity, but because you are anchored in something eternal. When your identity is rooted in Him, you are no longer defined by what surrounds you, but by what sustains you. His strength becomes your strength, His peace steadies your heart, and His Spirit fortifies you from the inside out. When God is your foundation, you are built upon a rock that cannot crumble. No matter what comes against you, you endure. You rise again. You press forward. Not in your own strength, but in His power working through you. And in that divine partnership, you become a living testimony that true strength is not about standing alone - it is about standing filled, sustained, and secured by the One who never fails.

| 16 |

"WHEN GOD FEELS SILENT"

There are seasons in every man's life when heaven feels quiet - when prayers seem to rise into silence and no immediate response comes forth. These are not moments of abandonment, but moments of refinement. God is not absent; He is often working in ways too deep for noise. In the silence, He strips away dependence on feelings and builds a faith that stands on truth alone. It is easy to trust when His voice is clear, but real strength is formed when the echoes fade and all you have left is His Word and your willingness to believe it. Silence is not rejection - it is an invitation to draw nearer, to seek Him not for what He says, but for who He is. This is where endurance is born. This is where a man learns to walk by faith and not by sight. And though it may feel like nothing is happening, heaven is not still - God is shaping your character, strengthening your spirit, and preparing you for what lies ahead. Stay the course. The silence will break, but the strength you gain in it will remain.

Silence from God is one of the deepest places your faith will ever be tested. It strips away the comfort of feelings and forces you to stand on what you truly believe. In those moments, it can feel as though heaven is closed and your prayers are echoing into emptiness. But what feels like distance is often divine intention. God is working beneath the surface, strengthening your trust, refining your character, and aligning circumstances in ways your eyes cannot yet perceive. When God is quiet, He is inviting you to walk by faith and not by sight. This is where trust becomes real - when you choose to believe He is near even when you cannot feel Him, when you hold onto His promises without visible proof. Waiting in silence is sacred ground where endurance is built and hope is purified. Stay steady. Stay faithful. The same God who spoke in the beginning has not stopped speaking - He is simply working in a deeper way, and in the right moment, His voice and His plan will become unmistakably clear.

There are seasons when heaven feels silent, when your prayers seem to rise but never return with an answer. You ask, you seek, you knock, and still, the door appears closed. In those moments, doubt quietly tries to take root, whispering that your faith is misplaced and your voice unheard. But do not be deceived - God's silence is not His absence. The enemy would have you believe you've been forgotten, but that lie is crafted to weaken your resolve and pull you away from the very One who is still working behind the scenes. So stand firm, even when you hear nothing. Keep praying, even when you see no movement. Faith is not proven when answers come quickly - it is proven when you remain steadfast in the waiting. Every unanswered prayer is a preparation, aligning your heart, your character, and your path with something greater than you can't yet understand. Hold your ground. Trust deeper and you will see that God was never distant - He was guiding, shaping, and preparing you all along.

God has never forgotten His sons - not once, not ever. A father does not abandon his child simply because he is silent; often, his silence carries purpose. God sees every step you take, every burden you carry, and every tear you try to hide. His silence is intentional, filled with wisdom beyond what you can yet understand. What feels like distance is often divine restraint, because He knows that timing is just as important as the blessing itself. While you are waiting for an answer, He is not idle - He is working within you. He is shaping your character so you can carry what you've been praying for, strengthening your endurance so you won't collapse under the weight of your calling, and aligning your heart so that when the answer comes, it won't destroy you but elevate you. Waiting is not wasted time in the kingdom of God; it is sacred ground where transformation takes place. So stand firm in the silence because when God finally speaks, you will realize He was never absent - He was preparing you all along.

Faith that depends on constant reassurance is easily unsettled. It rises and falls with circumstances, emotions, and visible outcomes. But real faith is not built on what can be seen - it is forged in what cannot. When the voice of God seems quiet and the signs you long for are absent, it can feel unsettling, even discouraging. Yet these moments are not signs of His absence; they are invitations into maturity. God is teaching you to stand, not on what you feel, but on who He is. In the silence, your roots go deeper, anchoring you in truth rather than temporary confirmation. Unshakable faith is born in these hidden places. It is the kind of faith that continues to pray when there is no immediate answer, that continues to believe when there is no visible evidence, that continues to walk forward when the path is unclear. When God feels quiet, He is inviting you to trust His character over your circumstances. As you choose trust over feeling you will discover a faith that is firm, steady, and immovable.

Many men walk away when heaven seems quiet. Silence can feel like absence, and absence can tempt a man to disengage. But what if the silence is not rejection, but invitation? What if God is not withdrawing, but deepening? The easy path is to step back when you feel nothing. The common response is to stop pursuing when there is no immediate reward. Yet silence is often where faith is proven - not in what is felt, but in what is chosen. The man of God does not measure his devotion by emotion - he measures it by commitment. When others pull away, he leans in. When feelings fade, his faith remains. He presses in - not because it feels good, but because God is worthy. In the quiet, he builds strength. In the unseen, he develops endurance.

He chooses prayer when it feels dry, worship when it feels empty, and obedience when it feels costly. And it is there, in that sacred persistence, that something powerful is forged within him - a faith that is no longer dependent on feelings, but anchored in truth.

Silence has a way of exposing what noise often hides. When God speaks clearly, it is easy to feel confident, directed, and secure - but when His voice seems quiet, the foundation of your faith is revealed. In those moments, you are faced with a deeper question: was your trust built on His voice alone, or on His unchanging nature? Silence calls you to walk not by what you hear, but by what you know to be true. God's character does not shift with your circumstances, and His presence does not fade when His voice grows still. In the quiet, faith is no longer sustained by reassurance - it is sustained by conviction. Real faith chooses trust over feelings, confidence over clarity, and endurance over doubt. It remembers every time God has been faithful before and anchors itself in that truth. Silence is where your faith matures, your trust strengthens, and your relationship with Him becomes rooted beyond emotion. So stand firm in the quiet. Keep walking, keep believing, and keep trusting.

There is a refining that only happens in quiet seasons when the noise fades, the striving settles, and the distractions that once filled your days are gently stripped away. In these moments, you are left face to face with what truly matters: your heart and your trust in God. It is here, in the stillness, that God does His deepest work - not through loud displays or sudden breakthroughs, but through steady, unseen transformation. What feels like emptiness is often sacred space, where He is clearing away the unnecessary so He can strengthen what remains. The quiet is not your absence from purpose; it is your preparation for it. Do not rush these seasons or try to escape them. What God is forming in you here cannot be rushed or replicated in noise. Depth is cultivated in the quiet decision to trust Him when nothing seems to be happening. Roots grow deeper in silence, anchoring you for the storms ahead. And when the time comes for you to rise, to speak and act, you will be grounded, steady, and strong.

God's timing is never hurried, never pressured, and never late. What feels slow to you is not slow to Him. In the quiet spaces where nothing seems to be happening, He is arranging, preparing, and aligning things in ways you cannot yet see. Every closed door, every waiting season, and every unanswered prayer is not neglect - it is intention. God is not reacting to your situation; He is orchestrating it with precision. So when you feel the weight of delay, do not mistake it for denial. Trust that behind the scenes, God is positioning people, shaping your character, and setting circumstances into place for the right moment. If He moved according to your urgency, you might step into something before you are ready or receive something before it can truly bless you. But because He loves you, He waits until everything is aligned with His perfect will. Stay faithful in the waiting. Stay anchored in trust. What is coming is being prepared perfectly, and when it arrives, you will understand why it could not have come any sooner.

Waiting is not wasted when it is surrendered - it is transformed. In the quiet places where nothing seems to be moving, God is doing His deepest work within you. What feels like delay is often divine development. Every moment you choose to remain faithful, even when you don't see results, is strengthening your character, refining your spirit, and anchoring your trust more firmly in Him. The world measures progress by visible outcomes, but God measures it by inward growth. And in His kingdom, what is built in hidden seasons carries eternal weight. Patience, then, is not passive—it is active trust in motion. It is the steady decision to believe God is working even when you cannot trace His hand. It is choosing obedience over frustration, hope over doubt, and surrender over control. In waiting, you are not standing still - you are walking by faith. And as you continue to trust

Him in the unseen, you are becoming the kind of person who can carry the very answers you are praying for.

Hope must be guarded most fiercely in those moments when heaven seems quiet and answers feel delayed. Disappointment will try to settle in, whispering that nothing is changing and nothing is coming. Like weeds in a garden, if disappointment is left unchecked, it will choke out the life of your faith and steal the confidence you once carried. Guard your heart with intention. Hold onto hope, even when your hands feel weak and your spirit feels tired. Hope is not denial; it is a declaration that God is still working, even when you cannot see it. It becomes the anchor that steadies you in uncertainty and the strength that carries you through the waiting. When you choose hope, you are choosing to trust God's timing over your own understanding. And in that trust, something deeper is formed within you - endurance, resilience, and unwavering faith. The answer will come, but until it does, hope will sustain you, strengthen you, and remind you that God has not forgotten you.

Some of God's greatest movements are born in the quiet places where nothing seems to be happening. It is in the stillness that He is working beneath the surface, aligning hearts, strengthening faith, and preparing what cannot yet be seen. Silence is not absence - it is often divine preparation. Just as the seed grows unseen beneath the soil before it breaks through, so God is moving in ways you may not yet recognize. In these moments, faith is not proven by what you hear, but by how you trust when you hear nothing at all. Before breakthrough, there is stillness. Before clarity, there is waiting. Before the promise is fulfilled, there is a process. Do not despise this season for it is shaping you for what is ahead. God is not delaying; He is developing. Every moment of waiting is building endurance, deepening your dependence, and refining your character. Hold steady. What feels like silence today will become the foundation of tomorrow's testimony.

The man who endures silence without quitting is being forged in a place few are willing to remain. He does not retreat, he does not compromise, and he does not allow temporary silence to rewrite eternal truth. In that quiet place, his faith matures beyond emotional dependence and becomes rooted in the unchanging character of God. He learns that God is still faithful when He is quiet, still present when He feels distant, and still working when nothing appears to be moving. This kind of man is no longer led by what he sees or feels - he is anchored in who God is. And that is what makes him dangerous in the Kingdom of God. He cannot be manipulated by fear, discouraged by delay, or shaken by uncertainty. He has learned to walk by faith, not by sight, and that kind of endurance produces a strength the enemy cannot break. A man like this becomes steady, bold, and unyielding because when you strip away everything else, what remains is a life fully anchored in God.

You may not hear God right now, but He hears you. In the silence, when your prayers seem to echo without reply and your heart grows weary from waiting, heaven is still listening. Nothing you have poured out before Him is lost or overlooked. What feels like silence is not neglect, it is often the sacred space where God is working beyond what your eyes can see and your ears can hear. He is near to the brokenhearted, attentive to every detail of your struggle, even when His voice seems quiet. Heaven is not ignoring you; it is preparing something for you. While you wait, God is aligning circumstances, strengthening your faith, and shaping your character for what is ahead. What you're walking through is holy ground where endurance is built and trust is refined. Hold on. Keep praying. Keep believing. The same God who hears you in the silence will answer in His perfect timing, and when He does, you will see that every moment of waiting had purpose, and every tear was part of a greater testimony.

Stay faithful in the unseen, for it is in the hidden places that God does His deepest work. What feels repetitive to you is often preparation in

His hands. Every quiet prayer, every unseen act of obedience, every moment you choose faith over feeling is building something eternal within you. You may not see immediate results, but heaven records every step of trust you take. Faith is not proven in what is visible - it is forged in the moments where nothing seems to be happening, yet you choose to believe anyway. Continue to pray, continue to believe, continue to stand. Even when your emotions grow weary and your circumstances remain unchanged, God is still moving behind the scenes. What feels like silence is not absence - it is divine timing at work. Do not walk away from what God has called you to stand in. Breakthrough often comes to those who refuse to quit. Hold your ground, fix your eyes on Him, and trust that in due season, what was done in secret will be revealed in power.

God often chooses the hidden places to do His deepest work - not the spotlight, not the noise, but the quiet, unseen corners of your life where transformation can take root without distraction. The silence you feel is not a void; it is a workshop. What feels like delay is often divine development, where roots are growing deeper so that what He builds in you can stand stronger. Do not mistake stillness for absence. Just because you cannot see God moving does not mean He has stopped working. Beneath the surface, prayers are being prepared for answers, doors are being positioned to open, and your spirit is being refined for what lies ahead. Faith is not proven in what you can see - it is revealed in what you choose to believe when you cannot. So remain steady in the hidden place. Trust Him in the silence. For when the season shifts and what was done in secret is revealed, you will realize that God was working all along - faithfully, powerfully, and perfectly on your behalf.

Do not confuse stillness with abandonment. There are seasons when heaven seems quiet, when the voice that once guided you so clearly now feels distant. The same God who spoke light into darkness, who whispered direction into your spirit before, has not stepped away from you now. He is still near, still working, still present in ways you may not immediately see. In the stillness, He is strengthening your faith beyond feelings, teaching you to stand not just on what you hear - but on who He is. He is calling you into deeper trust, deeper surrender, and deeper confidence in His timing and His ways. When the noise fades and the answers delay, it is not because God has forgotten you, but because He is maturing you. Faith grows strongest in the quiet places, where dependence replaces doubt and trust outlasts uncertainty. So keep believing. The God who spoke before will speak again and, when He does, you will recognize His voice even more clearly because you learned to trust Him in the silence.

One day, the silence will break. What felt like unanswered prayers will suddenly make sense, and what seemed like delay will reveal itself as divine timing. In the quiet seasons, when heaven felt still and your heart wrestled with uncertainty, God was at work beneath the surface. Like roots growing deep before a tree ever rises tall, He was strengthening your faith, aligning circumstances, and preparing what you could not yet see. His silence was intentional, precise, and filled with purpose. And when the answer comes you will look back and recognize His hand in every moment. You will see that nothing was wasted, no tear ignored, no prayer unheard. God was moving faithfully, weaving together every detail with perfect wisdom and timing. What you once questioned, you will now trust. What once felt uncertain will stand as testimony. So hold on in the silence, because the same God who promised is the One who fulfills and He is working even now, perfectly and faithfully, on your behalf.

Until that day, stand firm. God has not stepped away - He has simply shifted the way He is working. In the stillness, He is strengthening roots that cannot be shaken, forming character that cannot be rushed, and building faith that does not depend on constant reassurance. Trust His timing, even when it stretches longer than you expected. What feels like delay is often divine development. He is aligning things you cannot yet see, orchestrating outcomes you cannot yet understand, and shaping you into someone who can carry what you have been praying for. Guard your hope with everything in you. Do not let discouragement speak louder than truth. A silent God is not an absent God. He is a present God working in hidden ways, doing deep work beneath the surface. Silence produces endurance. It teaches you to walk by faith and not by sight. And when His voice breaks through and His promises unfold you will realize that the silence was full of purpose, full of transformation, and full of God Himself.

| 17 |

"CONQUERING FEAR"

Fear is one of the enemy's most subtle yet powerful weapons against a man's calling. It creeps in quietly, whispering lies that erode confidence and distort identity. It tells a man he is unprepared when God has already equipped him, that he is incapable when God has already called him, and that he is too weak when God's strength is made perfect in weakness. If left unchecked, fear will paralyze purpose, causing a man to hesitate at the very moment he is meant to step forward. It thrives in silence, feeding on doubt and magnifying uncertainty until the voice of God feels distant. But fear loses its grip when a man chooses faith over feelings and truth over lies. When a man anchors himself in God's promises, he begins to see fear for what it truly is: a barrier meant to be broken, not obeyed. Every step taken in faith weakens fear's voice and strengthens spiritual resolve. You are not called because you are ready - you are ready because you are called. Stand firm, move forward, and let faith rise louder than fear.

Fear is a master of distortion. It takes a moment and stretches it into a mountain, takes a shadow and shapes it into a giant. What God has spoken with clarity, fear clouds with doubt. It magnifies the obstacle until it dominates your vision, while quietly shrinking your purpose until it feels distant and unreachable. A man who listens to fear begins to question what he once knew was certain. He hesitates, delays, and eventually stands still not because he lacks strength, but because his focus has been redirected from God's calling to his own limitations. Fear does not have to defeat you to win; it only has to paralyze you long enough to keep you from moving forward. But God never called you to live frozen in the presence of intimidation. He calls you to see clearly again - to lift your eyes beyond the obstacle and fix them on His promise. The mountains fear creates are no match for the purpose God placed inside you. The giants that loom in your mind shrink when you step forward in faith.

Many men are not bound by visible chains, but by invisible fears that grip the mind and paralyze the spirit. Fear whispers lies that keep men standing still when God is calling them forward. Yet Scripture reminds us that God has not given us a spirit of fear, but of power, love, and a sound mind. Every time you choose faith over fear, you break another link of that unseen bondage. Movement begins the moment you trust God more than you trust your doubts. Purpose was never meant to be discovered in comfort - it is revealed in obedience. When you step forward despite trembling, when you speak though your voice shakes, when you stand firm in the face of opposition, you align yourself with the courage God has already placed within you. Fear may try to delay your calling, but it cannot destroy what God has ordained. So rise up. Take the step. Say the words. Stand your ground. Because on the other side of your obedience is the life you were created to live and fear has no authority to keep you from it.

Fear may knock, but it does not belong in the house of a man who knows his God. It may whisper lies, paint worst-case scenarios, and try to magnify the unknown, but its voice is not the voice of your Father. God does not plant fear - He plants power. He breathes courage into your spirit, steadies your mind, and anchors your heart in truth. When fear rises, it is not a signal to retreat - it is a call to remember who you are and whose you are. You are not governed by intimidation but by divine authority, shaped by love, and equipped with clarity of mind. So stand firm when fear comes knocking. Do not entertain it, do not negotiate with it, and do not give it a seat at your table. Instead, answer it with truth. Declare what God has spoken over your life. Walk forward even when your knees feel weak because a man anchored in God does not live by what he feels, but by what he knows. And what he knows is this: fear has no power over a life surrendered to God, filled with His love, and led by His Spirit.

Courage is not found in the absence of fear, but in the moment you choose to rise despite it. True courage is born in that sacred tension where your weakness meets His strength, where your hesitation is overcome by trust. It is there that you discover you were never meant to walk alone - God has gone before you to prepare the way, He stands beside you to steady your steps, and He works within you to give you the strength you thought you lacked. So step forward, even if your voice trembles and your path is unclear. The unknown is filled with the presence of the One who called you. Every act of obedience strengthens your spirit and silences the grip of fear. Courage grows each time you choose faith over feeling, each time you move when it would be easier to stay. And as you walk, you will begin to see that what once intimidated you now bows to the authority of God within you. For the same God who calls you is faithful to sustain you and, in Him, you are far stronger than your fear.

Faith is the foundation upon which courage is built, and without it, fear quietly takes root and grows. Faith does not deny the presence of fear; it confronts it with a greater truth. It reminds him that he is not alone, not abandoned, and not at the mercy of what could go wrong. Instead, he is held by a faithful God who sees the end from the beginning. In that assurance, fear begins to weaken, losing the authority it once claimed. With faith, a man's focus shifts from the instability of his surroundings to the sovereignty of his Creator. He no longer lives in reaction to every threat or possibility but stands firm in the confidence of who is in control. Faith lifts his eyes above the storm and fixes them on the One who commands the wind and the waves. And as his vision changes, so does his posture - no longer shrinking back, but stepping forward with boldness and resolve. Courage is no longer something he must manufacture; it becomes the natural outflow of a heart fully surrendered to God.

When a man truly believes that God is with him, something powerful begins to shift within his spirit. What once felt overwhelming now appears smaller in the light of God's presence. The same storm that once caused him to retreat becomes the very place where his faith is stretched and strengthened. He begins to see that every challenge is not sent to defeat him, but to deepen his dependence on God. Confidence rises and fear starts to lose its grip. In that place of trust, intimidation is replaced with quiet boldness. The battles that once caused trembling now become proving grounds where God's strength is revealed through him. He no longer measures the size of the obstacle; he measures the greatness of his God. Each step forward becomes a declaration of faith, each act of courage a testimony that God is faithful. And as he continues to stand, to trust, and to move forward, he discovers that what once threatened to break him has instead built him into a man who cannot easily be shaken.

Throughout scripture, the men who stood tallest were not those who felt no fear, but those who chose faith in the face of it. David stood before Goliath not with the confidence of a warrior seasoned in battle, but with the assurance of a shepherd who knew his God. Daniel faced the lions' den not because he was unafraid of death, but because he was unwilling to compromise his devotion. Their strength was rooted in a heart anchored in trust, a spirit surrendered to God. They did not stand firm because they were naturally bold, but because they were spiritually grounded. Likewise, when your confidence rests in God rather than in yourself, you can face overwhelming odds without being overwhelmed. The God who called you is the same God who equips you, strengthens you, and stands with you. So stand firm - not in your own ability, but in His unchanging power. For when faith rises, fear loses its voice, and the impossible becomes the very ground where God proves Himself faithful.

Facing giants is part of every man's journey, and the battlefield is often within. These giants may not carry swords or shields, but they are just as intimidating - fear of failure whispers that you're not enough, fear of rejection convinces you to stay hidden, fear of inadequacy tells you you'll never measure up, and fear of the unknown urges you to retreat. They rise up at the very moments when you are called to step forward. But understand this: just as David stood before Goliath not in his own strength but in confidence in God, so you too are called to face what towers over you with faith, not fear. Do not shrink back when the giant appears. Stand your ground. Move forward even when your voice shakes and your knees feel weak. Every giant you confront becomes a testimony of God's faithfulness in your life. And when you refuse to run, when you choose to stand, you will discover that what once seemed impossible is brought down not by your might, but by His power working through you.

Giants are not accidents - they are assignments. They do not appear to destroy you, but to draw something out of you that comfort never could. When fear rises and the obstacle looks too great, it is not a signal to retreat, but a call to remember who stands with you and what He has already deposited inside of you. God does not send you into battles empty-handed; He equips you with faith, courage, and authority long before the giant ever steps into view. What feels like intimidation is often revelation - an unveiling of strength you did not know you carried. So when you face your giant, do not measure its size—measure your God. The very thing that seems to threaten your progress is actually inviting your growth. It is calling you higher, deeper, and stronger. Rise to meet it, not in your own power, but in confidence that God has already prepared you for this moment. For every giant you confront is an opportunity to prove that what is within you, by God's design, is greater than anything standing against you.

Confidence is forged in confrontation. The giants you face are designed to draw out the strength God has already placed within you. When you choose to stand instead of retreat, to step forward instead of shrinking back, something shifts within your spirit. Fear begins to lose its grip, not all at once, but with every faithful step you take. Like David before Goliath, confidence is not the absence of intimidation - it is the presence of trust in a God who is greater than what stands against you. Each act of courage declares that your faith is louder than your fear. Every step of obedience builds a foundation that cannot be shaken. Confidence grows not from ease, but from endurance; not from avoidance, but from engagement. As fear's voice weakens, faith's voice becomes clearer, steadier, and stronger. And over time, what once intimidated you will no longer move you. You will stand firm, not because the giants disappeared, but because you have learned that with God, you are more than able to face them.

A man who faces his fears begins to awaken a strength he did not know he possessed. What once towered over him starts to shrink, not because the challenge disappears, but because his faith rises. With every step forward, he learns that fear was never meant to master him - it was meant to be mastered. In trusting God and moving anyway, he discovers that courage is not the absence of fear, but the decision to stand firm in the presence of it. As he continues to challenge what once held him back, something shifts within him. What once felt overwhelming becomes manageable, and what once seemed impossible becomes attainable. Confidence is built not in comfort, but in confrontation. And in that process, he begins to see himself the way God sees him - capable, called, and equipped. Fear no longer dictates his path; faith does. And the man who once hesitated now walks boldly, knowing that every fear he faces is another opportunity for God's strength to be revealed in his life.

Intimidation is fear wearing a louder voice. It magnifies the strength of your opposition while shrinking your sense of identity. When a man forgets who he is in God, he begins to measure himself against people instead of promises. Yet the truth remains: you were not called because you were the strongest - you were called because God is. And when He stands with you, no voice of intimidation has the authority to silence what He has placed inside you. So stand firm. Refuse to bow to pressure or shrink back in the face of opposition. The same God who called David before Goliath, who strengthened Moses before Pharaoh, now stands with you in your moment. Let intimidation lose its grip as you lift your eyes above the noise and fix them on God. Speak when fear says be silent. Step forward when intimidation says retreat. For the man who trusts in the Lord does not live small - he walks in authority, courage, and unshakable confidence.

Intimidation only gains ground when a man loses sight of his identity. It whispers lies, magnifies threats, and attempts to shrink purpose but its power is rooted in deception. Fear begins to lose its grip the moment a man remembers who he is and whose he is. Identity anchored in God is unshakable, because it is not built on circumstances, opinions, or opposition. It is built on truth. And truth stands firm when everything else trembles. When a man is rooted in that truth, intimidation has no authority over him. He may feel pressure, but he will not bow to it. He may face resistance, but he will not retreat. A man who knows his calling walks with quiet confidence, not because the path is easy, but because the One who called him is faithful. He stands steady when others waver, speaks boldly when others shrink back, and moves forward when others hesitate. Why? Because he understands that his life is not his own - it is a mission entrusted by God. And a man on assignment cannot be easily shaken.

Standing strong requires more than determination - it requires a foundation that cannot be shaken. A man who is grounded in truth does not drift with the opinions of the world, nor does he bend under the weight of cultural pressure. He is anchored in faith, rooted deeply in the unchanging promises of God, and built upon a rock that does not move when storms arise. When challenges come he does not collapse because his strength is not built on feelings or circumstances, but on conviction. Truth becomes his compass, and faith becomes his footing, keeping him steady when everything around him seems uncertain. He stands when others shrink back. He speaks when others stay silent. He moves forward when others hesitate. Not because he feels no fear, but because he refuses to be ruled by it. His courage is knowing that God is greater than anything he faces. This is how he becomes unshakable, steady, resolute, and unwavering in a world that desperately needs men who will stand.

Strength is not discovered in the absence of conflict, but in the presence of it. A man does not become strong by running from the battle - he becomes strong by standing in it, by refusing to be shaken when pressure rises and opposition surrounds him. The storms of life are inevitable, but when your roots are driven deep into God, when your identity is anchored in His truth and your confidence rests in His promises, you become unmovable. The wind may howl, the rain may fall, and the ground around you may tremble but the man who is planted in God does not collapse. He stands, not because the storm is weak, but because his foundation is strong. So when the battle comes, do not retreat but stand firm in your faith. Stand firm in your calling. Stand firm in the truth that God is with you and for you. Let every trial drive your roots deeper, not push you away. For it is in the storm that your strength is revealed, your faith is refined, and your life becomes a testimony of endurance.

Fear is relentless. It does not give up easily, and neither can you. While fear may be persistent, it is not powerful when it is confronted with truth. A man of faith does not pretend fear isn't there - he faces it head-on with the Word of God anchored in his heart. When fear rises, he responds. He speaks truth over his situation. He reminds his soul of who God is, what God has promised, and what God has already brought him through. Fear may knock at the door, but it does not get to live in a house where faith stands guard. Every time doubt begins to speak, it must be answered with conviction. You must rise up and declare what is true, even when your feelings say otherwise. Faith is active, vocal, and unyielding. It stands firm when everything tries to shake it. So when fear returns - and it will - meet it again with unshakable truth. Answer it again with bold conviction. Because a man who continually chooses faith over fear becomes a man who cannot be moved.

Each day presents new voices that whisper doubt, hesitation, and insecurity, but faith answers with quiet strength. It is in the daily choosing that courage is formed. You may not feel bold every morning, but when you rise and place your trust in God again, you are already overcoming. Fear loses its grip not in a single dramatic victory, but in the steady, persistent decision to believe that God is greater than whatever stands before you. Over time, those small decisions reshape the heart of a man. What once intimidated you begins to lose its power, and what once felt impossible becomes part of your testimony. Courage is not the absence of fear - it is the evidence of faith in motion. As you continue to choose faith over fear, day after day, you will find that courage is no longer something you strive for - it becomes who you are. And in that transformation, you walk not as a man controlled by fear, but as one led by the unshakable confidence that God is with you in every step.

So stand up. Face what you have been avoiding. The thing that has been looming over you only holds power as long as you keep your distance from it. Fear thrives in the shadows of avoidance, growing larger in your imagination than it ever could in reality. But when you step forward in faith, when you choose obedience over comfort, you begin to see clearly that what once intimidated you is not greater than the God within you. The moment you confront it is the moment its

illusion begins to break. You can confront what has been intimidating you because God has not given you a spirit of fear, but of power,
love, and a sound mind. The fear you refuse to face will always seek
to control you, but the fear you confront will bow before you because
it must submit to the authority of faith. Every step forward is a declaration that you will not be ruled by intimidation but led by purpose.
So rise with courage, move with conviction, and watch as what once
tried to stop you is forced to step aside.

| 18 |

"GUARD YOUR INTEGRITY"

Integrity is not forged in the spotlight - it is revealed in the shadows. It is proven in the quiet places where choices are made without applause or accountability. In those unseen moments, a man is either building strength or allowing compromise to take root. What is done in secret shapes the man he becomes in public. A life of integrity is not built in a day - it is formed decision by decision, choice by choice, in the stillness where character is tested and refined. A man who desires to walk with God must understand that integrity is not optional - it is essential. It is the foundation upon which trust is built, the guardrail that keeps him from drifting, and the quiet strength that sustains him when temptation comes. When a man chooses what is right, even when it costs him something, he aligns himself with truth and honors the God he serves. And in time, what was developed in the shadows will shine with undeniable strength in the light because a man of integrity does not just speak truth, he lives it.

The temptations a man faces in private often slip in quietly through a thought entertained too long, a compromise excused too easily, a moment of weakness justified by circumstance. What feels like a small indulgence or a harmless detour is often the seed of something far greater. The enemy of your soul does not need a loud victory - only a quiet agreement. And over time, those private agreements shape public outcomes. But God calls men to a higher standard - one of integrity that is consistent in both the light and the dark. A strong man is not merely one who stands firm before others, but one who stands firm when he stands alone. Private victories build public strength so guard your thoughts, protect your habits, and refuse the lie that small compromises don't matter. For in the quiet places, where battles are unseen, destinies are either weakened or strengthened. Choose to be the same man in private that you claim to be in public and you will become a man God can trust with greater things.

Private battles are never truly private. What a man tolerates in the hidden places of his life will eventually find a voice in the open. The thoughts he entertains in silence, the compromises he justifies when no one is watching, and the habits he feeds in secrecy all work together to form the man he becomes. A divided life cannot produce a stable foundation. Sooner or later, what is concealed will surface, because character is not built in the spotlight, but it is revealed there. Integrity is the bridge between who a man appears to be and who he truly is. It is choosing righteousness when there is no applause, and truth when there is no accountability. A man of integrity does not live two lives - he lives one consistent life before God. He understands that his hidden obedience shapes his visible authority. When what is unseen aligns with what is seen, there is power, peace, and credibility. Guard your inner life with vigilance, for it is the wellspring of everything you will become.

Many men fall into the trap of managing their image rather than guarding their character. They carefully curate how they are seen, polishing the outward appearance while neglecting the inward condition of the heart. But reputation shifts with opinion, rises and falls with circumstance, and can vanish in a moment. A man may be praised in public and compromised in private, celebrated by others while silently eroding within. God does not measure a man by the applause he receives, but by the integrity he maintains when no one is watching. What is hidden matters more than what is seen, for it is in the unseen places that true strength is formed. Integrity, however, is rooted deep. It is not built on performance, but on conviction. It is forged through daily choices - choosing truth over convenience, purity over compromise, and obedience over approval. While reputation seeks validation from people, integrity seeks alignment with God. And though it may go unnoticed by the world, it is honored in heaven.

A man of integrity lives with a deep awareness that his true identity is not shaped by applause or criticism, but by the unchanging gaze of God. Reputation may rise and fall with opinions, rumors, or moments of visibility, but integrity is forged in the hidden places where no audience exists and no recognition is given. It is in those quiet decisions, those unseen choices, that a man proves who he really is. While others may be fooled by appearances, God sees the heart with perfect clarity. A man anchored in integrity does not chase the approval of people, because he knows that standing right before God carries eternal weight. When a man prioritizes integrity, he builds his life on a foundation that cannot be shaken by shifting perceptions. He chooses truth over image, conviction over convenience, and obedience over popularity. Even when it costs him recognition, opportunities, or acceptance, he remains steady, knowing that what God knows about him matters far more than what the world says.

When a man drifts into isolation, he may convince himself that what he does in private carries no weight, but it is in those hidden moments that character is either strengthened or slowly eroded. Without accountability, the voice of conviction can become faint, and the heart begins to justify what it once resisted. Isolation feeds deception, allowing compromise to feel acceptable and even necessary. But what begins in secrecy shapes the man he is becoming. That is why guarding integrity is not a passive act, but a deliberate pursuit of connection. A man must stay anchored to God, inviting His presence into both public and private spaces, and surround himself with brothers who are unafraid to challenge, correct, and strengthen him. True accountability sharpens discernment, reinforces conviction, and keeps a man aligned with truth when temptation presses in. Integrity is preserved when a man refuses to walk alone, choosing instead to stand in the light, where honesty thrives and strength is sustained.

Integrity is not built in the spotlight - it is forged in the quiet, unseen decisions where no one is watching but God. It is in those moments that discipline rises as a guard over your soul, reminding you that not every desire deserves to be followed and not every opportunity is meant to be taken. When everything in you wants to say yes, discipline teaches you to pause, to weigh, and to choose what is right over what is easy. It calls you higher, beyond temporary satisfaction, into a life that reflects truth, strength, and unwavering character. Discipline is not a cage that confines you but is a shield that protects you. It preserves your calling, your peace, and your relationship with God. Every time you choose righteousness over convenience, you are building a foundation that cannot be shaken. Yes, integrity will cost you something - comfort, approval, or immediate gratification - but what it gives in return is far greater: a clear conscience, a steady heart, and a life that honors God.

Every man is building something beneath the surface of his life, even when no one else can see it. His moral foundation is formed in the quiet places through daily decisions, repeated habits, the voices he listens to, and the truths he chooses to believe. It is not built in moments of crisis, but long before them. When pressure comes what has been laid within him will be revealed. A weak foundation gives way to compromise but a strong foundation, rooted in truth and strengthened through obedience, holds firm when everything around him begins to shake. So build carefully. Guard what shapes your thinking and be intentional about what you allow to take root in your heart. Choose integrity when no one is watching. Choose truth when deception would be easier. Choose discipline when comfort calls your name for the strength of a man is not proven in ease, but in resistance.

When your foundation is anchored in God, pressure does not break you - it reveals you. And in that moment, you will not fall - you will stand.

Protecting that foundation requires intentional living. A man of wisdom understands that integrity is not lost in a single moment; it is worn down over time through small compromises. So he guards his heart, sets boundaries, and chooses what aligns with truth, because he knows that what shapes him today will define him tomorrow. A wise man is selective, not because he is fearful, but because he is focused. He understands the cost of becoming who God has called him to be, and he refuses to let distractions or corrupt influences derail that calling. He surrounds himself with voices that sharpen him, fills his mind with what is pure and strengthening, and walks away from anything that threatens his foundation. This kind of discipline is not weakness - it is strength under control. And in a world that constantly pulls at his convictions, the man who protects his foundation stands firm, unshaken, and ready to live a life marked by integrity, purpose, and honor.

Sin rarely announces itself with a crash - it whispers through compromise. What once felt wrong starts to feel tolerable, and what was once clear becomes blurred. This gradual drift is dangerous because it numbs the heart and dulls spiritual awareness. A man doesn't wake up one day far from God—he gets there one small step at a time, by ignoring the warning signs that once stirred his conscience. Guarding your integrity means refusing to overlook those small moments. It means confronting the thought before it takes root, honoring the boundary before it is tested, and responding to conviction without delay. Integrity is not built in the spotlight - it is forged in the quiet, unseen decisions of daily life. When a man chooses faithfulness in the small things, he builds a foundation that can withstand greater tests. Stay alert. Stay anchored. For the strength of your walk with God is not determined in the big battles alone, but in the countless small choices where your character is either protected or compromised.

Conviction is not meant to weigh you down - it is a sacred signal from God guiding you back to what is right. That inner check, that quiet but persistent prompting to turn away from compromise, is the hand of God guarding your integrity before damage is done, calling you to a higher standard because He has called you to a higher life. When you honor conviction, you are choosing strength over weakness, and truth over temporary satisfaction. But when conviction is ignored, something within begins to dull. The voice that once spoke clearly becomes quieter, not because God has stopped speaking, but because the heart has grown resistant. Yet the man who responds quickly and humbly finds his spirit growing sharper, stronger, and more sensitive to God's leading. He walks with clarity. He lives with peace. And he carries a quiet confidence that comes from knowing he is in step with God. Conviction is not your enemy. It is the evidence that God is shaping you into a man who walks in true freedom.

Integrity is forged in truth. A man who refuses to be honest with himself builds his life on unstable ground, because what is ignored cannot be healed, and what is hidden cannot be strengthened. God does not call you to pretend you are whole; He calls you to come as you are. The moment you acknowledge your weaknesses is the moment you take authority over them. Denial keeps you bound, but honesty breaks the chains. When you stand before God with nothing concealed, you create space for His truth to correct you, His wisdom to guide you, and His strength to uphold you. True transformation begins where pride ends. When a man humbles himself and brings his struggles into the light, he steps into a place where God can actively work in his life. Surrender is the decision to stop fighting battles in your own strength and to allow God to shape you from the inside out. In that place of openness, grace flows freely, and what once controlled you begins to lose its grip.

Living an honorable life is not built in a single moment of strength, but in the quiet, repeated decisions made when no one is watching. Anyone can do what is right when it is easy, but honor is revealed when it costs you something. It shows up when telling the truth risks your reputation, when standing firm invites opposition, and when obedience requires sacrifice. This kind of life is driven by a steady commitment to walk in truth, no matter the circumstance. Understand that honor does not demand perfection, it demands persistence. There will be moments you fall short, moments where you miss the mark, but an honorable man does not stay down. He rises, realigns, and chooses what is right again. Over time, these repeated choices forge a life of integrity that cannot be shaken. It is in this consistency - this refusal to compromise - that a man becomes trustworthy, dependable, and strong in spirit. Honor is not a destination you arrive at; it is a path you walk every day, one faithful step at a time.

Failure does not strip a man of integrity - it exposes the fractures that must be rebuilt. Every man will stumble, and there will be moments when he falls short of the standard he knows is right. But failure is not the end of his story; it is the moment where truth calls him back to alignment. Integrity is not proven in perfection, but in response. When a man refuses to hide, refuses to excuse, and instead brings his failure into the light, he begins the work of restoration. What could have hardened his heart instead becomes the very place where God reshapes it. A man of integrity does not defend his sin - he confronts it. He humbles himself, repents, and rises again with renewed conviction. He understands that strength is not found in pretending he never fell, but in the courage to stand back up and walk rightly again. Each time he chooses repentance over pride, he rebuilds what was broken and reinforces the foundation of his character. And in that process, he becomes stronger, wiser, and more anchored than before.

Your integrity is one of the most valuable things you possess. It is the quiet foundation beneath every decision, every relationship, and every step you take in life. It cannot be bought with success, borrowed from someone else, or replaced once it is lost. It is formed in the unseen places when no one is watching, when temptation whispers, and when compromise seems easier than conviction. In those moments, integrity becomes your shield, guiding you to choose what is right over what is convenient. Once integrity is compromised, it is not easily restored. It takes time, humility, and a steady commitment to walk upright again. That is why it must be guarded fiercely and treated as something sacred. Temporary pleasure may promise satisfaction, and momentary gain may seem rewarding, but neither can compare to the lasting strength of a clean conscience before God. When you choose integrity, you choose alignment with truth, with purpose, and with the character God is building within you.

There will be moments when it can seem like doing what is right is costing you everything. But heaven measures differently than the world. What you lose in compromise, you gain in strength. What you surrender in dishonesty, you receive in peace. Integrity anchors your soul when everything around you is uncertain. It quiets the noise of regret and replaces it with a steady assurance that your life is built on truth. When you choose what is right over what is easy, you are being established on a foundation that cannot be shaken. And what you gain is far greater than anything you give up. You gain a peace that does not depend on circumstances, a clarity that cuts through confusion, and a confidence that comes from walking in alignment with God. There is a deep, unshakable strength in knowing that your life reflects His truth, even when no one else sees it. Opportunities may come and go and people may misunderstand you, but the reward of a clear conscience and a life that honors God is eternal.

A man who guards his integrity becomes a man others can trust without hesitation. His words are not empty; they carry weight because they are backed by a life of consistency. His actions speak louder than promises, revealing a heart anchored in conviction rather than applause. While others may question his choices or fail to understand the path he walks, they cannot deny the steadiness of his character. There is a quiet authority about him - a strength that comes not from dominance, but from discipline and unwavering commitment to what is right. Over time, that kind of integrity builds something far greater than momentary success - it builds a legacy. Long after his voice is silenced, the impact of his life continues to speak through the lives he influenced, the standards he upheld, and the example he set. Integrity plants seeds that outlive a lifetime, shaping families, strengthening communities, and honoring God. A man who chooses integrity chooses eternal significance over temporary gain.

God honors integrity that stands firm when no one is watching. In the hidden places faithfulness is forged and character is proven. When a man chooses truth over convenience and obedience over ease, he is building a foundation that cannot be shaken. God sees what others overlook, and He measures a man by his private devotion. What is done in secret becomes the seed of what will be entrusted in the open. When a man proves he can be trusted in private, he is being prepared for public assignment. Integrity is not merely the avoidance of sin - it is the cultivation of readiness for purpose. God does not promote talent alone; He promotes trustworthiness. The weight of greater responsibility requires the strength of proven character, and that strength is developed behind closed doors. Every quiet act of obedience and every disciplined choice is shaping a man into someone God can rely on. So remain faithful in the hidden places, for they are not wasted - they are training grounds for destiny.

Guard your heart, for it is the wellspring of everything you will become. What you allow in will quietly shape your desires, your decisions, and your direction. Guard your mind, because battles are often won or lost long before they are ever seen. And guard your choices, because small compromises today can become strongholds tomorrow. Your integrity, your purity, and your calling are sacred, entrusted to you by a holy God. Protect them with intention. Defend them with conviction. Stand firm when no one is watching, because that is where true character is revealed. Live with the awareness that your life is always before God. He sees not just your actions, but your motives, your struggles, and your victories. And when you live with that awareness, you begin to walk differently. You become steady where others waver, strong where others fall, and faithful where others drift. This is the life of a man who understands that what is done in secret matters just as much as what is seen in the light.

Integrity is revealed in the decisions you make. A man may speak of honor, faith, and strength, but it is his daily walk that testifies to the truth within him. When he chooses honesty over convenience, purity over temptation, and obedience over ease, he is laying stones that form an unshakable foundation. Integrity is not built in a day - it is forged over time, through consistent faithfulness to what is right in the sight of God. Because in the end, integrity is not proven by what you say - it is proven by how you live. And a man who guards his integrity builds a life that cannot be shaken. Storms will come, pressure will rise, and trials will test every hidden place of the heart but the man who has anchored himself in truth will stand firm. His strength is not in appearance, but in alignment with God. His stability is not in circumstance, but in character. And when the winds have passed and the dust settles, his life will remain steady, grounded, and unmovable because it was built on integrity.

| 19 |

"THE STRENGTH OF CONVICTION"

Conviction is the backbone of a man who refuses to bend when the world bows. A man of conviction does not need to raise his voice to be heard, because his life speaks with authority. He is anchored in what is eternal, not swayed by what is popular. While others shift with culture, he remains steady, rooted in truth, grounded in faith, and guided by a higher standard that does not change. A man without conviction drifts, shaped by the opinions of others and the pressures of the moment. But a man of conviction stands, even when he stands alone. He does not chase approval, because he has already settled who he is and what he believes. His direction is clear, his purpose unwavering. When storms rise and voices oppose him, he does not retreat—he holds his ground. For conviction is not merely what he claims; it is what he lives. And in a world that constantly bends, the man who stands firm becomes a pillar - unshaken, unmovable, and unafraid to live for what is right, no matter the cost.

In a world where standards are constantly shifting and lines are easily blurred, conviction has become a rare and powerful force. Many men have traded truth for comfort, shaping their beliefs around what is easy rather than what is right. They bend with culture, adjust with pressure, and compromise when standing firm would cost them something. A man of conviction does not ask, "What is acceptable right now?" but rather, "What is right before God?" When a man roots his life in that truth, he becomes unshakable, even when everything around him is uncertain. Conviction produces courage. It builds a man who cannot be bought, silenced, or swayed by the opinions of others. He stands when others sit down, speaks when others stay silent, and holds the line when others retreat. This kind of life will always be respected in the eyes of God. In the end, it is not the man who blends in who makes an impact, but the one who stands firm and lives what he believes, no matter the cost.

Developing unshakable beliefs begins with knowing what you stand for and, more importantly, why you stand there. A man of conviction does not drift with the current of culture, nor does he shape his values based on what is popular or accepted. He roots himself in something eternal. The Word of God becomes his compass, his anchor, and his authority. When others shift with changing opinions, he remains steady, not because he is stubborn, but because he is grounded. He has settled in his heart that truth is not something to be negotiated - it is something to be lived. And in a world that constantly pressures men to compromise, his clarity gives him strength. Because his foundation is built on divine truth, his life can withstand pressure without collapsing. Storms will come - criticism, temptation, opposition - but they do not have the power to uproot him. Why? Because he is not standing on the fragile ground of approval or emotion, but on the unshakable rock of God's Word.

Conviction is forged in the hidden places where no applause is given and no audience is present. It is in those quiet moments, when a man chooses integrity over convenience, obedience over compromise, and truth over ease, that his foundation is laid. These unseen decisions are not insignificant; they are the very substance of who he is becoming. When no one is watching, heaven is. And in those sacred, private battles, strength is formed, character is refined, and a man learns to stand not for recognition, but for righteousness. When the pressure rises and the moment of testing comes, a man reveals what has already been built within him. Public courage is simply the overflow of private conviction. The man who has been faithful in the dark will stand firm in the light. He will not bend when it matters most because he has already settled his heart in the unseen places. So guard your private life. What you build in silence today will determine how you stand tomorrow.

Too many men drift through life assuming they will rise to the occasion when pressure comes. But pressure does not create conviction - it reveals it. When the moment of testing arrives, there is no time to build a foundation; you will stand on whatever has already been laid. If your beliefs are shallow, they will collapse. If your identity is unclear, you will waver. That is why conviction must be forged in the quiet place, long before the storm ever appears. It is in the unseen moments that a man settles who he is and what he stands for. Decide now. Settle it in your heart before the battle begins. Determine what truth you will live by, what lines you will never cross, and who you belong to. A man of conviction does not negotiate under pressure because he has already made his decision in peace. When temptation comes, when opposition rises, he stands strong. Not because the moment is easy, but because his foundation is firm. Build that foundation now, and you won't have to find your strength - you will reveal it.

Standing for truth in a compromising world will cost you something. When you choose conviction over convenience, you may lose approval from people who once applauded you. Doors that seemed open may quietly close. Relationships may grow distant when your standards no longer align with the crowd. But this is the price of integrity, and it has always been so. Truth has never been popular but it has always been powerful. The man who walks in it understands that he is not living for the applause of men, but for the approval of God. And when your foundation is anchored in Him, you are no longer shaken by what you lose, because you know Who you stand for. The man who stands firm sees beyond the temporary. He understands that comfort can be a trap, but strength is forged in resistance. Every time he chooses truth over compromise, something eternal is being built within him - character that cannot be bought, courage that cannot be broken, and faith that cannot be shaken.

There will be moments when the cost of standing firm seems too high, and the pressure to blend in feels overwhelming. In those moments, compromise whispers softly, convincing a man that a small step away from truth is no great loss. But truth is not something you drift from all at once - it is abandoned inch by inch. Every quiet surrender weakens conviction, every unspoken stand erodes courage, and every compromise reshapes the heart. What once felt clear begins to blur, and what once stood firm begins to bend. A man who continually yields in the small things will eventually find himself unable to stand in the greater ones. But a man of God is called to a higher standard - a life anchored in truth, not swayed by convenience or fear. Speaking truth may cost comfort, approval, and even relationships, but it preserves integrity, strengthens character, and honors God. The path of conviction is always right. When a man chooses truth in the small moments, he builds strength for the greater battles ahead.

A man of conviction does not bend with the shifting winds of culture because he is anchored in truth. While others chase approval and follow the noise of the crowd, he walks a narrower path marked by integrity, courage, and unwavering faith. His strength is not found in numbers, but in obedience. Even when the road grows lonely and the voices around him grow silent or critical, he does not retreat. His foundation is not built on the opinions of man, but on the unchanging character of God. Even if he is misunderstood, he remains faithful. There is a quiet power in a life fully surrendered to truth - a strength that does not need validation. This man is not driven by applause or shaken by rejection, because his identity is secure in God. He lives to please the One who called him, and that calling gives him the courage to endure, to lead, and to remain steadfast when compromise would be easier. In a world that constantly shifts, a man of conviction becomes a pillar - unmoved, unshaken, and unashamed.

Conviction is the anchor of a man's soul. It steadies him when emotions rise and pressures close in. When a man knows what is right, he is no longer tossed back and forth by opinions, fear, or uncertainty. He doesn't waste time negotiating with doubt or waiting for perfect conditions; he moves because his heart is fixed. Conviction reminds him who he is, what he stands for, and who he ultimately answers to. In that place of clarity, hesitation dies, and purpose takes its place. A man of conviction feels the same fear others feel, but he walks forward anyway - steady, resolved, and unshaken - because what he believes is greater than what he feels. Conviction gives him backbone in a bending world and boldness in moments that demand action. It transforms uncertainty into resolve and weakness into strength. When conviction is strong, courage becomes inevitable, and a man becomes the kind who does not retreat when it matters most but stands firm, speaks truth, and moves forward no matter the cost.

Fear loses its grip on a man who has already settled what he believes. A man anchored in truth is not easily moved, because his foundation is not built on feelings but on conviction. When you know who God is and who you are in Him, hesitation gives way to boldness. You may still feel fear, but it no longer controls your steps - it simply becomes noise in the background of a determined life. When the voice of God grows louder within you, the voices around you begin to lose their authority. The pressure to conform, the fear of rejection, and the weight of human opinion all begin to fade when compared to the certainty of His truth. Intimidation cannot dominate a man who has already decided whom he serves. He does not need approval because he is already accepted by God. This is the strength of a settled heart - it produces a quiet, unshakable confidence that does not need to prove itself. And in that place, fear has no throne, no command, and no lasting power.

History is filled with men who stood when others bowed, who held their ground when the pressure to compromise grew heavy. They were not always the loudest voices or the most celebrated names, but they carried something far greater within them - an unshakable conviction rooted in truth. When others drifted with the current of culture, they anchored themselves in what was right. Their strength did not come from physical power or social approval, but from a heart fully settled in God. And because they refused to move, even when it cost them comfort, reputation, or ease, they became pillars in moments where everything else seemed to collapse. Their legacy was not built in a day, but forged through quiet decisions to remain faithful when no one was watching and to stand firm when it would have been easier to walk away. Conviction gave them courage, and courage gave them endurance. And in the end, it was not talent or popularity that marked their lives - it was their unwavering obedience.

Becoming a man of conviction begins in the unseen places of the heart, where a man decides what he stands for and what he will never compromise. When your values are rooted in truth and anchored in eternity, they become immovable. Money loses its influence, recognition loses its shine, and the promises of comfort no longer have the power to sway you. You are no longer driven by what you can gain, but by who you are called to be. Integrity becomes your foundation, and righteousness becomes your path. Such a man walks with a steady confidence, not because life is easy, but because his soul is settled. He cannot be bribed by comfort, nor threatened by loss, because he understands that true gain is found in obedience to God. Even when standing alone, he remains firm. Even when the cost is high, he refuses to bend. His strength is not in his circumstances, but in his unwavering commitment to what is right. And in the end, it is this kind of man who leaves behind a legacy that cannot be erased.

The world will always try to negotiate your standards. It will whisper that a small compromise is harmless, that bending the truth is necessary, that lowering the bar will make life easier. It will dress shortcuts up as wisdom and disguise excuses as understanding. But a man of conviction recognizes the trap because he knows that every compromise, no matter how small, carries a cost. It may not be immediate, but it will erode character, weaken resolve, and dull the voice of truth within. What you allow today becomes what you tolerate tomorrow, and what you tolerate eventually becomes who you are. Conviction does not bargain - it stands firm. It does not shift with pressure or bow to convenience. It is rooted in truth and anchored in the fear of God, not the opinions of man. When your standards are settled in your spirit, you no longer debate what is right - you live it. You choose integrity when it costs you. You choose obedience when it isolates you. And in doing so, you build a life that cannot be shaken.

Integrity and conviction walk hand in hand, forming the backbone of a life that honors God. A man of conviction is the same in the quiet places as he is in the crowd. His character is not shaped by who is watching, but by what he knows is right. When conviction takes root in the heart, integrity becomes the fruit in his life. His words carry weight because they are backed by action. In a world where compromise is common, his consistency becomes a testimony. Such a man becomes dependable not because he is perfect, but because he is anchored. He does not shift with pressure or bend with opinion, for his foundation is deeper than circumstance. Trust follows him because he has proven, time and time again, that what he believes is how he lives. Integrity is a lifestyle of alignment between belief and behavior. And when conviction and integrity stand together, they form a strength that cannot be easily shaken, a life that speaks louder than words, and a legacy that endures beyond the moment.

This kind of man becomes a pillar in a collapsing culture, not because he is untouched by pressure, but because he refuses to bow to it.

While others bend under the weight of compromise, he stands anchored in truth. When confusion spreads like wildfire and truth is traded for convenience, he does not drift with the current. He brings clarity by the way he lives, speaks, and leads. His presence becomes a reminder that righteousness is still possible, and that integrity still matters. Day after day, decision after decision, he proves that standing firm is not a moment - it is a lifestyle. He does not need applause to remain faithful, nor does he require agreement to stay obedient. He knows who he serves, and that settles everything. In a world desperate for direction, his example points upward. And though the culture may continue to shift and crumble, the man who stands firm becomes a living witness that truth endures, and that those who build their lives upon it will not be moved.

When a man stands firm in what he believes, he creates a visible standard for others to follow. The next generation is always watching, always learning, not just from what is said, but from what is lived. A man of unwavering conviction teaches without needing a platform. His consistency becomes instruction. His obedience becomes direction. In a world filled with shifting values, his life provides something others can build upon. He becomes a living example that truth is to be lived out daily. His life becomes a blueprint, marking a path for those who come after him. Those within his influence begin to see what strength, integrity, and faithfulness truly look like. They learn that conviction is not loud, but it is immovable. It does not bend under pressure or fade in difficulty. And as they follow his example, they carry that same conviction into their own lives, extending its impact even further. In this way, one man's faithfulness becomes a legacy - shaping not just his own life, but generations to come.

God is not searching for flawless men - He is searching for faithful ones. A committed man does not wait until he has it all together before he steps forward; he answers the call even while God is still shaping him. When the pressure rises and the path narrows, he does not retreat - he stands. Not because he feels strong, but because he knows who he belongs to. In a world that rewards comfort and compromise, his life becomes a quiet rebellion rooted in truth, grounded in obedience, and strengthened by grace. This kind of man speaks when it would be easier to stay silent and obeys when it would be easier to walk away. He understands that following God will cost him something, but he also knows that anything surrendered to God is never truly lost. His commitment becomes his testimony. His obedience becomes his legacy. And while he may never be perfect, he becomes powerful in the hands of God because a man fully yielded is exactly the kind of man God uses to change the world.

Strengthen your convictions by anchoring them in truth that does not shift with culture, pressure, or circumstance. A man who is rooted deeply in what is right has settled it in his heart before the battle ever comes who he will be and what he will stand for. When your convictions are grounded in God's truth, they become more than beliefs; they become the foundation you build your life upon. Storms may rise, voices may challenge, and opposition may come, but a life rooted in truth stands firm when everything around it is shaken. So decide today that you will not be moved. Let your life be marked by faith that trusts God in every season, unshakable integrity that remains consistent in private and public, and courageous obedience that chooses what is right no matter the cost. This is the kind of life that leaves a legacy. When others compromise, you will stand. When others retreat, you will advance. And in doing so, your life will become a testimony that a man fully committed to God cannot be shaken.

There will be moments when the weight feels unbearable, when the voices around you grow louder, and when compromise seems easier than conviction. But this is where a man is revealed. Not in comfort, but in conflict. Not when everything is easy, but when everything is on the line. Stand firm when the pressure comes. Dig your heels into truth. Anchor your heart in what God has spoken. Let the storm rage, let the resistance rise, but refuse to bend to anything that opposes what is right. A man of conviction may be tested, but he will not be broken. He may feel the strain, but he does not surrender. He may be pressed, but he is not crushed. Why? Because he knows who he is, whose he is, and what he stands for. And when everything around him begins to shake, he remains steady - not because he is strong in himself, but because he stands on something eternal. So stand firm. Hold your ground. And let your life be a testimony that pressure does not destroy a man of God - it defines him.

| 20 |

"THE PRICE OF PURPOSE"

Purpose is never handed out cheaply because it carries eternal weight. It is not discovered in moments of ease but revealed in seasons where surrender stretches you beyond what is comfortable. The fire that refines a man is not meant to destroy him, but to shape him. In those moments when the cost feels greater than expected, God is forming something within him that cannot be produced any other way. Every calling that carries weight will demand something from you - your time, your pride, your plans, and sometimes even your security. But what it requires, it also prepares you to carry. The man who embraces that cost rather than running from it becomes stronger, clearer, and more anchored in who God has called him to be. Purpose is not proven in what you say yes to when it is easy, but in what you refuse to walk away from when it becomes difficult. And on the other side of that surrender is a life marked by impact, obedience, and the quiet strength of a man who chose purpose over everything else.

God, in His wisdom, does not overwhelm you with the full weight of your calling at the beginning. Instead, He invites you into it step by step. At first, you see the beauty of the vision. Your heart burns with excitement, and your spirit comes alive with purpose. But as you continue walking, He begins to uncover what that calling truly requires. The deeper you go, the more you realize that purpose is not just about what you gain - it is about what you must lay down. It will ask for your comfort, your pride, your plans, and sometimes even your understanding. Yet every layer He reveals is not meant to discourage you, but to prepare you - to strengthen your faith and anchor your obedience. Purpose is costly because it is sacred. God refines those He calls, shaping them through surrender and sacrifice. But hidden within the cost is a greater reward. Every step forward draws you deeper into the life God designed for you. You are not just fulfilling a purpose - you are becoming the man God intended you to be

Every man who has ever stepped into true purpose has first stood at the altar of surrender. Purpose will ask for your time when you would rather rest, your comfort when you would rather stay safe, your pride when you would rather be right, and even your plans when you would rather stay in control. Nothing is off limits, because God is not simply trying to use you - He is shaping you. The man who walks in purpose understands that what he lays down is never wasted; it is exchanged for something eternal, something stronger, something aligned with heaven's design. Purpose will always confront you with a defining question: What are you willing to give up to become who God has called you to be? Many admire purpose, but few embrace its cost. Yet on the other side of surrender is clarity, strength, and a life that carries weight and meaning. When a man releases his grip on lesser things, he makes room for greater things. When he dies to self, he comes alive in calling. So lay it down - whatever it is.

The cost of obedience is often misunderstood because many expect it to come wrapped in comfort and immediate reward. True obedience is revealed in the moments when it challenges everything within you. It is choosing God's direction when your emotions resist, when your plans must be surrendered, and when the outcome is uncertain. Obedience stretches you beyond what feels safe, not to harm you, but to shape you. Real obedience is forged in those defining moments when doing what is right comes with a cost. It may cost you convenience, recognition, or even relationships, but it always produces something far greater - spiritual strength, deeper faith, and alignment with God's purpose. What feels like loss in the moment becomes gain in eternity. God is not looking for comfortable agreement; He is looking for surrendered hearts that will follow Him wherever He leads. And in that surrender, you will discover that obedience, though costly, is the pathway to becoming who you were created to be.

Obedience will often take you beyond the boundaries of comfort and into the tension between what your flesh desires and what your spirit knows is right. In those moments, the battle is not external - it is deeply internal. Your flesh will crave safety, approval, and ease, while your spirit calls you toward truth, courage, and surrender. God's leading does not always feel convenient, but it is always purposeful. When He prompts you to speak, it may cost you acceptance. When He calls you to act, it may require risk. When He asks you to stand, it may mean standing alone. Yet it is in these very moments that obedience becomes real - not when it is easy, but when it demands something from you. Every act of obedience strengthens your spirit and weakens the grip of fear. What once felt intimidating begins to lose its power as you learn to trust God more than your own comfort. Obedience shapes your character, aligns your heart with His will, and positions you for greater purpose.

There is always a price attached to saying "yes" to God. It will cost you comfort, familiarity, and sometimes even the approval of others. It will stretch you beyond what feels safe and call you into places where your faith must carry you when your feelings cannot. But in that cost, there is life. Though the path may feel narrow and the resistance strong, there is a deep peace that comes from knowing you are walking in step with God. There is growth that shapes your character, impact that touches others, and fulfillment that cannot be manufactured by worldly success. Every sacrifice made in obedience becomes a seed planted into a greater purpose - one that outlives temporary discomfort and produces eternal significance. Saying "yes" may be costly now, but saying "no" will cost you later. One leads to becoming who God called you to be. The other leaves you wondering who you might have been. So when the tension rises and the easier path calls your name, choose obedience anyway.

Letting go of comfort is one of the fiercest battles a man will ever fight because comfort feels safe, familiar, and justified. It whispers, "You've done enough. Stay where you are. Don't risk what you have." But beneath that quiet voice is a slow erosion of purpose. A man who clings to comfort begins to shrink, trading calling for convenience and destiny for ease. Growth does not live in comfort zones - it lives where faith is required, where risk is real, and where dependence on God becomes necessary. The very thing that feels like protection can become the prison that keeps a man from becoming who he was created to be. Purpose, on the other hand, will always call you forward. It will stretch you, challenge you, and pull you into places your flesh resists. It says, "Step into what you were made for," even when the path is uncertain. Every man must choose: remain where it is easy or step into what is eternal. The men who make an impact are the ones who chose what is costly and step forward in obedience.

Comfort has a subtle way of disguising itself as security. It builds walls around your life that feel safe but over time those walls become a cage. You stop stretching, stop risking, stop growing. What once felt like rest becomes restriction. But purpose calls you beyond what is easy, beyond what is known, and into places that require faith. It will disrupt your routines, challenge your thinking, and pull you into deeper dependence on God. What feels uncomfortable is often the very place where transformation begins. A man who chooses purpose must develop the courage to leave what is familiar behind. He must be willing to walk away from comfort, even when it feels like loss, trusting that what God is leading him into is far greater than what he is leaving. Familiarity may offer peace for a moment, but purpose produces fulfillment for a lifetime. The step away from comfort is never easy but it is always necessary. Because on the other side of that step is growth, impact, and the life you were created to live.

Destiny is revealed in the moments that challenge you beyond what feels natural. It is in the stretching, when your strength feels insufficient, and in the pressing, when the weight seems heavier than you expected, that God begins to shape something deeper within you. The feeling of inadequacy is not a sign that you are unqualified; it is often confirmation that you are stepping into something greater than yourself. God will always call you into places where your dependence on Him must increase, because destiny is not built on human ability alone, but on surrendered obedience. That tension you feel - the pull between fear and faith, between comfort and calling - is the very ground where transformation takes place. It is there that your character is refined, your trust is strengthened, and your identity is anchored in who God says you are. If everything felt easy, there would be no need for growth, no reason to rely on His strength. But in the stretching, you expand. In the pressing, you are purified.

Many men stand at the edge of their calling, not because they lack ability, but because they are waiting for the perfect moment when it feels safe, when it makes sense, when it fits comfortably into their plans. But purpose was never designed to be convenient. It will interrupt your routine, challenge your comfort, and demand that you move forward even when you feel unprepared. The truth is, what God has placed inside you will always require faith to step into. If you wait for ease, you will wait forever. The longer a man delays his calling, the heavier it becomes to carry. That weight is not meant to crush you, but to awaken you. It is the tension between where you are and where you are called to be. So stop negotiating with comfort and start responding to conviction. Step forward, even if it costs you something. Because the price of obedience may be high, but the cost of delay is far greater - it is the slow erosion of the life you were created to live.

Choosing purpose over ease is a quiet, daily surrender. Each morning presents a new opportunity to align your life with what truly matters. The easy path will always call first, offering comfort, familiarity, and immediate relief. But purpose speaks with a deeper voice, calling you beyond convenience into commitment. It asks you to deny what feels good in the moment so you can embrace what is right for eternity. A man of purpose learns that greatness is built in consistent, intentional obedience. Every day, you stand at a crossroads. One path is wide, comfortable, and requires little sacrifice but it leads to stagnation. The other is narrow, often difficult, and demands discipline but it leads to growth, impact, and fulfillment. Choosing what is right over what is easy will stretch you, refine you, and sometimes even break your pride but it will never waste your life. Over time, these daily decisions shape your character and define your legacy. So choose purpose not because it is easy, but because it is worth it.

The men who leave a lasting mark are not those who chose comfort, but those who willingly carried the weight others avoided. They did not run from sacrifice - they leaned into it, understanding that every burden carried in obedience was shaping something far greater than themselves. While the world measures success by ease and convenience, these men measured their lives by faithfulness and surrender. They knew that sacrifice was not a sign of loss, but a pathway to purpose. They understood that the weight they carried was producing endurance, character, and eternal impact. Every sacrifice became a seed, planted in faith, destined to bear fruit beyond what they could see. So they pressed on not because it was easy, but because it was meaningful. And in doing so, they became men whose lives echoed into eternity. Let your life be marked the same way - not by what you kept, but by what you were willing to give up for the sake of something greater.

Sacrifice is not loss when it is tied to purpose. What feels like letting go is often the very thing that positions you to receive what God has already prepared. He takes what you place in His hands - your comfort, your plans, your desires - and He reshapes it into something that carries eternal weight. What you release in faith does not disappear; it is refined, multiplied, and redirected into purpose far greater than you could have produced on your own. God never wastes what is surrendered to Him. Every act of obedience, every quiet "yes," every costly decision becomes seed in His kingdom. Though it may feel like loss in the moment, heaven sees it as investment. In time, what was given up will reveal its true value - not always in what is regained, but in who you become and the impact your life carries. Trust that nothing laid at His feet is overlooked. He is a faithful steward of your sacrifice, and He will turn every surrendered thing into something that glorifies Him and strengthens you.

There will be moments when the weight of your calling presses against you so heavily that you begin to question everything. The sacrifice feels sharp, the path feels lonely, and the reward seems distant. In those moments, your flesh will whisper that it is too much, that the cost is too high, that comfort would be easier. But purpose was never designed to be easy—it was designed to be eternal. What God has placed inside of you is greater than the discomfort around you, and what He is calling you into will always demand more than what is convenient. When doubt rises, you must anchor yourself in this truth: you were not called to a life of ease, but to a life of obedience. Purpose is not measured by how comfortable the journey feels, but by how faithful you remain to the One who called you. The moments that feel the hardest are often the ones shaping you the deepest. So stand firm. Push forward. And remember that what feels costly now is producing something far greater than you can see.

The road of purpose is often marked by solitude, not because you are abandoned, but because you are set apart. When a man chooses obedience over approval, he steps onto a path that many will not understand. Some will question your decisions, others may withdraw their support, and a few may even oppose you. But purpose was never meant to be validated by the crowd. It is confirmed in the quiet place where your spirit aligns with the voice of God. The loneliness you feel is often evidence that you are walking where few are willing to go. Do not measure your calling by the applause of people, but by your faithfulness to God. Approval is fleeting, but obedience carries eternal weight. When you stand before God, it will not matter who agreed with your choices - it will matter that you followed His voice. So keep walking with God for in that obedience you will discover that what felt like loneliness was actually sacred ground, where God was shaping you for something far greater than the acceptance of men.

A man who truly lives for purpose begins to see life through a different lens. He understands that ease rarely produces growth, and convenience rarely produces transformation. Instead of asking what will make his life simpler, he asks what will make his life count. His mindset shifts from self-preservation to surrender, from temporary relief to eternal impact. He recognizes that every moment is an opportunity to build, to serve, and to obey, even when it stretches him beyond what feels natural. This kind of man is anchored by conviction and guided by responsibility. When faced with difficult choices, he does not retreat to what is comfortable - he rises to what is required. He understands that purpose demands discipline, sacrifice, and unwavering commitment. And in that pursuit, he becomes stronger, sharper, and more aligned with the will of God. His life becomes a reflection of obedience over comfort, impact over ease, and calling over convenience. And that is where true fulfillment is found.

When you fully embrace the price of purpose, something deep within you comes alive. The internal battle begins to quiet because the decision has already been made - you are no longer negotiating with comfort or consulting fear. What once intimidated you begins to lose its voice, because you have anchored yourself in something greater than feelings. You stop asking, "What will this cost me?" and start declaring, "Whatever it costs, it is worth it." That shift produces a man who walks steady, focused, and unshaken. His steps are no longer hesitant, because clarity has replaced confusion, and conviction has silenced doubt. In that place, resolve becomes your foundation. You are no longer pulled in every direction by emotion, opinion, or circumstance. Instead, you move forward with purpose etched into your heart and obedience guiding your steps. Comfort no longer controls you because you have seen beyond it. You have tasted the weight of calling and the significance of a life surrendered to God.

So count the cost and choose purpose anyway. Do not let the weight of what must be surrendered keep you from stepping into what God has prepared. Every calling requires a laying down of comfort, of control, of what feels safe and familiar. But what you release in obedience is never truly lost - it is transformed. God takes what you surrender and turns it into strength, clarity, and eternal impact. The path may narrow, and the road may grow lonely, but the deeper you walk in purpose, the more you realize that what you left behind was never equal to what lies ahead. Walk away from what must be left behind without regret. Do not cling to what cannot go with you into your calling. A life spent preserving comfort will always fall short of a life spent pursuing purpose. In the end, the true cost is not what you give up - it is what you miss if you refuse to move forward. So step boldly. Surrender fully. Live intentionally. Because the price of purpose is temporary, but the reward of obedience echoes into eternity.

| 21 |

"LESSONS FROM FAILURE"

Every man will face failure at some point in his journey. It is not a matter of if, but when. Plans will fall apart, doors will close, and moments you were certain would succeed will collapse under the weight of reality. But failure is not evidence that you are off course - it is often part of the course itself. God does not build strong men in places of constant success, but in moments where strength must be forged through disappointment. What feels like a breakdown is often the beginning of a deeper foundation. Failure has a way of stripping away pride, exposing weaknesses, and reminding you that your dependence must be on Him, not on your own ability. The danger is not in failing - it is in allowing failure to define you or stop you. A man who rises again after falling carries something different within him: humility, resilience, and a deeper trust in God. Setbacks are not the end of your story; they are chapters that shape it. God uses failure as a tool, not a termination.

Failure has a way of stripping away illusions that success can quietly sustain. When everything is going well, it is easy to overlook hidden weaknesses, ignore subtle pride, and assume strength where there is actually fragility. But failure exposes what was concealed, not to shame you, but to show you what needs refining. What feels like a collapse is often a divine invitation to confront what is real rather than what is comfortable. Instead of resisting that revelation, embrace it. The areas exposed in failure are not signs that you are finished - they are signs that God is working deeper than before. He is not interested in preserving appearances; He is committed to shaping character. When pride is broken, humility can grow. When weakness is revealed, strength can be built on a true foundation. So do not fear what failure uncovers. Lean into it, learn from it, and allow God to use it as a turning point. What feels like a breaking point may actually be the beginning of becoming who you were meant to be.

Many men fear failure because they confuse it with defeat. They see it as a final verdict stamped over their lives, rather than a temporary chapter in a much greater story. But failure does not have the authority to determine your ending - only your response to it does. What feels like a collapse is often a confrontation, exposing areas that need strengthening, humbling pride, and realigning your dependence on God. In those moments, failure shifts from being an enemy to becoming an instructor, revealing truths that success often hides. God uses those very moments to shape your character, deepen your faith, and prepare you for greater responsibility. The fall is not where your story ends - it is where your resilience is forged. A man who learns from failure walks forward with wisdom, not shame; with clarity, not confusion. So do not fear failure - embrace what it teaches, rise again with purpose, and trust that God is using even your setbacks to build something unshakable within you.

Every mistake carries instruction, but only the man who is willing to slow down long enough will receive it. Too often, failure is treated like something to escape rather than something to examine. But within every wrong turn is an opportunity to see what went wrong, what needs to change, and where growth is required. When a man humbles himself, he begins to uncover wisdom that success could never teach him. God often uses these moments not to condemn, but to correct, refine, and realign a man's path. Failure was never meant to be a prison—it was meant to be a classroom. It only becomes a place of captivity when a man refuses to learn from it. But when he leans in, listens, and allows the lesson to shape him, failure transforms into a powerful tool for growth. What once felt like a setback becomes preparation. What once felt like loss becomes instruction. And through it all, God is faithful to guide, teaching him how to move forward with greater strength, clarity, and purpose.

Failure it is a voice trying to teach you something your success never could. But when a man hardens his heart, avoids reflection, or blames everything around him, he silences the very lessons meant to shape him. He begins to repeat the same mistakes, the same frustrations, and the same outcomes while wondering why nothing changes. Growth is not automatic; it is chosen. And the man who refuses to learn from where he fell will continue to stumble over the same ground. But the man who pauses, reflects, and humbles himself before God turns every failure into a steppingstone. He asks, "What is this teaching me?" instead of "Why did this happen to me?" In that posture, wisdom is born, patterns are broken, and direction becomes clear. God does not waste failure, but He does require a willing heart to transform it. When you choose to learn, you break the cycle. You rise stronger, walk wiser, and step forward with a clarity that only comes from lessons embraced rather than ignored.

The man who leans into these lessons gains something far greater than relief - he gains wisdom. Instead of running from failure, he begins to study it. He asks God to reveal what was hidden, to expose what needs refining, and to teach what success never could. In that posture, failure loses its power to shame and becomes a tool that shapes him. What once felt like a setback becomes a sacred place of transformation, where pride is humbled, character is strengthened, and clarity begins to form. As his perspective shifts, so does his future. He no longer sees failure as something to escape, but as something to grow through. Each hardship becomes a steppingstone instead of a stumbling block. Where he once reacted with frustration, he now responds with faith. Where he once felt defeated, he now stands determined. These lessons build a man who is wiser, stronger, and more anchored in God. When a man learns to see through the lens of growth, even his failures begin to move him forward.

Quitting may feel like relief in the moment, like setting down a weight that has become too heavy to carry. But what feels like escape is often the very thing that steals what God is trying to build within a man. Failure is full of purpose. It exposes weaknesses that need strengthening, humbles pride that needs surrendering, and refines character that cannot be developed in comfort. When a man walks away too soon, he forfeits the growth that was waiting on the other side of endurance. Growth is rarely found in ease; it is uncovered in the very places a man is tempted to abandon. The struggle he wants to escape is often the classroom where perseverance is formed and faith is deepened. If he will press through instead of pulling back, he will discover that the breaking point was actually a building point. God does some of His greatest work in the moments a man feels like giving up. Instead of quitting, stand firm. What is being produced in you is far more valuable than the temporary relief of walking away.

When a man chooses to stand back up instead of walking away, something powerful begins to take place within him. What once felt like defeat becomes the very ground where resilience is formed. Each time he rises, he proves that failure does not have the final word - God does. Strength begins to take root in places that were once weak, and his character is no longer shaped by ease, but by perseverance. He becomes steady because he has learned to remain standing when everything around him says to quit. In those moments of choosing to continue, endurance is quietly being built. It is forged in the unseen decisions to keep going, to trust God again, and to take one more step forward. Over time, that endurance becomes part of who he is. He is no longer easily shaken, no longer quick to retreat. Instead, he carries a strength that has been tested and proven. And through it all, God is shaping a man who doesn't just start strong but a man who finishes with unwavering faith.

Every man will face moments where he stumbles, where plans unravel, and where strength seems to fail. But those moments are not the final word over his life. What truly defines him is what he does next. When a man chooses to rise again, even when it is difficult, even when it is humbling, he declares that failure will not have authority over his future. God does not measure a man by how many times he falls, but by the faith and courage he shows in getting back up. The line between defeat and development is drawn in the decision to stay down or to stand again. When a man rises, he steps into growth. He gains strength he did not have before, wisdom he could not learn any other way, and a deeper dependence on God. Rising is not just recovery - it is transformation. Each time he stands back up, he becomes more resilient, more refined, and more prepared for what lies ahead. The fall may have knocked him down, but the decision to rise is what moves him forward.

God has never been intimidated by failure. What overwhelms man does not unsettle Him. Throughout scripture, He consistently chose flawed men and met them in their weakest moments. Where others saw disqualification, God saw potential. Where men saw endings, God saw beginnings. Failure has never been a barrier to His purpose; in fact, it has often been the very place where His power is revealed most clearly. When a man places his broken pieces in God's hands, they are never returned the same. Time and again, God has taken imperfect stories and woven them into something eternal. He uses failure to strip away pride, to build dependence, and to reshape identity. The very moments a man would prefer to hide are often the ones God uses to display His grace. Nothing is wasted in His hands. What feels like a setback becomes a setup for transformation. So do not let failure convince you that your story is over. In God's hands, it may be the very chapter where your true purpose begins.

The moments that feel like failure are often the very places where God is building something deeper within you. When plans fall apart and expectations shatter, it can seem like everything is being lost but, in reality, something greater is being formed. God is not limited by your missteps or delayed by your detours. He works in the unseen, using disappointment to develop strength, using setbacks to refine character, and using broken moments to reshape your direction. What feels like an ending is often God clearing the ground for a stronger foundation. The truth is, many of the things you would have chosen for yourself could never produce what God is preparing you for. He sees beyond the moment, beyond the pain, beyond what you can currently understand. What you see as a setback, He sees as a setup for something greater than you imagined. So do not lose heart in the process. Trust that even now, in what feels uncertain or unfinished, God is preparing you for what is still to come.

God does not waste failure - He transforms it. What feels like a breaking point to you is often a building place in His hands. The very moments you wish you could erase are the ones He uses to reshape your heart, refine your character, and realign your direction. Failure may expose weakness, but it also creates space for grace. When surrendered to Him, your mistakes are no longer dead ends - they become turning points. God takes what was fractured and weaves it into something stronger, deeper, and more purposeful than before. Nothing given to God is ever lost. Every tear, every regret, every misstep placed in His hands is redeemed and repurposed. He doesn't just restore what was broken - He brings growth out of it, maturity through it, and purpose beyond it. Where you see ruin, He sees potential. Where you see wasted time, He sees preparation. Trust Him with your failures, because in His hands, even your lowest moments can become the foundation for your greatest calling.

Even in failure, God is active. What feels like a setback to you is often a sacred worksite to Him. In those moments where things fall apart,

He is carefully shaping your heart, exposing what needs to change, and refining your motives until they align with His purpose. What you thought was the end is often the beginning of transformation, where God is doing a quieter, deeper work that cannot always be seen but will eventually be revealed. What feels like loss is often construction happening beneath the surface. Just as a foundation must be strengthened before anything lasting can be built, God uses these hidden seasons to fortify your life from the inside out. He is reinforcing your character, stabilizing your faith, and preparing you to carry what you once were not ready to hold. Nothing surrendered to Him is wasted - not the pain, not the disappointment, not even the failure. In His hands, every broken piece becomes part of something stronger, something wiser, and something built to stand.

A man who understands this begins to walk differently. His steps are no longer hesitant, weighed down by the fear of getting it wrong. Instead, he moves with a quiet confidence - not in his own perfection, but in God's sovereignty. He realizes that failure is not a verdict over his life, but a moment within it. Where he once saw setbacks as endings, he now sees them as intersections where God can redirect, refine, and reveal something deeper. Fear loses its grip because he knows his story is not authored by his mistakes, but by a faithful God who is still writing. This understanding produces freedom. He is no longer paralyzed by the pressure to succeed at every turn, because he trusts that even when he falls short, God remains at work. So the man rises again, not discouraged, but strengthened. He walks forward with resilience, knowing that nothing surrendered to God is wasted. Every misstep becomes part of his making, and every trial becomes a tool in the hands of a God who finishes what He starts.

Rising again after falling requires humility - the kind that refuses to hide, justify, or shift blame. It is the strength to look honestly at where you missed the mark and say, "I was wrong," without trying to soften the truth. A humble man does not protect his pride at the cost of his growth; he lays it down so that God can rebuild him stronger. He understands that excuses delay progress, but responsibility unlocks transformation. In that place of surrender, God begins to reshape his character, not through perfection, but through honesty and obedience. When a man chooses humility, he also chooses forward movement. He stops dwelling in regret and starts walking in renewal. God does not ask for flawless men; He asks for willing ones. And the man who gets back up with a teachable spirit discovers that his fall did not disqualify him - it prepared him. What could have been a place of defeat becomes a turning point, where humility paves the way for growth, and grace carries him into a stronger, wiser future.

Rising again after failure requires more than determination - it requires faith. Faith that God is not finished with you, even when you feel like you've come to the end of yourself. It is the quiet confidence that your story is still unfolding, that what looks like a final chapter is only a turning page. When a man chooses to believe this, he refuses to let failure define him. Instead, he sees it through the lens of God's purpose, trusting that every setback is being woven into something greater than he can currently see. Faith allows a man to stand in the middle of disappointment and still declare that God is at work. It reminds him that failure is not a conclusion, but a continuation - a place where growth is forged and purpose is refined. What feels like an ending is often the beginning of a deeper, stronger, and more resilient version of who he is called to be. So he rises again - not because the path is easy, but because he believes the Author of his life is still writing, and the best parts of his story have yet to be revealed.

Each time a man rises after being knocked down, something within him is forged that cannot be produced any other way. Strength is not built in moments of ease, but in the decision to stand again when everything in him feels like staying down. With each rise, his faith deepens, his perspective sharpens, and his confidence shifts from himself to the One who sustains him. What once felt overwhelming begins to lose its power, because he has seen firsthand that falling is not the end - it is simply part of the process of becoming. The man who keeps rising develops a spirit that is not easily discouraged because he no longer measures his life by the moment, but by the mission. He understands that setbacks are not stop signs but steppingstones, and that endurance is what separates those who start from those who finish. With every comeback, he is being prepared, strengthened, and positioned for something greater. And when the next challenge comes, he will face it as a man who knows how to rise.

Over time, failure begins to lose its voice of intimidation in a man's life. What once felt like a stopping point becomes a steppingstone, and what once shook his confidence now strengthens his resolve. He realizes that failure is not an enemy sent to destroy him, but a tool God uses to shape him. He no longer measures his life by moments of success or failure, but by his willingness to keep moving forward in obedience. As this truth settles into his spirit, his walk changes. He no longer hesitates at the fear of falling, because he understands that falling is not final. Confidence rises within him - not because he believes he won't fail, but because he knows God will meet him even there. He gets back up quicker, walks forward stronger, and refuses to let past mistakes define his future. Failure becomes part of his process, not the end of his path, and with every step forward, he becomes a man who is no longer controlled by fear but led by faith.

In the end, the greatest men are not defined by a flawless record, but by a faithful response. They fell, but they did not stay down. They faced moments that could have broken them yet chose to rise instead. Each failure became a refining fire, burning away pride, strengthening character, and deepening their dependence on God. They did not allow their mistakes to write their identity - they allowed God's grace to rewrite their story. Where others saw endings, they saw opportunities to begin again with greater wisdom, humility, and resolve. These men learned to trust God not just in victory, but in the aftermath of defeat. They understood that falling was never the final word - God was. So they rose again, not in their own strength, but in faith. They grew through what they went through, allowing every setback to shape them into something stronger and more grounded. And in that rising, they became living testimonies that true greatness is not found in never failing, but in never surrendering to failure.

| 22 |

"THE WARRIOR SPIRIT"

Every man who chooses to follow God steps onto a battlefield, whether he realizes it or not. This fight is not fought with visible weapons, but in the quiet places of the heart and the hidden corridors of the mind. It is where truth confronts lies, where faith wrestles with fear, and where obedience stands against the pull of compromise. The unseen realm is active, and the pressures are real, but so is the presence of God within the man who chooses to stand. The warrior spirit begins to awaken in these moments - not when life is easy, but when resistance rises. It is in the tension of the fight that a man discovers who he truly is, and more importantly, whose he is. The warrior spirit is forged in conflict. Every challenge, every temptation, and every internal struggle becomes a training ground where strength is developed and conviction is solidified. Instead of running from the battle, the man of God learns to lean into it, knowing that each confrontation is shaping him into someone unshakable.

The enemy understands that if he cannot destroy a man outright, he can weaken him over time - numbing his conviction, dulling his spiritual awareness, and leading him off course without resistance. What feels harmless in the moment often carries deeper consequences, because the most dangerous battles are the ones you don't realize you're fighting. But a man who walks with God learns to recognize these quiet battles for what they are. He becomes alert, discerning the difference between comfort that refreshes and comfort that compromises. He refuses to accept ease at the cost of obedience. Instead, he leans into truth, even when it challenges him, and he guards his heart with intention. Victory in these moments is not found in dramatic displays, but in daily faithfulness - in choosing discipline over distraction, conviction over convenience, and purpose over passivity. Because in the end, it is not the loud battles that define a man's strength, but the quiet ones he refuses to lose.

A man with a warrior spirit realizes that many of the fiercest conflicts are fought in the mind, in the heart, and in the quiet moments where no one else is watching. He understands that if he can win the internal war, the external battles will not have the power to defeat him. So he stands guard over his thoughts, anchors himself in God's Word, and refuses to surrender ground in the places that matter most. Over time, he comes to recognize that true victory is often silent and deeply personal. It is the decision to choose obedience when compromise is easier, to walk in faith when fear is louder, and to remain steadfast when no one is applauding. These unseen victories shape his character and forge a strength that cannot be shaken by circumstance. Long before others see the results, the transformation has already taken place within him. And when the outward battles come, he stands firm, not because they are easy, but because he has already learned how to win where it counts most.

Fighting spiritual battles demands more than strength - it requires vigilance. A man must learn to stand guard over his thoughts, refusing to entertain what weakens him, and protecting his heart from influences that quietly pull him off course. When he becomes careless, he lowers his defenses without realizing it, leaving openings for doubt, compromise, and distraction. But the man who chooses to stay alert develops a sharpened spirit. He discerns what is right, rejects what is harmful, and walks with intentional focus. A watchful man is not easily defeated because he is not easily deceived. He anchors himself in truth, disciplines his mind, and stays connected to God through prayer and obedience. His awareness becomes his protection. His vigilance becomes his strength. And even when the battle intensifies, he stands firm because he is prepared. He understands that victory is not accidental; it is the result of a man who chose to stay awake when it mattered most.

A warrior is not defined by what he sees, but by what he is willing to face. There comes a moment when conviction must turn into action - when the things he has avoided can no longer be ignored. The fears he has hidden from, the habits he has excused, the responsibilities he has delayed are the very battlegrounds calling his name. And in that moment, he must choose: retreat into comfort or rise into courage. Stepping into the fight requires honesty, humility, and boldness. It means admitting where you've been weak and deciding that weakness will not define you. It means standing firm when everything in you wants to run. Transformation begins when a man stops making peace with what is holding him back and starts taking ground in the areas he once surrendered. God meets a man in that place of decision, empowering him to stand, to endure, and to win the battles that matter most. The fight you've been avoiding may be the very place where your strength is forged and your calling is revealed.

The pressure you feel is not meant to break you, but to build you. God uses resistance to forge endurance where there was once weakness, to build discipline where there was once inconsistency, and to grow faith where there was once doubt. What feels like opposition is often divine construction, forming a man who is steady, grounded, and unshakable. So do not run from resistance - lean into it. Embrace the struggle as part of your becoming. The challenges you face today are preparing you for the responsibilities of tomorrow. They are teaching you how to stand when life pushes back, how to remain faithful when the outcome is uncertain, and how to press forward when your strength feels depleted. A man who understands this stops asking, "Why is this happening to me?" and begins asking, "What is this producing in me?" Because in the hands of God, resistance is never wasted - it is the very place where strength is forged, character is refined, and a man is transformed into who he was created to be.

Too many men ask God for strength, yet quietly resist the very circumstances designed to produce it. They pray for endurance but avoid hardship, ask for courage but retreat from challenge, and seek growth while clinging to comfort. But God does not build strong men in easy places. Strength is not something handed over in moments of convenience - it is forged in the tension of resistance, in the weight of responsibility, and in the fire of adversity. The very trials a man wishes away are often the tools God is using to shape him into someone unshakable. What feels like pressure is often preparation. What feels like opposition is often opportunity. A man becomes strong when he chooses to stand in the moment he feels like sitting down, when he pushes forward despite fear, fatigue, or doubt. Strength is built in those quiet, unseen decisions to keep going, to hold the line, to trust God when the outcome is uncertain. It is developed when he refuses to run from difficulty and instead leans into it with faith.

The warrior spirit understands that resistance is not an obstacle to avoid, but a force that forges strength within. Where others see discomfort, the warrior sees development. Where others see struggle, he sees opportunity. He knows that God often uses pressure as a tool, shaping endurance, refining character, and building a resilience that cannot be shaken. Instead of asking for an easier path, he chooses to become a stronger man, trusting that every moment of resistance is preparing him for something greater. This kind of man does not interpret battles as punishment, but as preparation. He recognizes that every trial carries purpose, every hardship carries instruction, and every challenge carries the potential to transform him. The fire does not consume him - it refines him. The weight does not break him - it builds him. With faith in God and determination in his spirit, he leans into the process, knowing that on the other side of resistance is strength, clarity, and a man who has been shaped for greater impact.

Over time, something begins to shift deep within a man who chooses to walk with God. The fears that once paralyzed him begin to lose their voice, and the battles that once seemed overwhelming no longer carry the same weight. What used to make him retreat now calls him forward. Not because he suddenly feels stronger in his own ability, but because he has seen the faithfulness of God in his weakness. With every step of obedience, his spirit grows steadier, and what once felt impossible becomes another opportunity for God to prove Himself faithful. He knows where his strength comes from, and because of that, he is no longer shaken by what stands against him. There is a calm resolve in his heart, a steady assurance that no matter the challenge, he is not facing it alone. God is working through him, strengthening him, guiding him, and sustaining him. What once intimidated him now becomes the very ground where his faith is proven and his calling is fulfilled.

Each time a man chooses to stand firm when it would be easier to compromise, something powerful is being developed inside him. What once shook him begins to lose its grip because he has become stronger through God's work in him. These repeated moments of resistance are the shaping of a man who is learning to trust God over his feelings, his fears, and his circumstances. Over time, those decisions form a foundation that cannot be easily broken. Character is no longer something he hopes for - it becomes something he walks in. Each act of obedience and each choice to stand when others fall becomes a brick laid into the structure of his life. And though the progress may feel slow, it is sure. God is building something unshakable within him - a strength that is not dependent on emotion but anchored in truth. What is formed through consistency will stand through adversity, and the man who refuses to give in will one day realize he has become the very thing he once struggled to be.

Eventually, he becomes a man who refuses to surrender. His strength is no longer dependent on circumstances but is rooted in a spirit that has been tested, stretched, and anchored in God. What once felt overwhelming now becomes an opportunity to stand. He learns that endurance is not about avoiding hardship, but about remaining unshaken in the middle of it. And with every challenge he understands that surrender is not an option when purpose is at stake. There is too much on the line - too much calling, too much responsibility, too much God-given potential to walk away. So he stands his ground, not in his own power, but in the strength that comes from trusting God fully. Even when the path is difficult and the outcome uncertain, he presses forward with conviction. Because a man who knows his purpose cannot be easily moved. He may bend, he may be tested, but he will not break. And in that unwavering commitment, he becomes the kind of man who not only endures but a man who overcomes.

This kind of man is not driven by comfort, but by conviction. When the weight of life presses in and the path grows steep, he does not retreat to what is easy - he leans into what is right. He understands that difficulty is not a signal to quit, but often a confirmation that he is walking in purpose. Though the pressure may cause him to bend, it does not have the authority to break him, because his strength is not rooted in circumstances. It is rooted in God. His foundation is built on truth that does not shift with emotion, fear, or fatigue. And because of that, he remains standing long after others have walked away. There is a quiet strength within him that cannot be shaken by temporary storms. He has learned that feelings come and go, but truth remains. So when doubt whispers and exhaustion sets in, he remembers who God is, and in doing so, he remembers who he is called to be. He keeps going because he has already settled in his heart that quitting is not an option when truth is leading the way.

Living with a warrior spirit is not about being fearless - it is about being faithful in the face of fear. A man with a warrior spirit recognizes that courage is a choice, not a feeling. He does not wait for fear to disappear before he acts; he moves forward while his heart is still pounding. Instead of surrendering to fear, he confronts it with truth, reminding himself that God has not given him a spirit of fear, but of power, love, and a sound mind. This kind of man does not allow fear to dictate his direction. He may feel it, but he does not follow it. He steps into challenges, responsibilities, and callings with boldness because he knows that growth, purpose, and victory are always found on the other side of resistance. Each time he chooses courage, he strengthens his spirit and deepens his trust in God. Over time, he becomes a man who advances when others retreat, stands when others shrink back, and lives with a quiet, unshakable confidence rooted not in himself, but in the One who goes before him.

Determination is no longer something he visits in moments of crisis - it becomes the way he lives. He rises each day with purpose already set in his heart. His steps are not random; they are directed. His decisions are not careless; they are intentional. He walks with conviction because he knows who he belongs to, and that identity fuels his direction. Even when the path is uncertain, he does not hesitate because his confidence is not in perfect conditions, but in a faithful God who orders his steps. He no longer drifts with the current of culture or circumstance. He advances steadily, focused, and unshaken. Every challenge becomes a battleground where his faith is proven, and every victory, no matter how small, becomes a reminder that progress is being made. He stands with authority not because life is easy, but because his spirit has been strengthened through resistance. Battle by battle, he is being formed into a man who does not retreat, does not compromise, and does not quit.

There will be days when exhaustion presses in from every side - when his strength feels drained, his mind clouded, and his spirit stretched beyond what he thought he could endure. In those moments, it would be easy to step back, to loosen his grip, to convince himself that rest should become retreat. But deep within him, something stronger begins to stir. It is not loud, but it is steady. The warrior spirit God placed inside him refuses to be silenced by fatigue. It reminds him that his identity is not rooted in how he feels, but in who he has been called to be. So he rises not because the battle has become easier, but because his resolve has become stronger. The warrior spirit reminds him that quitting is not in his nature, because perseverance is being forged into his character. And step by step, even when weary, he moves forward again. Because a true warrior is not defined by how he feels in the moment, but by his decision to keep standing when everything in him wants to fall.

He begins to understand that true victory is not always loud, immediate, or visible. It is often quiet, forged in the unseen moments where he chooses to keep going when everything in him wants to stop. He learns that enduring faithfully is its own kind of triumph - that staying committed when progress feels slow is evidence of a deeper strength at work within him. God is not only honored in the breakthrough, but in the perseverance. Every step forward, no matter how small, becomes a declaration that his faith is stronger than his circumstances. Over time, he realizes that refusing to give up is not weakness - it is power under control. It is the steady decision to stand when others fall away, to press on when the path is unclear, and to trust God when results are delayed. In those moments, his character is refined, his spirit is strengthened, and his foundation is secured. What once felt like a struggle becomes a testimony: that endurance produces strength, and faithfulness leads to a victory that cannot be shaken.

When a man chooses to remain steady, to keep trusting God when answers are delayed and the path is unclear, something deeper begins to take root. His faith is no longer shallow or dependent on circumstances; it becomes anchored, unshakable, and alive. What once would have discouraged him now develops him. In enduring, he discovers that strength is not built in ease, but in persistence through difficulty. And as that endurance continues, his life begins to carry a weight that others can see and feel. His words hold substance because they have been tested. His character stands firm because it has been proven. There is a quiet authority about him. People are drawn to it, not because he seeks attention, but because they recognize something real. This is the power of a life shaped by endurance: a man who has walked through fire with God does not come out the same - he comes out stronger, deeper, and marked with a strength that cannot be ignored.

In the end, the warrior spirit is not about aggression - it is about perseverance. It is forged in the quiet decisions to stand when it would be easier to walk away, to trust when circumstances feel uncertain, and to keep moving forward when progress seems slow. This kind of strength comes from a deep-rooted confidence in God. It is the steady resolve that says, "I will not surrender what God has called me to," even when opposition rises and the battle feels relentless. In those moments, a man is not defined by how loudly he fights, but by how faithfully he endures. True spiritual strength is revealed in the ability to remain anchored when everything around you is shaking. It is choosing to trust God in the middle of the storm, believing that He is working even when you cannot see it. The warrior spirit refuses to abandon purpose, not because the path is easy, but because the calling is worth it. It understands that perseverance is not just about surviving the battle - it is about becoming stronger through it.

So stand your ground. Not every battle is worth your strength, but the ones that shape your character, your calling, and your faith are worth everything. There will always be pressure to compromise, to drift, to take the easier road but a man of God recognizes that ease is often the enemy of purpose. He plants his feet firmly, anchored in truth, and refuses to be moved by fear, culture, or circumstance. He fights with disciplined conviction choosing what is right over what is easy, every single time. Fight the battles that matter. Resist what seeks to weaken you whether it comes through distraction, doubt, temptation, or fatigue. These are the quiet wars that determine the strength of your life. And as you refuse to back down, something powerful is formed within you. You become steady. You become unshakable. You become the man God designed you to be not because life got easier, but because your spirit grew stronger. With God, you were never meant to retreat - you were built to stand, to endure, and to overcome.

"STANDING FIRM IN YOUR IDENTITY"

There is a strength that rises in a man when he knows he belongs to God, that he is called and chosen to do a mighty work on the earth. He no longer chases validation because he already carries identity. And in that place, his strength becomes immovable like a foundation set deep beneath the surface. Storms may come, opinions may shift, and expectations may rise and fall, but he remains grounded because his identity is not built on what is temporary, but on what is eternal. From that identity flows a different kind of life. He walks with confidence because he knows the source of his strength. He makes decisions with clarity because he is not trying to become someone, he already knows who he is. When challenges come he does not crumble under pressure because his identity is not up for negotiation. It has already been established. This is the strength that cannot be shaken - the strength of a man who is anchored in God, defined by truth, and unmoved by the shifting winds of the world.

Knowing who you are in Christ anchors your life in something that cannot be shaken by failure, success, or the shifting opinions of people. Your identity is not something you earn - it is something you receive. God has already spoken over you. He has called you His own, set you apart, and given your life meaning long before you ever accomplished anything. When a man truly grasps that he is known by

God, chosen with intention, and called with purpose, he stops striving to prove his worth and begins living from a place of confidence and peace. His foundation is no longer built on what he does, but on who God says he is. And from that place, everything changes. His decisions carry clarity. His steps carry conviction. He is no longer easily shaken by rejection or inflated by success, because his identity is settled. He walks with quiet authority because he understands that his life is rooted in something eternal. When a man knows who he is in Christ, he is living as the man God has declared him to be.

Too many men exhaust themselves as they strive to prove their worth, comparing their strength, success, and status against others. But identity in Christ was never meant to be earned through performance - it is received through grace. You are not defined by what you accomplish, but by what God has already spoken over you. In Him, you are chosen, accepted, and established. That truth does not fluctuate with your failures or rise with your victories. It is settled. It is secure. It is not up for negotiation. When a man begins to live from that place instead of striving for it, everything changes. He no longer fights for approval - he walks in it. He no longer competes for significance - he carries it. Confidence is no longer rooted in comparison, but in calling. And from that secure identity, he stands firm, moves with purpose, and lives with quiet authority. The man who knows who he is in Christ is no longer trying to become someone - he is finally free to live as the man God has already declared him to be.

When a man truly understands who he is in God, something deep within him settles. The restless striving fades. The need to prove, to compete, and to measure up begins to lose its grip. He no longer wakes up trying to earn worth that has already been given to him through Christ. Instead, he rises with a quiet strength, rooted in truth. Confidence replaces insecurity, not because life becomes easier, but because his identity becomes clearer. He knows he is chosen, called, and equipped, and that knowledge steadies his steps. His words carry weight because they are anchored in conviction, not fear. His leadership becomes steady and trustworthy because it flows from purpose, not ego. In moments of pressure, he stands firm in who he is. When a man stops striving to become what other people want him to be and starts living as the man God has already declared him to be, his life begins to influence others - not through force, but through the quiet, undeniable power of a man who knows who he is.

The world never stops trying to reshape a man into its image. It speaks through culture, media, and expectation, offering a version of manhood built on appearance, power, and outward success. It tells him that his worth is measured by what he has, how he looks, or how much influence he can command. These voices are relentless, persuasive, and often disguised as truth. And if he is not firmly rooted, he will begin to absorb these definitions without even realizing it, slowly conforming to a standard that was never designed by God. But a man grounded in truth learns to recognize the difference between what is loud and what is right. He anchors himself in God's definition, not the world's distortion. He understands that real strength is found in character, not comparison; in obedience, not applause; in purpose, not performance. When his identity is rooted in Christ, he walks with clarity and conviction, living out a manhood that is not borrowed from culture, but built by God - steady, secure, and unshakable.

Rejecting the world's definitions of manhood is a daily act of spiritual resistance. Culture will always try to redefine strength, reshape identity, and lower the standard of what a man should be. But a man anchored in truth does not drift with shifting opinions. He measures himself not by popularity, but by alignment with God's Word. When the world celebrates compromise, he chooses conviction. When it promotes comfort, he embraces calling. This kind of life requires awareness, discipline, and the courage to stand when standing alone would be easier to avoid. A man who refuses to conform is not trying to prove something; he is protecting something sacred. He understands that character is not formed by following the crowd, but by walking faithfully with God. So he resists the pressure to blend in. He chooses obedience over approval, and conviction over convenience. And in doing so, his life makes a powerful statement that real manhood is not defined by the world, but by the One who created him.

The world teaches men to compete, to outperform, to prove themselves in order to matter. But a man grounded in Christ understands that his value was settled long before he ever had the chance to earn it. He is not defined by another man's strength, success, or recognition. He is defined by the unchanging Word of God. Because of this, he walks with a steady confidence. He knows who he is, and that knowledge silences the need to compete. While others chase identity, striving to become enough, he lives from a place of already being enough in Christ. He does not wrestle for position, because he has been given a position. He does not fight for approval, because he has already been accepted. This produces a quiet strength within him - a stability that cannot be shaken by comparison or threatened by another man's success. Instead of striving, he abides. Instead of competing, he grows. And from that place of rest, his life begins to bear fruit - not out of pressure, but out of purpose.

This does not make him passive - it makes him powerful. When his identity is rooted in Christ, there is a steady strength within him - a quiet confidence that comes from knowing who he is and whose he is. That confidence sharpens his focus. It redirects his energy away from striving for validation and toward living with intention. He becomes disciplined, not distracted; anchored, not anxious; purposeful, not performative. What once drained him - comparison, approval-seeking, and fear - no longer has authority over his life. Now his strength is invested where it truly matters. He pours himself into obedience, trusting that God's way produces lasting fruit. He commits to purpose, even when it requires sacrifice. And he lives for impact, understanding that his life carries weight beyond the moment. This is

the power of a secure identity. It frees a man to walk boldly in his calling without hesitation or apology. He is not trying to become someone - he is living as the man God has already called him to be.

Living confidently in God's design means you begin to see that your
strengths are not random and your temperament is not a flaw. God
did not assemble you carelessly - He formed you with precision, purpose, and intention. When you embrace that truth, you no longer feel
the need to compare, compete, or conform to someone else's path. Instead, you stand firmly in who God created you to be, trusting that His
design carries both wisdom and direction. This kind of confidence
produces a quiet strength. You move with clarity because you know
your life is not an accident - it is an assignment. Your calling is not
something you have to chase desperately; it is something you grow
into faithfully. As you walk in obedience, your design begins to reveal its full power. What once felt uncertain becomes purposeful, and
what once felt ordinary becomes significant. When you live this way,
you honor God not by trying to be someone else, but by fully becoming the man He intentionally created you to be.

Confidence in God's design is the settled assurance that your life is not
random, your calling is not accidental, and your path is not a mistake.
When a man is aligned with how God made him, he stops striving to
prove himself and starts living with purpose. He no longer borrows
identity from the opinions of others, because he is rooted in something deeper and unshakable. This confidence is quiet but powerful.
It does not shout for attention, because it does not need validation. It
simply stands firm, steady, and grounded in the truth that God's design is enough. And in that alignment, there is freedom from comparison, freedom from insecurity, and freedom from the exhausting need
to perform. A man walking in God's design moves with clarity, acts
with conviction, and carries a presence that speaks without words. He
becomes unmovable not because life is easy, but because his founda-

tion is secure. He stands, not to impress the world, but because he knows who he is and whose he is.

There will be moments when doubt tries to creep in - quiet whispers that question who you are and what you're capable of. Circumstances may shift, people may misunderstand you, and situations may not reflect the truth you carry inside. These moments are not the measure of your identity. They are only tests of what your identity is built upon. When your foundation is rooted in Christ, you are not defined by what you feel in a moment, but by what God has spoken over your life. His truth stands when everything else feels uncertain. Feelings rise and fall, but His Word remains steady and unchanging. When doubt presses in, you don't have to collapse under it. You can stand firm, knowing that your worth, your purpose, and your calling were established long before the challenge appeared. You are not at the mercy of temporary conditions. You are grounded in a permanent truth. And because of that, you can move forward with quiet confidence, unshaken and unwavering.

Feelings can be powerful, but they are not always reliable. They rise and fall with circumstance, pressure, and fatigue. Truth, however, stands firm. When a man anchors himself in what God has spoken, he steps onto solid ground. He remembers who he is, what he is called to, and what is ultimately unshakable. This return is not weakness - it is alignment. It is the deliberate decision to silence confusion and stand on what is eternal. This is where strength is reinforced - by choosing truth over emotion, again and again. Each time he does, something within him is fortified. His mind becomes steadier. His spirit becomes more resilient. He is no longer led by impulse, but by conviction. Over time, this discipline shapes him into a man who cannot be easily moved, because his foundation is not built on how he feels in the moment, but on what God has declared from the beginning. And in that place, he finds a strength that does not waver - a quiet, unshakable confidence rooted in truth.

Walking with a secure identity anchors a man in a place that circumstances cannot shake. When failure comes, he does not crumble under its weight or allow it to rewrite who he is. He learns from it, stands back up, and keeps moving forward because his worth was never tied to his performance. At the same time, when success finds him, he does not lose himself in pride or become dependent on achievement for validation. His foundation is rooted in who God says he is, not in what he accomplishes. This kind of stability produces a quiet strength that endures through every season. He becomes consistent, not because life is easy, but because his identity is settled. Storms may come, but they do not uproot him. Praise may come, but it does not control him. He walks with a steady confidence and in that place, adversity loses its power to define him, and success loses its power to distract him, because he is already secure in something greater.

When a man is secure in who God has called him to be, he no longer leads to prove himself, but to serve a purpose greater than himself. Fear no longer drives his decisions, and control is no longer his method. Instead, clarity guides him because he knows his assignment. Conviction anchors him because he trusts the truth God has placed within him. And humility shapes him because he understands that leadership is stewardship, not ownership. He is not striving to be seen as strong; he is simply walking in the strength that has already been established in him through Christ. His presence carries weight because it is grounded in truth, not ego. He listens, he discerns, and he leads with a steady hand, even when pressure rises. His leadership creates stability, not fear - direction, not confusion. Because when a man knows who he is, he no longer leads from insecurity - he leads from identity. And that kind of leadership does not just influence people, it transforms them.

Relationships are transformed when a man is no longer driven by the need to be filled by others but instead is filled by God. He stops approaching people as a place to draw identity, approval, or worth, and begins to show up as someone grounded, steady, and secure. And from that place of stability, he becomes a refuge to others. His life begins to strengthen those around him rather than strain them. Instead of taking, he gives. Instead of constantly looking to be affirmed, he becomes the one who lifts others up. Encouragement flows from him because he is no longer empty - he is anchored. He sees people through the lens of purpose, not performance, and calls out the best in them. This is where true strength is revealed - not in dominance, but in contribution. Not in needing to be upheld, but in becoming someone who upholds others. And in doing so, his relationships are no longer transactional - they become transformational, marked by strength, selflessness, and the quiet power of a life rooted in God.

This kind of man is not easily swayed, because his life is anchored deeper than circumstances. He is not driven by approval, fear, or the need to fit in. Instead, he stands firm in what he knows to be true. He has settled his identity in something unchanging, and because of that, shifting winds do not move him. While others adjust themselves to match the moment, he remains consistent, steady, grounded, and sure. He does not compromise under influence because his roots run deep. Like a tree planted by living water, he draws from a source that does not run dry. When everything around him feels uncertain, his identity holds him in place. He knows who he is, and more importantly, whose he is. That truth becomes his foundation, reinforcing him in moments where others might fold. His life becomes a quiet testimony of strength - not loud or forceful, but unshakable. And in a world that constantly changes, his rootedness becomes a light, showing others what it means to stand firm in God.

The world constantly offers competing definitions of worth, success, and manhood, but God's voice remains steady and unchanging. A man who stands firm learns to return to that voice again and again. He reminds himself of who God says he is - not based on performance, approval, or circumstance, but rooted in divine purpose. This daily reinforcement becomes the anchor that keeps him steady when everything else feels uncertain. Over time, these repeated choices build a life that cannot be easily shaken. He begins to recognize the difference between truth and suggestion, between conviction and pressure. He no longer drifts with culture or bends under expectation, because his identity has been reinforced through consistency. And in that discipline, he transforms into a man who walks with quiet confidence, grounded strength, and unwavering clarity because he has trained his heart to believe God, no matter what surrounds him or what others may say.

And as he does, something powerful begins to take shape within him. What was once inconsistent becomes steady. What was once shaken by circumstances becomes rooted in truth. His walk with God produces a quiet strength that shows up day after day. He becomes a man who can be counted on, not because life is easy, but because his foundation is secure. Consistency is no longer forced - it is the natural result of a life surrendered and aligned. In that place, his life begins to carry weight. Not the weight of performance or achievement, but the weight of presence, character, and conviction. When he speaks, there is substance behind his words. When he leads, there is integrity in his steps. People begin to trust him not because he is perfect, but because he is anchored. He knows who he belongs to, and that identity shapes everything he does. And in a world full of instability, his grounded life becomes a steady light - quietly powerful, deeply impactful, and impossible to ignore.

When a man truly understands who he is in Christ, his life begins to reflect a deeper reality. He no longer strives to prove his worth, because his worth has already been established at the cross. This kind of identity produces stability. It anchors him in truth when culture shifts, when opinions change, and when circumstances try to redefine him. He becomes a man who is not easily shaken, because he is not built on what is temporary - he is grounded in what is eternal. And when a man stands firm in that identity, his life begins to mirror the character of Christ in how he speaks, leads, serves, and loves. In a world filled with confusion, compromise, and misplaced identity, that kind of clarity stands out. It brings direction to the lost, strength to the weary, and truth to the uncertain. His presence carries weight because it points to something greater than himself. And in that reflection, he becomes living evidence that when a man knows who he is in Christ, everything changes.

| 24 |

"STRENGTH TO KEEP GOING"

When the road stretches longer than you expected and the weight presses deeper than you prepared for, something sacred is being formed within you. This is the place where surface-level strength gives way to something far more enduring. Passion may have started the journey, but it is perseverance that carries you through it. God often does His deepest work not in the moments of excitement, but in the quiet, grinding seasons where continuing requires faith, not feeling. It is here that character is refined, where dependence on Him grows stronger, and where a man learns that true strength is not loud - it is steady. When everything in you wants relief, but you choose to remain faithful, you step into a strength that is not your own. Endurance is not simply about surviving the moment - it is about becoming the kind of man who cannot be stopped by it. The strength to keep going is built decision by decision, step by step, long after the emotions have faded.

God does not call you to begin boldly only to abandon the path when it becomes hard; He calls you to finish with the same conviction you started with. Every step forward, no matter how small, is a declaration that quitting is not an option. And in that persistence, victory is being shaped even before you see it. Because the man who refuses to give up is the man who will ultimately overcome. A man anchored in conviction does not rely on how he feels in the moment

- he relies on what he knows to be true. Conviction pushes him forward when progress feels painfully slow because conviction is not built on circumstances - it is built on truth. And when a man is rooted in truth, he becomes unmovable. He endures not because it is easy, but because it is right. And in that endurance, something powerful is formed within him - a strength that cannot be manufactured by emotion, a resilience that only comes from standing firm when everything in him wants to walk away.

Endurance is the decision to rise again when motivation is gone, to keep moving when progress feels invisible, and to remain faithful when results seem delayed. What looks like weakness from the outside is often the deepest form of strength within. God does some of His greatest work in those hidden spaces, shaping a man's character through consistency, humility, and trust. It is there, in the unseen effort, that resilience is developed and faith is refined. And while the world celebrates sudden victories and visible success, heaven honors persistence. Every small step taken in obedience matters. Every moment you refuse to quit is a declaration of who you are becoming. Endurance is not about speed - it is about staying power. It is about trusting that even when you cannot see progress, God is still producing something powerful within you. So keep going. Keep showing up. Because in the quiet struggle, God is building a strength in you that cannot be shaken.

The exhaustion you feel is not evidence that you are failing - it is often proof that you are being stretched beyond your old limits. Just as muscles are strengthened through resistance, your character is being formed in the tension you are walking through right now. What feels heavy at the moment is building endurance in you, shaping your faith, and developing a strength that cannot be produced in ease or comfort. What you feel is not the signal to retreat, but the sign that something deeper is being formed within you. So don't walk away in the middle of the process. The very place where you feel like quitting may be the place where breakthrough is closest. If you release the pressure too soon, you risk missing what God is trying to produce through it. Stay planted. Stay faithful. Lean into Him because His strength is made perfect in your weakness. What feels like your breaking point may actually be your building point. Keep going - not because it's easy, but because it's worth it.

God never intended for you to carry the weight of your life alone. The moments when you feel stretched, exhausted, and unable to keep going are invitations to shift your dependence. Your natural strength was never meant to be the foundation; it was meant to lead you to a deeper realization that true strength comes from Him. When you reach the end of yourself, you are not at a dead end - you are at a doorway. It is there, in that place of surrender, that God begins to do what your effort never could. So do not fear the moments when your strength fades. Embrace them. When your energy is gone and your resolve feels thin, that is when His strength rises within you in a way that is unmistakable. You begin to move not by striving, but by grace. Not by pressure, but by power. And in that place, you discover a truth that changes everything: you were never meant to do this on your own - you were meant to walk it out with Him.

Renewal is the result of surrender. The more a man tries to force strength from within himself, the more he discovers how limited that strength truly is. But when he turns his heart back to God, he is no longer striving to produce what he cannot sustain. Instead, he is receiving what God freely gives. In that quiet return, strength begins to rise again not as a burst of human effort, but as a steady flow of divine supply. What once felt heavy becomes manageable, not because the burden disappeared, but because God is now carrying it with him. The confusion and fatigue that once clouded his vision are replaced with truth and direction. God does not just comfort - He restores. He rebuilds what pressure has worn down and refuels what has been emptied. There is a well in His presence that never runs dry, a strength that does not fade with time or circumstance. When a man learns to return again and again, he discovers that renewal is not occasional - it becomes a way of living.

There is a divine exchange that unfolds when a man chooses to lean fully into God. In place of what you lack, He supplies what you need. Your weakness is an invitation for His strength to be revealed. Your exhaustion becomes the very place where His renewal flows, and your doubt becomes the ground where His truth takes root. God does not ask you to arrive strong; He asks you to come willing. And in that willingness, He begins the exchange that changes everything. This exchange requires letting go of self-reliance and choosing, again and again, to depend on Him. Surrender opens the door, trust keeps it open, and faith walks through it daily. As you lean into Him consistently, you begin to experience a strength that is not your own, a clarity that does not come from circumstances, and a peace that cannot be shaken. This is the life shaped by divine exchange - a life where what you give to God is never lost but always returned transformed into something greater.

The man who endures understands that moments of exhaustion, doubt, and pressure are invitations to draw closer to God. When weakness comes, he does not run from it or try to mask it; he brings it before the One who supplies what he lacks. Instead of retreating into isolation, he presses into God's presence. Instead of allowing discouragement to take root, he lifts his eyes higher. And in that upward focus, his weakness becomes the very place where God's strength begins to flow. Endurance is fueled by divine connection. The man who looks up discovers that what he needs - strength, clarity, courage, perseverance - is not something he has to manufacture; it is something he receives. And as he continues to press forward, not in his own power but in dependence on God, he becomes stronger than he ever could have been on his own. This is the secret of endurance: not avoiding weakness but meeting it with faith and finding that God has already provided everything needed to keep going.

Perseverance is not merely the act of surviving hardship - it is the process through which God reshapes a man from the inside out. Your character is being refined. Your faith is being strengthened. Your perspective is being elevated beyond comfort and into purpose. What feels like resistance is often the very tool God is using to build resilience within you. In those moments when quitting seems easier, choosing to press forward becomes an act of transformation. You are not just advancing through challenges - you are becoming someone who can carry greater weight, greater responsibility, and greater impact. Every difficult step is depositing strength into your spirit and wisdom into your decisions. The man who refuses to stop, even when progress feels slow, is the man who is being prepared for something more. God does not waste the struggle; He uses it. So keep moving forward, not just to reach the destination, but to embrace the transformation that is taking place within you along the way.

There is a reason perseverance produces victory. It is not just about getting through difficulty - it is about being refined by it. The pressure strips away what is shallow, exposing what is real. It reveals whether your foundation is built on convenience or conviction, on comfort or calling. What cannot endure is removed, but what remains is strengthened. Over time, perseverance forges something solid within you - a faith that has been tested, a character that has been proven, and a strength that is no longer dependent on circumstances. This is the quiet work of God, shaping a man from the inside out until he becomes unshakable. Victory, then, is not simply about reaching a goal, but about becoming the kind of man who can carry what he has been given without collapsing under its weight. Many desire the outcome, but few are willing to endure the process that prepares them to sustain it. True victory is stable because it is built on endurance. It is lasting because it has been tested and forged over time.

Many people are drawn to the idea of victory, but far fewer are willing to walk the road that leads to it. The truth is, victory is not found in moments of ease - it is formed in seasons of resistance. It is in the long days when motivation fades, when progress feels slow, and when quitting seems justified that true strength is revealed. God does not build enduring men through comfort, but through commitment. Every step you take when it would have been easier to stop is shaping something that cannot be produced any other way. Real victory is built through consistency when no one is watching, through faith when results are not visible, and through obedience when emotions are unreliable. The process refines you, strips away what is shallow, and strengthens what is lasting. What you gain at the end is a man who has been proven. So do not despise the resistance. Embrace it because the very struggle you are in is working for you, preparing you to carry the victory you are pursuing.

What feels heavy in the moment is actually sharpening your vision, cutting away distractions, and aligning your heart with what truly matters. Pressure has a way of exposing what is weak and strengthening what is real. It forces you to decide what you believe, what you stand on, and who you will trust when comfort is no longer an option. In that place, your resolve is not just tested - it is built. Your faith is no longer theoretical - it becomes lived, active, and unshakable. What you may be calling a burden is actually a tool in the hands of a Master Craftsman. God is forming something in you that cannot be developed any other way. He is shaping your character, reinforcing your endurance, and calling out a strength that you didn't know you possessed. The pressure is not there to break you - it is there to build you. If you remain faithful in it, you will come out refined, focused, and stronger than before. You are not being crushed - you are being crafted into the man you were created to be.

When the weight of the journey makes you want to stop, go back to the moment God stirred something inside of you that would not let you stay the same. That calling was placed within you by a God who sees the end from the beginning. Difficulty does not erase purpose; it reveals it. The resistance you feel is not proof that you are off track, but often confirmation that what you are pursuing matters. The same God who called you is the One who sustains you, and He has not changed His mind about your assignment. So when your strength feels low and your motivation begins to fade, remind yourself that your purpose is greater than your present discomfort. You did not start this journey just for ease - you started it in obedience. And obedience is not proven in moments of excitement, but in moments of endurance. Reconnect with the vision God gave you. The calling is still alive. The purpose is still waiting. And every step forward is a declaration that you will not quit on what God has placed in your hands.

Determination is the quiet resolve to rise each day and take another step, even when no one is watching and nothing feels easy. It is built in choosing discipline when distraction calls, choosing purpose when comfort tempts, choosing obedience when convenience offers another way. This kind of determination is not driven by emotion, because emotions fade - it is anchored in conviction. And conviction keeps a man steady when everything else tries to pull him off course. Over time, this steady determination begins to shape something deeper within you. It strengthens your character, sharpens your focus, and aligns your life with God's calling. What feels like slow progress is often the most meaningful kind, because it is building something that lasts. God honors persistence that refuses to quit, even when the results are not immediate. So keep moving forward. Keep choosing what is right over what is easy. Because every step taken in determination is a step closer to becoming the man you were created to be.

Pressing forward requires a disciplined focus that refuses to be scattered by every obstacle along the way. Life will present delays, resistance, and moments that try to steal your attention, but a man of purpose learns to lock his eyes on what truly matters. He understands that not every battle deserves his energy and not every distraction deserves his response. Instead of being consumed by what stands in front of him, he is driven by what is ahead of him. With his gaze fixed on God and his calling, he moves forward with clarity, not confusion. He is anchored in truth rather than shaken by circumstances. Distractions will always compete for your attention, but determination is what keeps you aligned with your purpose. When your focus is rooted in Him, you gain the ability to filter out what is temporary and stay committed to what is eternal. So guard your focus because the man who refuses to be pulled off course is the man who ultimately reaches the destination God has prepared for him.

There will be seasons when your effort feels unnoticed and your progress feels invisible. You show up, you remain faithful, you keep moving forward and yet nothing seems to shift. But what you cannot see is not the same as what is not happening. Beneath the surface, God is at work. Roots are growing deeper. Your character is being strengthened. Your faith is being refined. Just as a seed spends time hidden in the soil before it ever breaks through the ground, so too does your growth develop in unseen places before it is revealed in visible ways. Do not mistake silence for stagnation or delay for denial. Every step of obedience, every moment of perseverance, and every act of faith is building something far greater than what you can measure right now. The seeds you have planted are not wasted - they are being prepared for a harvest in the right time. Stay steady. Stay faithful. What feels like nothing today is often the foundation for something powerful tomorrow.

Do not underestimate the power of consistency. The quiet, daily decisions you make are the very things shaping your future. God often works through what seems small and ordinary, building strength, character, and endurance one step at a time. Just as a seed grows unseen beneath the soil before it ever breaks the surface, your faithfulness in the small moments is preparing something greater than you can currently see. What feels insignificant today is not wasted - it is being woven into something purposeful. Faithfulness is not about how fast you move, but about how steady you remain. There is power in simply showing up again, choosing obedience again, and taking one more step forward when it would be easier to stop. Progress in God's kingdom is often quiet before it becomes visible, but it is always meaningful. Stay committed to the process. Keep moving forward with trust, even when results feel distant. In time, what you have been faithfully building will begin to speak for itself.

There will be days when your energy is low, your emotions are stretched, and your progress feels slow. But strength is not the absence of weariness; it is the refusal to surrender to it. It is the quiet, steady decision to rise again when staying down would be easier. It is choosing to trust God again when doubt whispers louder, to take another step when your legs feel heavy, and to move forward when everything in you wants to stop. This is where true endurance is formed. And as you keep going, you begin to realize something powerful - you were never meant to carry this journey alone. God walks with you in every step, strengthening what feels weak and renewing what feels drained. His presence meets you in your persistence. His power shows up in your weakness. What felt impossible begins to shift as you lean into Him, drawing from a source that does not run dry. So keep rising. Keep trusting. Keep moving. Because every step you take in faith is supported by a strength far greater than your own.

So keep going. When the road stretches longer than you expected and every step feels like effort, keep going. Turn your heart toward God in those moments, not away from Him. It is in your weakness that His strength becomes real, not just something you speak about, but something you experience. The journey was never meant to be carried by your strength alone. Every step forward, even the slow and difficult ones, becomes an act of faith when you choose to trust Him in the middle of the struggle. Because on the other side of perseverance is victory - but not just a victory you reach, a victory you become. The man who refuses to quit is being shaped with every step he takes. He is being refined, strengthened, and established in ways that comfort could never produce. Quitting may promise relief, but endurance produces transformation. So keep moving because the man who presses forward when everything in him wants to stop is the man who will not only see victory but will be ready to carry it.

| 25 |

"THE POWER OF QUIET CONFIDENCE"

Quiet confidence is strength that has been tested, refined, and brought under control. A man who walks in quiet confidence is not driven by the need for recognition or approval; he is anchored in something greater than the opinions around him. His strength is steady, not sporadic. His presence is calm, not chaotic. In a world that often equates volume with power, quiet confidence stands as a different kind of authority. There is something unmistakable about a man who is at peace with who he is in God. He does not waver under pressure because his foundation is not external - it is eternal. His words carry weight because they are not many. His actions carry impact because they are intentional. And when he leads, he does so with a steady hand and a clear heart. Quiet confidence is not about being seen - it is about being rooted. And when a man is rooted in God, he becomes unshakable, not because life is easy, but because his strength is no longer his own.

True strength is not found in how loudly a man speaks, but in how firmly he stands. A man who is grounded in God does not need to raise his voice to be heard, because his life already speaks with authority. His peace in pressure, his restraint in conflict, and his steadiness in uncertainty reveal a strength that cannot be manufactured. While others strive to be noticed, he remains focused on being faithful. And in that faithfulness, his strength becomes undeniable because it is evident in everything he does. There is a power in quiet confidence that the world often overlooks. It is the strength to remain calm when chaos surrounds you and to trust God when outcomes are unclear. This kind of man knows who he is, and more importantly, whose he is. And because of that, he leads without forcing, speaks without striving, and stands without shaking. His life becomes a reflection of a deeper strength that does not need to prove itself, because it has already been established.

There is a difference between being heard and being effective. A man can raise his voice and still lack influence, but a man who is grounded carries weight without needing to prove it. Quiet confidence is not concerned with being noticed - it is concerned with being rooted. While others chase recognition, the grounded man pursues truth. He does not need the approval of the crowd because he has anchored himself in something greater than their opinion. His strength comes from knowing who he is before God, and that identity produces a steady, unshakable presence. Quiet confidence listens more than it speaks, observes more than it reacts, and moves with intention rather than impulse. When this kind of man speaks, his words carry clarity. When he acts, his actions carry purpose. When pressure comes, he remains steady because he is anchored. In a world that rewards noise, be the man whose life speaks louder than his voice, and whose faith in God makes him effective wherever he stands.

A man who operates in quiet confidence does not draw his strength from the shifting voices around him - he draws it from an unshakable foundation within him. He understands that opinions are temporary, but truth is eternal. Because of this, he is not easily pulled in different directions by praise or criticism. His identity is not formed by the crowd, and his worth is not determined by applause. Instead, he is anchored in what God has spoken over his life, and that truth becomes the steady ground beneath his feet. This kind of man does not need to prove himself to everyone, because he already knows who he is. He moves with purpose, speaks with intention, and stands with conviction. Even when misunderstood, he does not panic. Even when criticized, he does not crumble. There is a quiet strength in him that comes from trusting something greater than human opinion. Because his foundation is rooted in God, he is not easily shaken - he is established, grounded, and unwavering no matter what comes his way.

This kind of strength is built in the quiet places where only God sees. It is formed in the early moments of obedience and in the steady commitment to do what is right when there is no recognition. In those hidden spaces, character takes root. Integrity is established. Faith is deepened. A man who learns to be faithful in private is preparing himself for moments in public that will require strength, clarity, and conviction. What may feel small and unnoticed is actually sacred ground, where God is shaping something that cannot be easily shaken. And when the time comes for that strength to be revealed, it will not need to announce itself - it will be evident. The decisions made in private will surface in public moments of pressure. The discipline developed in secret will sustain him when others falter. This is the power of a life built with God behind the scenes. What is built in secret becomes the foundation for a life that stands firm, leads boldly, and reflects the strength of the One who formed it.

Calm leadership is not revealed when everything is easy - it is revealed when everything is uncertain. When pressure rises and others begin to react out of fear, the quietly confident man stands firm. His steadiness is not accidental; it is anchored in something deeper than emotion. While others are moved by what they see, he is grounded in knowing that God is still in control. Because of that, he does not rush, he does not panic, and he does not lose direction. His calm becomes a covering for those around him, a visible reminder that stability is still possible even in the middle of chaos. This kind of leadership carries weight because it is rooted in trust, not circumstance. The quietly confident man has already settled the question of who he depends on, so when storms come, he is not shaken by them. Instead of reacting, he responds with wisdom. Instead of spreading fear, he releases peace. His presence alone begins to shift the atmosphere, because people can sense that he is anchored.

While others react, he responds. He does not allow the urgency of the moment to dictate the posture of his spirit. In a world that moves quickly and reacts loudly, he stands apart, choosing to pause, to discern, and to act with purpose. His strength is not found in how quickly he reacts, but in how clearly he sees. And because his vision is shaped by truth, his actions carry weight and direction. While others are overwhelmed, he is anchored. Not because life is easier for him, but because his foundation is stronger. His calm is the evidence of a heart that trusts God even when the situation is uncertain. Fear may knock, pressure may rise, and chaos may surround him, but he does not surrender his peace. He leans into God and finds stability that the world cannot offer. This kind of man becomes a steady presence in unstable times - a voice of clarity in confusion, a source of strength for others. Because when a man is anchored in God, he does not drift with the storm, he stands firm in the middle of it.

In moments of pressure, when everything feels uncertain and unstable, people are drawn to the man who does not panic, who does not crumble under the weight, who remains steady when others are shaken. Quiet confidence becomes that anchor. It does not shout or demand attention, yet its presence is undeniable. It is the calm in the storm, the steady hand in chaos, the unshakable posture of a man whose trust is rooted deeper than circumstances. In a world filled with noise, fear, and reaction, there is something powerful about a steady spirit. It reassures, it stabilizes, and it brings clarity where confusion once ruled. When pressure rises, the man grounded in God does not absorb the chaos - he diffuses it. His peace speaks louder than panic ever could. His presence reminds others that strength is not always loud, and stability is not always seen - it is often felt. And in that stillness, God's strength is revealed, not through force, but through unwavering, quiet confidence.

A calm leader does not need to fill every silence or control every conversation because he understands that true authority is not proven by volume, but by presence. While others rush to be heard, he takes time to listen. While others react impulsively, he responds with intention. There is a steadiness about him that brings clarity into confusion and peace into pressure. His words carry weight because they are not wasted, and his actions speak with a quiet confidence that does not need validation. This kind of leadership reflects a deeper trust in God. His identity is settled, his purpose is clear, and his direction is steady. When he speaks, it is with wisdom. When he moves, it is with conviction. And when challenges arise, he remains composed, knowing that God is not shaken and neither is the man who walks closely with Him. In a world that equates loudness with strength, the calm leader stands as a powerful reminder that true leadership is not announced - it is revealed.

A man who is rooted in clarity does not scramble when decisions arise, because he has already settled who he is before the moment ever came. His identity is not shifting with opinions, emotions, or circumstances; it is anchored in truth. Because he knows what he stands for, he does not need to pause in uncertainty or wait for approval. His steps are guided by conviction, not confusion. And in a world filled with hesitation and compromise, that kind of clarity becomes a steady light that others are drawn to. His conviction makes him reliable. There is a calm strength in a man who has already counted the cost and chosen his path. He does not waver under pressure or bend to the weight of expectation. Instead, he stands firm, not in pride, but in purpose. His leadership carries authority because it is backed by consistency, and his decisions carry weight because they are grounded in truth. This is the kind of man others can trust not because he is perfect, but because he is unwavering in what he believes.

Confidence that is rooted in God carries a strength that is not shaken by circumstances or dependent on outcomes. When a man anchors his confidence in God, he is no longer at the mercy of those fluctuations. His identity is not defined by what he achieves or what he lacks, but by who God says he is. Because God does not change, the foundation of his confidence does not change either. It becomes steady, reliable, and deeply rooted - able to stand firm in both victory and adversity. This kind of confidence produces a quiet assurance. It does not need to prove itself, compare itself, or defend itself. It simply stands. When challenges arise, it does not collapse under pressure, because it knows its source is greater than the situation. When success comes, it does not become prideful, because it understands where its strength truly comes from. A man who lives this way walks with a calm, unshakable presence. He trusts God knowing that his worth, his purpose, and his strength are secure.

When a man draws his confidence from God, he is no longer carried by the highs of success or crushed by the weight of failure. His security is not tied to visible results, but to an unchanging source. Even when doors seem closed and progress feels slow, he remains steady, because he knows that God is still at work behind the scenes. What he cannot see, God is already shaping. What he cannot understand, God is already orchestrating. And in that assurance, fear begins to lose its grip. This kind of trust produces a peace that cannot be manufactured by circumstances. It is not the absence of challenges, but the presence of confidence in the One who is greater than them all. A man who trusts God learns to rest without becoming passive and to move forward without becoming anxious. He does not rush ahead in panic, nor does he retreat in doubt. Instead, he walks with quiet confidence knowing that every delay has purpose and every outcome is ultimately held in God's hands.

This peace becomes his strength. It steadies his heart when everything around him feels uncertain. He stands firm without anxiety, rooted in a confidence that is not shaken by circumstances. While others are driven by pressure or controlled by outcomes, he is guided by a settled assurance that God is present, working, and faithful. This peace quiets the noise of doubt and silences the urgency of fear. It is a quiet strength, but it is powerful. It does not need to prove itself or demand attention, because its source is secure. This kind of strength enables him to lead without insecurity, to make decisions without hesitation, and to remain steady when challenges arise. It becomes a foundation beneath his life - unseen, yet unshakable. And as he walks in that peace, others begin to notice. Not because of loud words or bold displays, but because of the calm authority and steady presence he carries. In a restless world, his peace becomes a testimony that true strength is found in trusting God completely.

Confidence in God does not inflate a man - it anchors him. When he truly understands that his strength, wisdom, and opportunities all flow from God, there is no room for pride to take root. He no longer strives to prove his worth or elevate his image, because he knows his identity is already secure in the One who called him. This kind of confidence is steady and quiet. It frees him from comparison and self-promotion, allowing him to walk with a calm assurance that does not need validation from others. Instead of exalting himself, he lives with a deep sense of gratitude. He recognizes that every victory is a gift, every step forward is guided, and every ability is entrusted to him by God. This realization keeps his heart grounded and his spirit teachable. He remains humble not because he thinks less of himself, but because he thinks rightly about his source. And in that humility, he becomes stronger because a man who stays low before God can be trusted to stand tall in the world.

Humility and confidence are allies working together in a man who understands who he is in God. Confidence gives him the strength to stand, to lead, and to move forward without hesitation, while humility reminds him that his strength is not self-made. He can walk boldly without becoming arrogant, and he can serve others without feeling diminished. In him, strength is steady and rooted in truth. This balance creates a man who is both firm and compassionate, both strong and approachable. He stands his ground when it matters, but his heart remains open. He leads with conviction, yet he listens with grace. People are drawn to him not just because of his strength, but because of the peace and humility that shape it. In a world that often separates power from compassion, this kind of man reflects something greater. He shows that true strength is not about elevating yourself above others, but about walking with God in a way that lifts others up while standing firmly in who you were created to be.

Steady conviction is the quiet strength of a man who has already settled his values before the pressure comes. When difficulty rises, he does not scramble to decide what he believes - he stands on what he has already committed to. He understands that truth does not change based on circumstances, and neither should his character. Even when compromise seems like the easier path, he resists it, because he knows that integrity is built in moments like these. What is tested in the fire is either weakened or proven, and the man of conviction chooses to be proven. Choosing what is right over what is popular may cost him approval, opportunities, or comfort, but it will never cost him his identity. He does not lead for applause - he leads from purpose. And in doing so, he becomes a steady voice in unstable times, a firm foundation when others are shifting. His life sends a clear message that a man who refuses to bend will ultimately stand stronger than the pressure that tried to move him.

A man of quiet confidence does not drift with every wind of opinion or pressure of circumstance. He is anchored. His purpose is something he lives. Because his confidence is rooted in God, he is not easily swayed by distraction, fear, or the need for approval. He knows where he is going, even when the path is not fully visible. His direction is clear because it has been settled in his heart. And that clarity gives him a steady footing that the world cannot shake. His steps are intentional, not rushed or reckless, but deliberate and consistent. He does not rely on bursts of motivation because he is built on discipline and conviction. Day by day, choice by choice, he moves forward with purpose, trusting that God is guiding his path. Even when progress feels slow, he does not abandon his course. He understands that faithfulness over time produces strength, and strength produces impact. So he keeps walking, not loudly, but steadily because a man who refuses to drift is a man who will ultimately arrive.

In the end, quiet confidence is about becoming unshakable. It is the kind of strength that is built in private, formed through prayer, tested through trials, and anchored in truth. A man who carries this kind of confidence does not need to prove himself to others, because he has already been established by God. His identity is settled. His direction is clear. And because his foundation is firm, his presence brings stability wherever he goes. He does not chase recognition - he walks in purpose. This kind of man leads without noise but leaves a lasting impact. His words are measured, his actions are intentional, and his life reflects a deep and steady trust in God. In moments of chaos, he brings calm. In times of uncertainty, he stands firm. His strength speaks, not through volume, but through consistency. And over time, it becomes evident that this is a man who has been shaped by something greater than himself. A man whose quiet confidence is not weakness, but power under control.

| 26 |

"PREPARING FOR GREATER RESPONSIBILITY"

God does not elevate a man based on potential alone - He elevates him based on what has been proven in private. Before greater responsibility is entrusted, there is always a season where a man is examined, stretched, and refined. These tests are not designed to destroy him, but to reveal what is truly within him. They uncover the hidden places of his heart - his motives when no one is watching, his discipline when no one is applauding, and his character when pressure is applied. In these moments, a man begins to see himself clearly, and more importantly, he learns to rely fully on God rather than his own strength. If a man embraces this season instead of resisting it, the testing becomes preparation. What feels like delay is actually development. What feels like pressure is actually positioning. God is not trying to keep him from something - He is getting him ready for something. Because when the weight of responsibility comes, it will rest on the foundation that was built in those unseen moments.

Many men desire promotion, but few embrace preparation. They are drawn to the spotlight, yet they avoid the shaping that happens in the shadows. But God does not promote based on outward readiness - He looks at the condition of the heart. In the quiet places, where no one is watching, character is formed, faith is tested, and integrity is proven. It is there that a man learns obedience, humility, and dependence on

God. What feels hidden is holy ground where God is building a foundation strong enough to carry what is coming. What a man becomes in private will always determine what he can sustain in public. Platforms do not create strength - they reveal it. If there is no depth beneath the surface, the weight of influence will eventually expose it. But the man who has allowed God to refine him in secret will not be shaken when he is seen. He will stand with quiet confidence, not because of his own ability, but because he has been prepared by God. So do not rush the process. Embrace it.

Testing rarely announces itself with clarity. It shows up in the form of inconvenience, delay, and unexpected pressure, in moments that feel small, frustrating, and easy to overlook. Yet these are the very places where a man is being formed. What feels like interruption is often instruction. What feels like resistance is often refinement. In these hidden moments, God is not measuring performance - He is shaping character. Heaven pays attention to what man often dismisses. Every decision to remain patient, every choice to respond with integrity, every act of quiet obedience is building something far greater than the moment itself. Trust is not handed over in a moment - it is built layer by layer through consistent integrity, proven character, and faithfulness over time. And the man who proves faithful in what seems small is preparing himself for what is significant. The pressure is not pointless; it is purposeful. It is forging a man who can carry weight, handle responsibility, and stand firm when it truly matters.

Faithfulness is not proven in comfort - it is revealed under pressure. When everything within a man urges him to compromise, to take the easier path, or to justify a lesser standard, yet he chooses to stand firm, something powerful is established. His commitment becomes more than words; it becomes substance. Integrity in those hidden, difficult moments is what separates a man who merely desires purpose from a man who is truly prepared to carry it. Pressure does not weaken a faithful man - it exposes the strength that God has been building within him all along. These are the moments that heaven honors. Not the public victories that draw attention, but the private decisions that require conviction. When a man chooses integrity over convenience, he aligns himself with the character of God, and in doing so, he becomes someone who can be trusted with greater responsibility. The approval that matters most is not found in applause, but in knowing that he has remained faithful where it counted.

When a man remains faithful in the middle of strain, resistance, and uncertainty, he is showing that his commitment is not built on ease but on conviction. Anyone can stand firm when the path is smooth, but it takes a grounded spirit to hold the line when the cost is real. In those moments when no one is watching, when shortcuts are available, when compromise would be easier, his choices speak louder than words ever could. Integrity becomes his testimony, and faithfulness becomes his strength. He is not performing for recognition; he is living from a place of truth. These are the moments that carry eternal weight. God is not measuring a man by public applause but by private obedience. When he chooses what is right over what is easy, heaven takes notice. Trust is not granted through intention - it is proven through consistency under pressure. And as a man continues to walk in integrity, even when it costs him something, he is being shaped into someone who can carry greater responsibility.

Faithfulness is forged in the quiet places where no one is watching and nothing seems remarkable. The small assignments, the unseen responsibilities, and the unnoticed acts of obedience are where a man's character is truly built. It is there that discipline is strengthened, integrity is tested, and commitment is proven. What feels minor in the moment is actually laying a foundation that will either support or collapse under the weight of greater responsibility. God does not overlook these moments; He uses them. Every small act of faithfulness is preparation for something more, shaping a man into someone who can be trusted when it truly matters. There is no shortcut to becoming trustworthy. It is developed step by step, decision by decision, in the consistent choosing of what is right over what is easy. A man who honors the small things positions himself for greater things, because he has already proven that his character does not depend on the size of the assignment.

A man who neglects the small responsibilities of his life is quietly shaping a pattern that will follow him into greater opportunities. The way he manages his time, honors his word, and handles what has been placed in his hands today is revealing who he is becoming tomorrow. God does not build leaders on moments of sudden greatness; He builds them through daily faithfulness. What a man consistently does in private is what he will inevitably display in public. Character is forged through repetition, discipline, and obedience over time. The same consistency required to steward the small is the consistency required to sustain the great. When a man learns to be faithful with little, he develops the stability, humility, and strength needed to carry more without compromise. Leadership is not about rising quickly - it is about standing firmly when the weight increases. And the man who has been disciplined in the hidden places will not crumble under pressure, because his foundation has already been proven.

God often entrusts a man with assignments that seem small, hidden, or even beneath what he believes he is capable of. What appears insignificant is often deeply intentional. In those moments, God is shaping the inner life, refining motives, stripping away pride, and building a foundation that can sustain greater responsibility. When a man chooses to serve without recognition, he steps into true humility. He learns that his value is not found in applause, but in obedience. It is here, in the unseen places, that character is formed and a man becomes steady, grounded, and trustworthy. There is also a quiet strength that is developed when a man continues faithfully without immediate reward. It is easy to be committed when progress is visible and praise is present but real strength is revealed when neither is guaranteed. These seasons anchor a man in something greater than results. In time, the man who endured the quiet will be ready to carry the weight of more.

If a man cannot be trusted with little, he cannot be trusted with much. This is not a harsh judgment - it is a divine principle. The small things are not tests to be rushed through; they are the proving grounds of character. How a man handles what is unnoticed, what is inconvenient, and what seems insignificant reveals the true condition of his heart. Faithfulness in the little things is where integrity is formed, discipline is strengthened, and trust is established. These moments may feel ordinary, but heaven measures them with eternal significance. Greater responsibility is not given to potential - it is given to proven character. When a man consistently shows up, follows through, and honors what has been placed in his hands - he is building something solid within himself. And when the time comes for greater opportunity, he will not be overwhelmed by it, because he has already been prepared for it. What is done in the small places is never wasted - it is the very thing that qualifies a man for what comes next.

Growing into leadership is about becoming accountable before God and others. A man is not proven by how many people follow him, but by how faithfully he carries what has been entrusted to him. True leadership is formed in the quiet decisions to take responsibility, to admit when you are wrong, and to do what is right even when no one is watching. God shapes leaders through accountability, because a man who cannot govern himself cannot be trusted to guide others. Leadership is a responsibility to be carried with humility and restraint. It is not about elevating yourself above others, but about lifting others up with integrity and care. A true leader understands that leadership is not about being seen - it is about being dependable. When a man embraces this calling, he reflects the heart of Christ, who led through service and strength. And in that place, leadership is no longer about power - it becomes a calling to protect, to guide, and to faithfully carry the weight of others with honor.

A man who is prepared for leadership recognizes that every word he speaks carries weight, and every action he takes creates direction for those who are watching. He does not lead carelessly, because he knows people are shaped by what they see in him. His integrity becomes a compass. His consistency becomes a foundation. He does not seek to be admired - he seeks to be dependable, knowing that true leadership is measured not by status, but by the impact he has on others. Leadership, when done right, becomes a sacred trust before God. It is a calling that requires humility, responsibility, and a heart that is willing to serve rather than be served. A man who understands this does not take his role lightly. He leads with intention, aware that his example can either build or break those who follow. He prays for wisdom, walks in accountability, and chooses faithfulness even when no one is watching. Because in the end, leadership is not about being in front - it is about being worthy of being followed.

God is not in a hurry to expand a man's assignment. Before influence is given, identity must be secured. Before authority is entrusted, character must be proven. In the quiet seasons where little seems to be happening, God is doing His deepest work. He is strengthening integrity, refining motives, and teaching obedience because when the weight of influence comes, it will not be sustained by talent or ambition, but by the strength of what has been built within. This is why the foundation matters. When authority is rooted in righteousness, it produces lasting impact. A man who has been developed by God does not misuse what he has been given; he stewards it with humility and wisdom. He understands that leadership is not about elevating himself, but about serving others well. And because his life is built on a solid foundation, what God builds through him will not collapse under pressure; it will stand, endure, and make a difference that outlives him.

Stewardship of influence is one of the greatest tests a man will face because it reveals not only his strength, but his character. What a man does with that influence matters, but how he carries it matters even more. If he leads with pride, it will corrupt him. If he leads with selfish ambition, it will damage others. But when he walks in wisdom and humility, he becomes a vessel through which God can move. He understands that influence is not ownership - it is stewardship. A man who truly grasps this lives with a constant awareness that he is accountable before God. He does not take lightly the impact he has on others, because he knows that influence can either build or break, guide or mislead. So he chooses humility over ego, service over status, and faithfulness over recognition. In doing so, he honors the trust placed in him. And when influence is stewarded well, it does more than elevate a man - it multiplies good, strengthens others, and leaves a legacy that reflects the heart of God.

A man who leads well carries his position with a deep sense of reverence. He does not see leadership as a platform for recognition, but as a responsibility entrusted to him by God. He understands that every decision he makes has weight, and every word he speaks has influence. Because of this, he leads with intention, humility, and care. He knows that true leadership is not about being served - it is about serving faithfully, even when no one is watching. His strength is not found in control, but in his willingness to lay himself down for the good of others. He recognizes that the people around him are not stepping-stones to his success, but souls entrusted to his stewardship. He leads to protect, to guide, and to build - not to manipulate or dominate. His example becomes a source of direction, his integrity becomes a place of safety, and his consistency becomes a foundation others can stand on. In this way, his leadership reflects the heart of God - firm yet compassionate, strong yet selfless.

Responsibility stretches a man beyond convenience and calls him into a higher level of discipline, awareness, and sacrifice. It demands more of his time, more of his energy, and more of his focus than he may have ever given before. And without preparation, that weight can become overwhelming. It can expose weaknesses, reveal cracks in his character, and press him to the point of breaking. But this is why preparation matters. God does not increase the weight without first developing the man. The seasons of training, testing, and quiet growth build the strength required to carry what is coming. But when a man embraces preparation, the weight that once felt heavy begins to build endurance. The pressure that once felt overwhelming begins to produce clarity and strength. He learns to rely not on his own ability, but on God's sustaining power. And through that process, he is transformed. He becomes steady under pressure, focused in the midst of demands, and faithful in the responsibilities entrusted to him.

God's preparation process is precise, purposeful, and deeply intentional. Every challenge you face is shaping your endurance. Every delay is refining your patience. Every hidden season is strengthening your character in ways that visibility never could. God does not waste moments, and He does not overlook details. He is forming a man who can carry weight, handle responsibility, and remain steady under pressure. What feels unclear to you is completely clear to Him. What feels like restriction is often His protection, keeping you from stepping into something you are not yet ready to sustain. What feels like waiting is often Him building a stronger foundation beneath you. In these seasons, God is not holding you back - He is preparing you to move forward with strength, wisdom, and stability. If you trust His process, you will see that nothing you walked through was unnecessary. Every moment was shaping you into the man you need to become for what lies ahead.

The man who embraces the process refuses to let delay turn into disappointment or hardship turn into bitterness. Instead of measuring his life by missed opportunities, he begins to measure it by growth, by maturity, by the quiet strengthening of his character. He realizes that every closed door and every unseen battle is shaping him into someone who can stand when the weight finally comes. He is no longer fighting the process - he is being formed by it. And with that realization, his questions begin to change. He no longer anxiously asks, "When will my opportunity come?" but honestly asks, "Am I becoming the man who can carry it?" That shift replaces impatience with intention, and pressure with preparation. He leans into the work God is doing within him, knowing that timing and capacity must meet for purpose to be fulfilled. And when the moment finally arrives, he will not just step into it - he will be ready for it, strengthened by the very process he once struggled to understand.

When the time for promotion comes, it will not feel overwhelming to the man who has been prepared. The weight that might crush another will rest naturally on his shoulders, because he has been carrying it in smaller measures all along. When the door finally opens, he does not panic or strive to prove himself. He walks through it with steady confidence, not because he suddenly became ready, but because he has been becoming ready all along. This is the beauty of God's process - He aligns the man with the moment. Promotion does not introduce pressure that a man cannot bear; it reveals the strength that has already been formed within him. Instead of scrambling to become something new, he simply steps into the reality of who he has already become in private. His identity is not built in the spotlight but is established long before it. And because of that, he carries the responsibility with humility, clarity, and peace, knowing that the same God who prepared him in obscurity will sustain him in influence.

So do not rush the process. What feels like delay is often divine design, forming strength where weakness once lived and building character where there was once impatience. Do not despise small beginnings, because the daily decisions to honor God when no one is watching are the moments that carry eternal weight. Testing will come, not to break you, but to prove you. It reveals what is real, strengthens what is weak, and anchors you in something deeper than emotion or circumstance. God is not holding you back; He is setting you up. He is aligning your heart, refining your motives, and strengthening your foundation so that what He places in your hands will not destroy you, but flow through you. The man who remains faithful in this season is becoming someone who can be trusted with more. And when the time for greater responsibility arrives, he will be ready for it. Not because it came suddenly, but because he has been steadily becoming the man who can carry it.

| 27 |

"A LIFE WORTH IMITATING"

A man others can follow is shaped in the quiet, repeated decisions that define his character over time. He is forged in consistency when no one is watching, when there is no applause, when the easier path is calling his name. His convictions are proven under pressure, tested in difficulty, and strengthened through obedience. This kind of man does not drift with culture or bend with convenience. He is anchored in truth because his life is surrendered to God. And in that surrender, he finds the strength to remain steady when everything around him is shifting. Leadership begins long before a title is ever given. It starts in the unseen places where integrity is chosen, discipline is practiced, and faith is lived out daily. A man may not realize it, but people are always watching - learning not just from what he says, but from how he walks. His patience teaches. His perseverance speaks. His humility sets a standard. Before he ever gives direction, his life is already pointing the way.

True leadership is forged in the private decisions a man makes when compromise would be easy, and no one would ever know. In those moments, integrity becomes his foundation. A man who leads well does not react out of emotion, pride, or frustration - he responds with steadiness, wisdom, and restraint. His strength is not loud, but it is unshakable because it has been built in the hidden places where God has shaped him. Before a man can lead others, he must first learn to submit his life to God's voice, God's Word, and God's ways. This kind of surrender is the source of true authority. A man who follows God with humility and obedience develops a clarity that guides others, a conviction that steadies others, and a faith that strengthens others. His life becomes a pattern worth imitating, not because he seeks influence, but because he has been transformed in the presence of God. And when the time comes for him to lead, he simply walks out what has already been formed within him.

People are not drawn to a man who appears untouchable - they are drawn to a man who is real. Perfection creates distance, but authenticity builds connection. A man others can follow does not pretend to be strong in every moment; he chooses to remain steady in his trust in God. In his honesty, others find hope. In his consistency, others find direction. His life becomes a living reminder that strength is not found in having no weaknesses, but in refusing to let those weaknesses define him. Instead, he allows God to meet him in those places, shaping him, refining him, and proving His faithfulness again and again. This kind of man does not point people to himself - he points them to God. When he remains faithful in difficulty and continues forward despite uncertainty, he reveals something greater than personal resilience. He reveals dependence. His testimony is not, "Look at what I have achieved," but "Look at what God has sustained." That is what inspires others. That is what calls men higher.

Leadership through example is forged in consistency. What he proclaims with his mouth, he proves with his life. In the quiet places where no one is watching, he chooses the same standard he displays in public. There is no hidden compromise, no secret life that contradicts his message. His strength is not in perfection, but in alignment. And that alignment produces credibility. When a man lives this way, his life speaks louder than anything he could ever say. This kind of consistency builds trust, and trust is the currency of true influence. People are not drawn to titles or positions - they are drawn to authenticity they can believe in. When others see a man whose private character matches his public image, it gives them confidence to follow, to listen, and to grow. His life becomes a steady example in an unstable world. He does not have to demand respect; it is given because it has been earned. And through that trust, his influence expands not for his own glory, but as a reflection of the One he follows.

A life worth imitating is not measured by talent, applause, or outward success. Talent may open doors, but it cannot keep them open without integrity. A man can impress a crowd with his abilities, but only his character will hold their trust when the spotlight fades. What he does may gain attention, but who he is determines whether that attention turns into lasting influence. God is far more concerned with the condition of a man's heart than the display of his gifts. Gifts can be given but character must be developed, refined, and proven over time. In the end, people do not follow perfection - they follow truth, consistency, and integrity. They watch how a man responds under pressure, how he treats others when there is nothing to gain, and how he lives when no one is watching. A man of character becomes a firm foundation in a culture of compromise. And over time, his life begins to speak louder than his words - calling others higher, inspiring them to live with the same strength and unwavering integrity.

A man who understands the weight of his influence does not live carelessly. He realizes that his decisions echo into the lives of others. The way he speaks, the way he responds under pressure, the way he treats people in both public and private become a silent instruction to those watching. This awareness does not burden him - it anchors him. It calls him higher. It reminds him that his life is not just his own, but a living example that is constantly teaching something. Because of this, he chooses to walk with intention. He does not compromise in small moments, knowing that small compromises create large consequences. Instead, he leans into integrity, even when it costs him. He understands that leadership is not about position, but about example - and example is built daily, decision by decision. Such a man becomes a steady force in an unstable world. His life speaks before his words ever do. And over time, he becomes the kind of man others trust, follow, and quietly aspire to become.

Living a life worth imitating is forged in decisions where doing right costs something. It is choosing integrity when no one is watching, choosing truth when silence would be safer, and choosing obedience when compromise would be more comfortable. The easy road will always invite you with convenience, but it never produces strength. The narrow path, though difficult, shapes a man into someone steady, trustworthy, and grounded in conviction. This kind of life speaks louder than words ever could. It becomes a blueprint for others who are watching, searching for something real in a world full of compromise. When you stand firm, you give others permission to do the same. When you walk the narrow path, you show that it is possible and worth it. A life worth imitating is not perfect, but it is consistent. It is marked by courage, guided by truth, and sustained by faith. And in the end, it is not the crowd that defines a man's direction, but his willingness to follow what is right, no matter how few choose to walk that way.

Courage carries a ripple effect. When a man stands firm in his convictions, refusing to bend under pressure or compromise under fear, something powerful is released into the atmosphere around him. Others begin to see what is possible. They recognize that strength is not reserved for the extraordinary, but available to anyone willing to stand. His boldness becomes a living testimony that truth is worth holding, that integrity is worth the cost. In a culture that often rewards silence and compromise, his unwavering stance becomes a light that exposes a better way to live. Courage is contagious because it awakens what has been dormant in others. The man who stands gives permission for others to rise. Quiet men find their voice. Fearful hearts discover strength. Those who once hesitated begin to move with conviction. What started as one man's decision to stand becomes a chain reaction of boldness, integrity, and purpose. When one man refuses to bow, he doesn't stand alone for long.

A man ignites boldness in those around him by how he lives in moments of pressure. When he refuses to compromise truth, even when it costs him, he becomes a visible standard. When he remains steady while others panic, he becomes an anchor. When he keeps moving forward through difficulty instead of retreating into comfort, he proves that strength is available to any man who is willing to stand. His life begins to speak louder than any words ever could. And in that quiet, unwavering example, something powerful happens - others begin to believe. They see his resolve and realize that fear does not have to control them. They watch his endurance and understand that quitting is not their only option. His life becomes a testimony that courage is not the absence of pressure, but the decision to stand in the middle of it. Without demanding attention, without seeking recognition, he becomes a catalyst for strength in others. Because when one man stands firm, he gives permission for others to rise.

There will be moments when leadership feels heavier than expected - when the responsibility presses in and the results seem distant. In those times, a man may wonder if his efforts matter, if anyone is truly paying attention, or if his example is making a difference at all. But true influence is rarely loud or immediate. It works beneath the surface, shaping hearts in ways that cannot always be seen in the moment. Just as seeds are planted quietly in the soil before they ever break through the ground, the impact of a faithful life is often hidden before it is revealed. So do not measure your effectiveness by what you can see right now. Measure it by your consistency, your integrity, and your obedience to what is right. Every steady decision, every act of patience, every moment of courage is leaving a mark. In time, what was planted in quiet faithfulness will grow into visible fruit. Lives will be shaped, paths will be redirected, and strength will rise in others because you chose to lead well when it was not easy.

A man others can follow wakes up each day asking how he can be faithful. His focus is not on building his own name, but on honoring God in the way he lives, speaks, and leads. While others may chase recognition, he quietly pursues obedience, knowing that heaven measures differently than the world. His strength is not found in applause, but in alignment with God's will. And because of this, his life carries a weight that is formed through surrender, discipline, and truth. Whether he stands in the spotlight or walks in obscurity, he remains the same. His integrity does not shift with the crowd, and his commitment does not depend on who is watching. He understands that true influence is not built on visibility, but on consistency. Over time, people begin to notice because his life reflects something real, something steady, something worth following. In a world that rewards performance, he chooses obedience. And in doing so, he becomes the kind of man others trust, respect, and are inspired to follow.

Raising up the next generation is essential. Truth was never meant to stop with one man; it was meant to flow through him. A man who has been shaped by God understands that what he has learned carries weight beyond his own life. His experiences, his victories, his failures, and his faith all become tools for building others. He does not hoard wisdom - he invests it. He speaks life, demonstrates integrity, and models what it means to walk with God. He knows that someone is always watching, always learning, always being influenced by the way he lives. Because of this, he becomes intentional. He pours into others not out of obligation, but out of purpose. He teaches what is right, corrects with humility, and leads by example even when no one seems to notice. He understands that legacy is not built through words alone, but through consistent action over time. The seeds he plants today may not bear fruit immediately, but he trusts that God is working beneath the surface.

A man who understands his calling does not leave growth to chance - he pursues it with purpose. He invests his time where it matters, speaks truth when it is needed, and creates space for others to rise. He does not rush the process, because he knows that real strength is built over time. With patience, he teaches. With wisdom, he guides. And with consistency, he models what it means to live with integrity. He understands that every conversation, every correction, and every opportunity given is shaping someone else's future. True leadership is measured by how many are strengthened, equipped, and sent forward with confidence. A man who leads well is humble enough to step back and allow others to grow, even if that growth comes through mistakes and hard lessons. He does not need to hold the spotlight, because his goal is not to be elevated, but to elevate others. In doing so, he is raising up, building up, and preparing the next generation to stand strong when their time comes.

The next generation is not looking for flawless men - they are looking for real ones. They need to see conviction in action, not just spoken from a distance. They are watching how a man responds when he falls short, and whether he has the humility to rise again. Your life becomes their blueprint. When you choose integrity over convenience, faith over fear, and obedience over approval, you give them something tangible to follow. Perfection creates distance, but authenticity builds connection. More than words, they need a consistent example. They need to see a man trust God when the outcome is uncertain, remain steady when emotions fluctuate, and stay faithful when no one is applauding. It is in the quiet, repeated choices that a legacy is formed. Every time you get back up, every time you keep your word, every time you walk with God when it's hard - you are teaching them what strength truly looks like. And in time, they won't just hear your message - they will become it.

A man who truly understands leadership does not measure his worth by how long he remains at the top, but by how many he helps rise beside him. Where insecurity would feel threatened, he feels fulfilled. Where pride would compete, he chooses to cultivate. He knows that strength is not proven by standing alone, but by building others who can stand just as firm. So he teaches, he equips, and he invests, even when it means others may one day go further than he has. And instead of fearing that moment, he looks forward to it because it means his labor was not wasted. This kind of man sees legacy differently. He understands that what he builds with his own hands may fade, but what he builds into others will endure. His impact multiplies through the lives he has touched. Every lesson shared, every example lived, every opportunity given becomes a seed that continues to grow long after he is gone. And in that, he finds deep satisfaction.

Inspiring others to follow is about building a pathway to God. A man who leads with the right heart understands that he is not the destination, but a guide. His words, actions, and decisions consistently point beyond himself, directing others toward the One who never fails. His life becomes a signpost, quietly but clearly pointing others toward something greater than himself. This kind of leadership requires humility and intentional focus. It means resisting the temptation to take credit and instead giving glory where it belongs. It means reminding others, both in word and example, that their dependence must be on God and not on any man. When a leader lives this way, he creates something lasting. He raises up people who are not attached to his presence but anchored in God's truth. And in doing so, his influence multiplies far beyond what he could accomplish alone, because he has led others not to follow him, but to follow the One who leads them all.

A life of a man who chooses to live with integrity becomes a steady example, and that example begins to shape those closest to him. His family sees it first. They witness consistency, strength, humility, and trust in God lived out daily. And from that foundation, something greater begins to grow because integrity is contagious, and faith, when lived authentically, cannot be contained. Over time, that influence extends outward in ways he may never fully measure. A strengthened family becomes a light within a community. A community marked by truth and conviction begins to shift the direction of a generation. What started as one man simply choosing to surrender his life to God becomes a ripple that touches countless others. This is the power of faithful leadership. It reminds us that no act of obedience is small, and no life surrendered to God is without eternal impact. What begins in one heart can echo through many, leaving a legacy that reaches far beyond what was ever imagined.

Become the man others can follow by committing to obedience. True influence is not built on visibility, but on consistency before God. When a man chooses integrity in private, courage in pressure, and humility in success, he becomes a steady foundation others can trust. He does not need to announce his convictions for his life reveals them. In a world full of noise and self-promotion, quiet obedience stands out. It carries weight, it builds trust, and it honors God in a way that draws others not to the man, but to the One he follows. Live with integrity. Stand with courage. Walk with humility. As you walk this path, your life becomes a guiding light. Others will see that it is possible to live with purpose, to remain strong without becoming hard, and to hold faith without wavering. Your example will remind those around you that a life surrendered to God is transformational. What begins as personal obedience will become a testimony that leads others toward strength, truth, and unwavering faith.

| 28 |

"THE LEGACY OF A GODLY MAN"

A faithful man does not live with his eyes fixed on what he can gather, but on what he can give. He understands that possessions fade, titles are forgotten, and achievements eventually lose their shine, but character endures. So he invests where it matters most. He pours truth into others, models integrity when no one is watching, and walks in obedience even when it costs him something. He is driven by a deeper calling to live in a way that honors God and strengthens those around him. Because of this, his legacy is not built in a moment, but over a lifetime of steady devotion. Long after his voice grows silent, the impact of his life continues to speak. The wisdom he shared, the example he set, and the faith he lived become seeds planted in the lives of others. Generations may rise who never knew his name yet still walk in the strength he helped cultivate. And in the end, he leaves behind a path marked by faith, a standard of truth, and a legacy that points others toward God.

The legacy of a godly man is never measured by what he accumulates, but by what he imparts. Every word of wisdom he speaks, every act of integrity he models, and every life he encourages becomes a seed planted for eternity. Through quiet moments of guidance, steadfast example, and unwavering faith, he strengthens others to stand, to grow, and to walk in truth. His life becomes a living blueprint, showing that real success is found in lifting others closer to God. Long after he is gone, the evidence of his life continues to speak. It is seen in stronger families, in men who choose courage over comfort, and in hearts that remain anchored in faith because of his influence. His testimony does not end at the grave - it echoes through generations. A godly man lives with this understanding: that every decision, every action, and every moment matters far beyond himself. And because he lives with eternity in mind, his legacy is not temporary - it is eternal, carried forward in the lives of those he faithfully poured into.

A faithful man understands that his life is a living blueprint for others to follow. He does not drift through his days, but walks with intention, knowing that every decision is laying stones in a path someone else may one day travel. His obedience to God becomes a visible pattern of truth, integrity, and purpose. Long after his voice is gone, the direction he established continues to speak. In moments of uncertainty, others can look back at his life and find clarity, because he chose conviction over convenience and faithfulness over ease. A faithful man may never fully see the reach of his impact, but heaven records every step, and generations feel the result. His life becomes a guiding line, helping others avoid confusion and walk with confidence. Because he stayed true, others can stand firm. Because he followed God wholeheartedly, others can follow with greater understanding. His legacy is not just remembered - it is lived out, carried forward in the strength and direction he left behind.

Character is the unseen structure that holds a man's life together when pressure comes. Without it, influence may rise quickly, but it cannot stand for long. It collapses under the weight of compromise, pride, or inconsistency. But when a man commits to integrity, even in the smallest matters, he lays a foundation that can carry real weight. His words begin to matter because they are backed by truth. His actions carry authority because they are consistent. A man of character becomes a reference point for others, a steady example in a shifting world. Because he is rooted in truth rather than opinion, his legacy is not easily erased or redefined. It lives on in the principles he upheld, the lives he influenced, and the standard he refused to lower. Influence built on image may impress for a moment, but influence built on integrity multiplies across generations. In the end, it is not what a man gained that defines him - it is what he faithfully built within that continues to stand long after he is gone.

The influence of a godly man is not always loud or immediately recognized, but it carries a depth that echoes far beyond what can be seen. His life speaks in steady, consistent ways through integrity, kindness, and unwavering faithfulness to God. In the way he lives his life he is shaping hearts and setting direction. His influence is built on truth, and truth has a way of enduring long after moments have passed. Though he may never fully witness the reach of his impact, nothing done in faith is ever wasted. Seeds planted through prayer, through example, and through sacrifice take root in ways that time alone reveals. Long after he is gone, those seeds begin to rise. They are seen in lives changed, in courage strengthened, and in generations choosing a better path because he once walked it faithfully. A godly man may not always see the harvest, but he can trust that God does. And in that trust, he finds peace, knowing his life is part of a greater story still unfolding.

A faithful man understands that legacy is built in the quiet, daily decisions that shape his character. The way he speaks when no one is applauding, the way he leads when no one is watching, and the way he responds when pressure rises are forming a testimony that will outlive him. He knows that every word carries weight, every action sets a direction, and every choice plants a seed. Because of this, he lives intentionally, aware that even the smallest moments are threads being woven into something far greater than he can see. He understands that consistency in the unseen is what produces impact in the seen. When challenged, he chooses integrity over convenience.

When tested, he chooses faith over fear. And when the moment would allow compromise, he chooses obedience instead. In the end, what he leaves behind will not simply be remembered in words but revealed in the lives that were shaped by the steady, unwavering example he chose to live every day.

A man of real faith does not need to announce it - he lives it. His belief shows up in the way he treats people, in the way he responds when things do not go his way, and in the quiet choices he makes when no one is watching. It is not a performance designed to impress others, but a consistency that reflects what is truly rooted in his heart. Day after day, decision after decision, his life becomes evidence of what he believes. And because it is genuine, it carries a quiet authority that words alone could never achieve. This kind of authenticity is what gives a man's legacy its weight. People may forget what he said, but they will remember how he lived. They will remember his steadiness, his integrity, and the way his faith held firm under pressure. His life becomes a pattern others can follow not because he was perfect, but because he was consistent. In the end, it is not loud declarations that shape generations, but a faithful life that leaves behind a clear and undeniable testimony of truth.

A godly man understands that leadership is not proven by words alone, but by the consistency of his life. He does not set expectations for others that he avoids himself. Instead, he walks the path first by choosing integrity when compromise is easier, choosing discipline when comfort calls, and choosing obedience when no one is watching. His example carries weight because it is real. It is forged in daily decisions, quiet sacrifices, and a steady commitment to honor God in all things. Those around him do not just hear what he believes - they see it lived out in a way that is both strong and sincere. In this, his strength is balanced by humility. He does not lead to be seen, but to serve. He does not elevate himself, but points others toward God through the way he lives. His life becomes a visible testimony that a man can be firm in conviction while remaining gentle in spirit. And long after his words are forgotten, the example he set continues to guide, challenge, and inspire those who choose to follow it.

Legacy is shaped in the quiet, consistent choices a man makes every day. It is built in how he speaks when no one is listening, how he responds when no one is watching, and how he remains faithful when there is no recognition. The ordinary moments are the very tools God uses to form something lasting. Each act of obedience, each decision rooted in truth, and each step taken in faith becomes a brick in the foundation of a life that will stand long after he is gone. What is done in the unseen places carries more weight than what is done in the spotlight. Faithfulness in private develops strength for public responsibility. A man who chooses integrity in the hidden places is building something that cannot be easily shaken. Over time, those daily decisions form a clear and powerful legacy that others will see, follow, and be strengthened by. What may feel small today is shaping something eternal, and in God's timing, what has been built in secret will be revealed with purpose and impact.

A faithful man does not measure his life by what can be seen, counted, or applauded. He invests in what will outlive him. He pours his time into relationships that strengthen and uplift, into truth that anchors the soul, and into the things of God that carry eternal weight. While others chase recognition and temporary success, he quietly builds something that cannot be shaken by time or circumstance. He understands that the most valuable work is often unseen, formed in conversations, in prayers, and in consistent obedience. These are the investments that shape lives, including his own. He knows that what is built in the spirit endures beyond this life. Every act of love, every word of truth, every moment surrendered to God becomes part of a legacy that cannot decay. A faithful man lives with eternity in mind, choosing what is lasting over what is immediate. And in doing so, he builds a life that not only stands firm now but continues to bear fruit long after he is gone.

The impact of a godly man does not end when his life on earth does - it multiplies. What he has spoken in truth, lived in integrity, and demonstrated in faith continues to move through the lives of others. His words become anchors in moments of uncertainty. His example becomes a reference point when difficult decisions arise. Even when he is no longer present, the imprint of his life remains, guiding, strengthening, and reminding others of what it looks like to walk with God. His influence is not confined to time - it is carried forward through the lives he has touched. This is the power of a life rooted in faith. Long after his voice is no longer heard, his faith still speaks. It speaks through the courage of those he encouraged, the convictions he helped shape, and the paths he helped straighten. What he built in obedience does not fade - it echoes. And in ways he may never fully see, his life continues to point others toward truth, toward strength, and ultimately, toward God.

A godly man does not live for applause - he lives for purpose. He is not driven by recognition, nor does he measure his worth by the opinions of others. He understands that what is seen by people is temporary, but what is seen by God carries eternal weight. So he serves without needing credit and remains steady whether he is celebrated or overlooked. His focus is not on building a name for himself, but on fulfilling the calling placed on his life. He is not concerned with being remembered for greatness, but for faithfulness. He knows that true impact is not measured by how loudly his name is spoken, but by how consistently his life reflects truth. And in that faithfulness, true greatness is found - not in moments of recognition, but in a lifetime of obedience. When the applause fades and the crowds move on, what remains is the substance of his character and the legacy of his devotion. A godly man may not always stand in the spotlight, but he stands approved where it matters most and that is enough.

A godly man understands that legacy is not built on flawless performance, but on faithful consistency. He does not measure his life by moments of perfection, but by the steady rhythm of returning to what is right. When he stumbles, he does not stay down - he rises, corrects his course, and continues forward. There is humility in his walk, because he knows that growth is a process. Each decision to realign with truth, each step back toward obedience, becomes a brick in the foundation he is laying day by day. Over time, that perseverance begins to speak louder than any single success or failure ever could. Those who watch his life see not a man who never struggled, but a man who never quit. His endurance becomes part of the inheritance he leaves behind - a pattern of resilience, a testimony of faithfulness. Long after he is gone, his example will remind others that it is not perfection that defines a life, but the unwavering commitment to keep returning to God until that consistency becomes legacy.

A faithful man builds with eternity in mind. He understands that what is seen is temporary, but what is unseen carries lasting weight. While others may be consumed by immediate results or discouraged by present struggles, he remains steady, anchored in a greater purpose. He does not measure his life by comfort or convenience, but by obedience and impact. Even in seasons of difficulty, he continues to sow what is right knowing that seeds planted in faith will produce a harvest that outlives him. He refuses to be distracted by what is fleeting. Temporary setbacks do not shake him, because his vision extends beyond the moment. He lives with an awareness that his choices echo into eternity, shaping not only his life but the lives of those who follow. With quiet determination, he builds character, truth, and faith that cannot be erased by time. And though he may not see the full reward of his labor, he walks forward with confidence, knowing that a life lived for God is never wasted.

The integrity of a man of character creates a place of safety for others. His consistency builds trust that people can stand on. In a world that often shifts with emotion and circumstance, his steady walk with God provides stability for those around him. He does not need to control or dominate to lead; his life speaks with quiet authority. Because he is anchored in truth, others find direction. Because he is grounded in faith, others find strength. His presence becomes a refuge, not because he is perfect, but because he is faithful. His responses under pressure teach resilience. His humility teaches wisdom. His obedience teaches others how to walk with God in real and practical ways. What he carries internally begins to cover others externally. His life becomes a living example that influences decisions, strengthens convictions, and steadies hearts. In this way, his character does more than define him - it becomes a gift to others, a source of guidance and strength that extends far beyond his own life.

A godly man's legacy is not built on talent, success, or recognition - it is built on faith. His trust in God becomes the anchor of his life, steadying him in uncertainty and strengthening him in adversity. He does not rely on his own understanding, but leans into the wisdom of God, allowing His Word to shape his decisions and direct his steps. This unwavering faith becomes the foundation upon which everything else is built, giving his life a stability that cannot be shaken by circumstance. Because his life is rooted in God, what he builds carries eternal weight. His influence extends beyond what can be seen, touching lives in ways he may never fully realize. The truth he lives and the example he sets create a legacy that outlives him. Long after his voice is silent, his faith continues to speak through the lives he impacted. A legacy rooted in faith does not fade with time; it multiplies through generations, because it is built on the unchanging foundation of God Himself.

Legacy is never formed by accident - it is shaped by intention. A man who understands this does not drift through life, hoping something meaningful will emerge. He lives with purpose, recognizing that every decision is a brick in what he is building. Discipline becomes his foundation, focus becomes his direction, and obedience to God becomes his guide. While others chase momentary success, he invests in what carries eternal weight. A faithful man makes this choice daily. He does not wait for perfect conditions or dramatic moments but builds through consistency in the unseen places. In his words, his actions, and his quiet obedience, he is constructing something far greater than himself. He understands that legacy is not about what he gains, but about what he leaves behind. And because his life is anchored in faith, what he builds is not temporary - it endures. Long after he is gone, the strength of his choices, the depth of his character, and the faith he walked in will continue to speak.

In the end, the legacy of a godly man is not measured by what he accumulates, but by what continues because he lived. His life becomes a seed planted in obedience, watered by perseverance, and sustained by faith. Long after his voice is no longer heard, the impact of his choices remains - growing quietly in the lives he touched, strengthening those who follow his example. His faith becomes a foundation others can stand on, and his devotion becomes a path others can walk. A life lived with God is never wasted because God redeems every act of faithfulness and weaves it into something eternal. The faithful man may not always see the full harvest of what he has sown, but that does not diminish its power - it confirms it. Generations are shaped by seeds he planted in trust, integrity, and truth. His life stands as a testimony that surrender to God produces significance that outlives him. And in that, his legacy is still alive, still growing, and still pointing others toward the One he followed.

| 29 |

"GRATITUDE FOR THE JOURNEY"

There comes a moment in a man's life when the pace slows just enough for him to see what he could not see while he was in the middle of it. The struggles that once felt random begin to line up with quiet precision. The closed doors, the delays, the seasons of isolation - none of them were wasted. God was present in every step, shaping, refining, and directing, even when it felt like nothing was happening. What once felt like abandonment is revealed as protection. What once felt like confusion is uncovered as divine order. In that moment of reflection, a man realizes that he was never wandering but was being led by God Himself. And with that clarity comes a deep sense of gratitude. Not just for the victories, but for the valleys. Not just for the breakthroughs, but for the breaking points that built his character. He begins to understand that the lonely road was not empty - it was sacred. It was where his faith was strengthened, his dependence on God was deepened, and his identity was forged.

The journey did not happen to him; it happened for him. There were moments when progress felt slow, when prayers seemed unanswered, and when the path ahead looked uncertain. Yet even in those places, you were not abandoned. What felt like aimless movement was actually intentional leading. God does not waste steps. Every detour carried purpose. Every delay held meaning. Even when you could not see His hand, His guidance was steady, quietly directing your steps in ways your understanding could not yet grasp. Now, as you begin to look back, you may start to see what you could not see then - that the wandering was never wandering at all. It was preparation. It was positioning. It was refinement. God was shaping your character, strengthening your faith, and aligning your heart with His will. What once felt confusing is becoming clear. What once felt empty is revealing its value. You were never lost - you were being led with precision, with care, and with purpose.

Looking back at the lonely road, you begin to recognize that what once felt like abandonment was actually intentional separation. God was drawing you away from noise, from distraction, and even from dependence on others so that something unshakable could be formed within you. In those quiet places, your faith was being purified, your character was being strengthened, and your identity was being rooted in God rather than in approval. What felt like silence was not absence - it was divine focus. Those hidden seasons were sacred because you learned to keep going without encouragement, to stand firm without support, and to trust God without visible evidence. That kind of strength cannot be taught in crowds - it is forged in solitude. And now, as you look back, you realize that the quiet was not wasted time; it was preparation. God was building a man who would not be moved by opinions or shaken by pressure - a man whose strength was formed in silence and sustained by Him alone.

There were nights when everything felt uncertain, when the silence was loud, and the path ahead seemed hidden in shadow. You questioned your direction, your purpose, even whether you were making any real progress. But those moments were not evidence that you were failing; they were evidence that you were being stretched. God was not abandoning you in the unknown - He was inviting you deeper into trust. Faith is not formed when everything makes sense; it is forged when nothing does. In those quiet, wrestling nights, God was teaching you to rely not on what you could see, but on who He is. What felt like confusion was actually construction. What felt like delay was actually development. God was creating in you a steady, unshakable trust that does not depend on circumstances. Walking by sight requires clarity, but walking by faith requires surrender. And every time you chose to keep going without answers, you took a step into a stronger, deeper relationship with Him.

What once felt like abandonment was never God turning His back on you - it was His hand redirecting you. In the moment, it felt like loss, like something was taken without explanation. Doors closed without warning. Opportunities slipped through your hands. People you expected to walk with you disappeared. But what you could not see then, heaven saw clearly. God was not removing something good - He was preventing something harmful. He was shielding you from paths that looked promising but carried consequences you were not meant to bear. Now, with time and perspective, you can begin to see the wisdom in what once confused you. Those closed doors guarded you from wrong environments. Those broken connections freed you from misplaced attachments. What left your life made room for what truly belongs in it. God was preserving your future and the same God who protected you then is still guiding you now. Trust Him. What He removes, He replaces with something greater.

As you reflect, what once felt like unnecessary delay now reveals itself as intentional design. Every pause, every closed door, every season where nothing seemed to move was God working in your life. In those quiet and often uncomfortable places, He was strengthening your character, deepening your faith, and removing what could not go with you into what He has prepared. What felt like standing still was actually sacred progress. You begin to understand that the weight of your calling demands a man who has been stretched, humbled, and anchored in God. If it had come sooner, you may have stepped into it unprepared, but now you are becoming someone who can carry it with strength and integrity. So you no longer resent the process - you honor it. Because now you see that every delay had purpose, every challenge had meaning, and every moment was part of God forming you into the man who can not only receive the promise but sustain it.

There were battles you walked through that did not make sense in the moment. The resistance felt unnecessary, the pressure felt excessive, and at times you questioned why it had to be so hard. You could not see the purpose while you were in it - you could only feel the weight of it. But what felt like opposition was not random, and what felt like delay was not wasted. Every difficult moment was stretching your capacity, strengthening your spirit, and teaching you how to stand when everything in you wanted to quit. The battle was not there to break you - it was there to build you. Now, with clearer vision, you can see what God was doing all along. Those seasons were forging an endurance that cannot be shaken by pressure or fear. You are stronger now, steadier now, and more prepared than you realize. So do not regret the battles - honor them. They trained you to keep going when it's hard, to trust when it's unclear, and to stand firm when others would fall.

God was not merely escorting you through difficult seasons - He was shaping something far deeper within you. Every trial you faced carried a lesson designed to refine your thinking, strengthen your faith, and anchor your identity in Him. Nothing was wasted. Every tear, every setback, every moment of uncertainty was being used with precision. While you were focused on getting through it, God was focused on building you through it - forming endurance where there was weakness, courage where there was fear, and wisdom where there was once confusion. The resistance you experienced was not always meant to stop you - it was meant to strengthen you. God was laying a foundation that could carry greater weight, shaping a man who would not collapse under future responsibility. So when you look back, don't just see the hardship - see the handiwork. You were not being held back; you were being built up. And what God builds through the fire is not fragile - it is unshakable.

You begin to recognize that God was working in ways you could not always see. In the victories, it was His wisdom that guided your steps and His favor that opened doors no man could shut. In the struggles, it was His strength that held you together when you felt like falling apart. And in the waiting, when nothing seemed to move and prayers felt unanswered, He was shaping your character, refining your faith, and preparing you for what was ahead. Even in the silence, God was speaking - just not always in ways you expected. Looking back, you begin to see that He never wasted a single moment. The delays were not denials, the hardships were not punishment, and the quiet seasons were not abandonment. They were all part of His faithful work in your life. And now, with clearer vision, your confidence grows - not in circumstances, but in Him. Because the same God who was present then is present now, and He will continue to lead, sustain, and develop you in every season ahead.

The moments you once labeled as wasted were never empty in the hands of God. In seasons that felt slow, unseen, or even insignificant, He was laying the groundwork for something that required depth, strength, and stability. What looked like delay was actually development. What felt like repetition was reinforcement. God does not rush what He intends to last. Every quiet step, every unseen sacrifice, every choice to remain faithful were the building blocks of a life being shaped with purpose. God was weaving together details you could not yet understand, aligning pieces you could not yet see, and preparing outcomes you could not yet imagine. What seemed ordinary was part of something extraordinary in His hands. And in time, you will realize that what you thought was wasted was actually essential because God was not just bringing you through moments, He was building something through you that would stand long after the season had passed.

Understanding the purpose of trials has a way of reshaping your entire perspective. What once looked like random hardship begins to reveal itself as intentional development. The pain you questioned, the delays you resisted, and the pressures you wished away were not meaningless - they were molding you. God was not wasting your time; He was building your strength, refining your character, and deepening your dependence on Him. When you see your past through this lens, regret begins to lose its grip, and gratitude begins to take its place. You start to recognize that every trial carried something you needed. Without the pressure, you would not have developed endurance. Without the breaking, you would not have discovered what was truly within you. The man you are becoming is not in spite of those moments - it is because of them. And when you fully understand that, you stop resenting the process and start respecting it, knowing that God never allows a trial without attaching a purpose to it.

The fire did not come to consume you - it came to purify you. What felt like loss was actually the removal of what could not go where God is taking you. The heat exposed what was weak, but it also revealed what was real. In those moments, when you thought you were being undone, you were actually being refined into something stronger, steadier, and more resilient. The pressure that pressed against you did not crush you - it built endurance within you. It taught you how to stand when it would have been easier to fold, how to trust when you could not trace, and how to remain when everything in you wanted to run. And the process you questioned was never a delay - it was divine positioning. God was aligning your character with your calling, your strength with your assignment, and your spirit with His purpose. What lacked explanation still carried intention. Every closed door, every difficult season, every unseen battle was shaping your capacity for what lies ahead.

You begin to realize that God's priority was never your comfort - it was in who you would become. While you were asking for ease, He was establishing endurance. While you were seeking relief, He was cultivating resilience. Every uncomfortable moment carried intention. Every stretch of pressure was adding strength. What felt like inconvenience was actually investment. God was shaping a character that would not collapse under pressure but stand firm when the weight increased. In that understanding, your perspective shifts. You stop resisting the process and start embracing it. You recognize that shallow strength cannot carry deep responsibility, and surface-level faith cannot endure real trials. So God builds depth quietly, consistently, and often painfully. He forms a man who is steady, grounded, and unshaken. And in the end, you see clearly: God was not withholding ease from you - He was preparing you for something greater than comfort could ever sustain.

There is a quiet humility that settles into a man when he realizes that his journey was never about proving his worth, but about surrendering his will. What he once tried to accomplish through effort, striving, and self-reliance, God was accomplishing through shaping, refining, and teaching him to trust. He begins to understand that his value was never determined by what he could produce, but by who he was becoming through obedience. Surrender becomes strength, and humility becomes the foundation on which true manhood is built. The strength he carries now was formed in quiet places, in moments of dependence, in seasons where he had no choice but to lean on God. What once felt like weakness became the very source of his endurance. He no longer fights to stand alone; he stands because he is upheld. And in that posture, he becomes unshakable not because of his own power, but because he has learned to draw from a strength far greater than himself.

Gratitude begins to take root when you realize that every step of your journey carried purpose. What once felt like obstacles now reveal themselves as instruments of growth. The hardships that frustrated you were not there to stop you - they were shaping you, strengthening you, and drawing you closer to God. Instead of wishing the road had been easier, your heart shifts to thankfulness, because you can now see that an easier path would have produced a weaker man. The very things you would have removed are the things God used to refine you. Every challenge, every delay, every moment of pressure played a role in forming your character and deepening your faith. You understand now that who you have become is worth what you went through. So you stop resisting your past and start honoring it, recognizing God's hand in every season. Gratitude replaces frustration because you see clearly that this path, with all its difficulty, was not against you. It was for you.

There comes a point in a man's journey where he no longer resents the seasons that once stretched him - he reveres them. The lonely seasons, though quiet and heavy, became sacred training grounds where God stripped away dependence on people and anchored you in Himself. The difficult seasons, though painful and demanding, built endurance deep within you. They taught you how to keep moving when everything in you wanted to quit, how to remain faithful when the outcome was unclear, and how to carry weight without collapsing under it. When you couldn't see the way forward, you learned to follow the One who could. When answers were delayed, your faith was strengthened. What once felt unstable has become the very place where your confidence in God was solidified. So now you stand with gratitude not because the journey was easy, but because it was necessary. Every season was shaping you into a man who can stand, endure, and trust no matter what comes next.

What once left you questioning now leaves you standing stronger. The seasons that didn't make sense, the moments that felt uncertain, and the paths that seemed unclear have all become part of a greater testimony within you. You begin to see that God was active, even in the silence. His hand was guiding, protecting, and shaping you with a precision you could not recognize at the time. What felt like confusion was often divine construction, building a faith that would not collapse under pressure. Now your perspective has changed. You no longer measure God's faithfulness by your understanding, but by His consistency. You see that He never wasted a moment - every delay had purpose, every challenge carried weight, and every unanswered question was working something deeper within you. His hand was steady and sure when your footing was not. And because of that, your faith is no longer fragile - it is anchored, rooted in the truth that even when you could not trace Him, you can now trust Him.

There comes a moment when you quietly look around and realize you are standing in the very place you once cried out to God about. The prayers that felt unanswered were not ignored; they were being worked out in ways you could not yet see. The delays were not denials, and the struggles were not setbacks. They were shaping, stretching, and strengthening you for this very moment. And now, even without having every answer, you carry a deep assurance in your spirit that God was faithful then, and He is faithful now. The journey makes sense not because every question has been resolved, but because every step has revealed His consistency. He never left you in the waiting and never abandoned you in the struggle. What you see now is the evidence of His hand - steady, intentional, and full of purpose. And as you stand here, you no longer need full understanding to trust Him. You have lived enough to know that wherever He leads next, His faithfulness will meet you there just as it always has.

| 30 |

"READY TO SOAR"

The man who stands firm will, in time, begin to notice that the very weight that once threatened to break him begins to build him. What once pressed him down now strengthens his stride, because his spirit has been conditioned to carry what it could not carry before. What once felt like resistance now feels like lift, because every challenge has trained his faith, sharpened his endurance, and deepened his dependence on God. This is the result of quiet, consistent perseverance. It is the evidence of a man who refused to quit, a man who trusted God even when the process felt heavy. He no longer fears the weight, because he understands it is shaping him for greater purpose. He no longer resists the pressure, because he recognizes it is producing strength that cannot be developed any other way. What once felt like a burden has become part of his power. And now, with steady confidence and refined faith, he rises, not just surviving the journey, but walking in the strength it has produced.

Perseverance is rarely celebrated in the moment it is being formed. It is not built on stages or in seasons of applause, but in the quiet places where discipline is chosen over comfort and faith is held without visible reward. It is found in early mornings when a man rises before the world does, in long nights when he refuses to quit, and in silent prayers whispered when no one else hears. These are the moments that shape him - not the recognition of others, but the refinement of his spirit. What feels unnoticed is often the very place where God is doing His deepest work, strengthening what cannot be seen so that it will stand when it finally is. And when perseverance has done its work, it produces something unshakable. It builds a man who is not moved by pressure, not broken by delay, and not dependent on approval. His endurance is not rooted in emotion, but in conviction. He has learned to keep going when it is hard, to remain faithful when it is quiet, and to trust God when there is no immediate evidence.

Many men walk away in the very moment their breakthrough is closest. The waiting feels too long, the pressure too heavy, and the silence from heaven too loud. But what they cannot see is that beneath the surface, God is working with precision. Every delay is strengthening endurance. Every challenge is refining character. Every unseen moment is building a foundation strong enough to carry what is coming. What feels like stagnation is often sacred preparation. But the man who refuses to quit begins to realize that the struggle was never sent to stop him, but to shape him. It trained his spirit, deepened his faith, and anchored his identity in God rather than circumstances. When the breakthrough finally comes, he is not overwhelmed by it - he is ready for it. He has become the kind of man who can carry the weight of blessing, steward the responsibility, and walk in purpose with strength and humility. What once felt like resistance becomes the very reason he rises.

Every trial you faced was not random - it was intentional. What looked like resistance was actually refinement, shaping your strength in places no one else could see. The delays that frustrated you were not wasted time; they were moments of divine preparation, aligning your heart, sharpening your character, and deepening your dependence on God. While you may have felt like you were standing still, heaven was actively at work within you, reinforcing the very foundation that your future will stand on. What seemed like opposition was not sent to stop you, but to strengthen you for what lies ahead. You were never being held back - you were being built up. God was developing endurance in your spirit, stability in your walk, and resilience in your faith. Now, as you look back, you can see that those difficult seasons were not barriers but building blocks. And because of what you have endured, you are stronger, wiser, and more prepared to step into the purpose God has designed for you.

The reward of perseverance is far greater than what can be seen on the outside. It is not measured only in doors opened, goals achieved, or victories gained - it is revealed in the man you become along the way. Through pressure, delay, and resistance, your character was strengthened and your resolve became unshakable. What once would have caused you to quit now becomes the very thing that refines you. Perseverance shapes your spirit until stability replaces inconsistency, and conviction replaces hesitation. As you endure, you are transformed into a man who can carry weight without collapsing under it. Steadiness becomes your posture, not just your intention. You learn to stand firm when others waver, to continue when others retreat, and to remain faithful when the outcome is uncertain. This is the true reward - becoming a man God can trust with greater responsibility. Not because you chased strength, but because you allowed the process to build it within you.

There is a difference between achieving something and becoming someone. Achievements can be gained quickly, but character is formed slowly, often in unseen and uncomfortable places. God is not impressed by what a man can accumulate if his foundation cannot support it. He is shaping your integrity, your discipline, and your humility because these are the qualities that will carry you when success arrives. Without that transformation, even the greatest accomplishments will eventually collapse under the weight of who you are not. God's focus is not temporary gain, but lasting strength. He is building a man who can carry responsibility without being crushed by it. When your identity is rooted in who you are becoming, not what you are achieving, you are no longer shaken by outcomes. You become steady. You become grounded. And in time, what God allows you to gain will match the man you have become because you will finally have the strength, maturity, and faith to sustain it.

When a man commits to the process, something deeper than progress begins to take place. The desire to prove himself fades, replaced by a desire to become who God has called him to be. He begins to pursue what carries eternal weight - character, obedience, and faithfulness. In doing that, his life begins to reflect something greater than his own ambition. As his focus shifts, so does his definition of success. Temporary rewards lose their grip, and lasting significance becomes his pursuit. He understands that what he builds in the spirit will outlast anything he could accumulate in the natural. His life is no longer measured by applause, status, or achievement, but by impact, by how he lives, how he leads, and how he honors God in every season. This is the transformation that comes through commitment. He becomes a man no longer driven by what he can gain, but by what God can do through him. And in that shift, he discovers a life that is not only meaningful, but eternal in its influence.

Living fully in God's purpose is not about achieving perfection - it is about daily surrender. It is choosing to lay down your own agenda and pick up His direction, even when it challenges your comfort or stretches your faith. A surrendered man is teachable, correctable, and willing. He does not resist conviction - he embraces it knowing that God's refinement is not rejection, but preparation for something greater. When a man truly trusts that God's plan is better than his own, he stops clinging to comfort and starts walking in calling. He no longer measures his life by ease or convenience, but by obedience and impact. Even when the path feels uncertain, he moves forward with confidence, knowing that God wastes nothing and leads faithfully. In that place of surrender, purpose becomes clear not because everything is easy, but because everything is aligned. And the man who lives this way will discover that the life he once tried to control is far less fulfilling than the life God is building through his surrender.

Purpose gives direction to your strength. Without it, even the strongest man can drift - expending energy but going nowhere meaningful. Strength without purpose becomes scattered, misused, or even destructive. But when a man aligns his life with God's design, his strength finds its assignment. His decisions carry weight, his discipline has direction, and his steps begin to move him forward with clarity instead of confusion. What once felt like striving now becomes steady progress. When your life is anchored in God's purpose, everything begins to work together with meaning. The trials you endure build endurance for your calling. The discipline you develop strengthens your capacity to carry responsibility. Even the quiet seasons become preparation instead of frustration. And as you walk in alignment with Him, your life gains focus, your actions gain power, and your journey gains significance. Purpose doesn't just guide your strength - it multiplies its impact.

You were not created to drift aimlessly through life, carried by whatever current feels easiest in the moment. You were designed with intention, formed with purpose, and called to rise above passivity. There is something within you that was meant to build, to strengthen, to lead with conviction, and to stand firm when others fall away. This calling challenges you to reject distraction and to embrace discipline. When you give your full attention and full commitment to that calling, your strength gains direction and your decisions gain purpose. Your life begins to carry meaning far beyond temporary success. You stop living reactively and start living intentionally. Even in difficulty, you remain steady because you know you are building something that matters. You begin to stand firm in seasons of pressure. And as you stay faithful to what God has placed before you, you rise into the man you were created to be - one who does not drift, but one who leads, builds, and stands with unwavering conviction.

The seasons of loneliness you walked through were sacred. In those quiet places, God was doing a deep and intentional work within you. He was strengthening your foundation, teaching you to depend on Him instead of external affirmation, and forming a character that could stand firm without constant support. In the stillness, He was speaking, refining, and rebuilding parts of you that could not be shaped in crowded or comfortable seasons. Those moments were not wasted - they were transformative. God was developing an inner strength that does not break under pressure, a faith that does not waver when no one is watching, and a clarity that comes only from walking closely with Him. What felt like being set apart was actually being set up for something greater. Now, you carry a depth, a resilience, and a spiritual maturity that could only be forged in solitude. The man you are becoming is not dependent on the presence of others but anchored in the presence of God and that is where true strength is found.

Lonely seasons are where a man learns to stand on what is real. When there is no encouragement and no one reminding him who he is, his foundation is exposed. It is in those quiet, stretching moments that his faith is tested and refined. What he truly believes rises to the surface. If his strength depends on others, he will waver but if his strength is rooted in God, he will remain steady. These seasons are not meant to break him, but to build him into someone who can stand alone if necessary. The strength formed in solitude cannot be borrowed, imitated, or transferred - it must be developed. In the absence of affirmation, he learns to encourage himself. In the silence, he learns to hear God more clearly. And in the stillness, he becomes grounded in identity, not opinion. When he emerges, he is no longer dependent on external validation, because he has been anchored internally. What once felt like loneliness becomes the very place where strength was forged and a man was made steadfast.

In those moments when everything around you grew quiet and support seemed distant, God was teaching you to have a deeper dependence on Him. When there was no one else to lean on, you discovered that His presence was not only near, but sufficient. He met you in the stillness, in the questions, in the waiting. And there, you began to realize that what you truly needed was not more affirmation from people, but a stronger connection with Him. His voice became clearer, not because life got easier, but because you learned to listen more closely. Through those seasons, your foundation was strengthened in ways that cannot be shaken. You found that His strength does not waver when yours runs out. He does not grow tired, and He does not step away when things get hard. In those hidden moments you gained endurance, confidence in His faithfulness, and a quiet assurance that no matter what you face, you are not alone. His presence is enough, and it always will be.

Now you begin to see the evidence of what God has been doing all along. The man you are today did not appear overnight - he was forged through pressure, shaped in hidden places, and strengthened through seasons that demanded more than you thought you could give. You are not who you used to be. The old patterns, the weaker mindset, and the unstable foundation have been refined by fire. What remains is something stronger, steadier, and more grounded in truth. You now carry a weight that you once could not handle - a weight of responsibility, clarity, and spiritual maturity. This is not a burden meant to break you, but a strength that proves you have grown. The testing did not destroy you - it developed you. The pressure did not crush you - it sharpened you. And now, you stand as a man who has been prepared, not just for where you are, but for where God is taking you. Walk forward with confidence, knowing that what has been built within you cannot be easily shaken.

This is what it means to rise into the man God created you to be - not a man molded by the shifting opinions of culture, but one anchored in unshakable conviction. This kind of man does not ask what is popular - he asks what is right. He is not easily swayed because his foundation is not external, it is spiritual. God forms this man through truth, through testing, and through a deep alignment with His Word. And not a man driven by comfort, but a man directed by purpose. Comfort will always call you to settle, to stay where it is easy, to avoid the weight of responsibility but purpose calls you higher. It demands sacrifice, discipline, and a willingness to walk difficult paths. The man who embraces purpose understands that his life is not his own; it is an assignment. He wakes up with intention, he moves with clarity, and he endures with strength because he knows he was created for more. This is the man who rises not because life is easy, but because his calling is greater than his comfort.

You are no longer the man who bends under pressure - you are the man who is strengthened by it. What once intimidated you now sharpens you. You have been forged in unseen battles, shaped in quiet seasons, and refined through trials that demanded your faith to grow deeper roots. Now, when weight is placed on your shoulders, you do not panic - you stand. You do not retreat - you engage. You are no longer chasing every open door - you are walking with intention toward the right one. Distraction has lost its grip because purpose has taken its place. You have clarity that comes from surrender, strength that comes from obedience, and direction that comes from listening to God's voice above all others. This is what maturity looks like - not movement for the sake of motion, but alignment with divine assignment. And when a man reaches this place, he becomes steady, effective, and impactful - no longer scattered, but anchored, moving forward with conviction into everything God has called him to be.

And now, you are ready to soar. Not because life has suddenly become easy, but because something within you has changed. The weight that once pressed you down has been strengthening you all along. Every trial you endured stretched your faith, sharpened your focus, and deepened your dependence on God. You are no longer the man who was shaken by every storm - you are the man who has learned to stand in it. You didn't escape the pressure - you grew through it. And because of that, you carry a strength that cannot be easily broken. The same challenges may still exist, but they no longer define your limits - they reveal your growth. You are no longer confined by fear, doubt, or past struggles. You are lifted by purpose, anchored in truth, and strengthened by experience. This is what it means to soar - not to avoid the winds, but to rise above them. And as you do, you step into the man God created you to be - unshaken, prepared, and ready for what lies ahead.

So keep going. What you are stepping into is the fruit of a life that chose obedience when it was hard, discipline when it was inconvenient, and faith when it was tested. Every unseen sacrifice and every moment you refused to quit when no one would have blamed you - God saw it all. And now, you are beginning to see what He was building in you. The height you are reaching is not just about where you are going, but who you have become along the way - a man strengthened by pressure, refined by process, and anchored in purpose. You are soaring higher than you ever imagined, not because the path was easy, but because you endured it. You did not settle. You did not turn back. You allowed God to shape your character until your capacity matched your calling. And now, you rise with clarity, with strength, and with conviction. So do not slow down now. The same obedience that brought you here will carry you forward. Keep walking. Keep trusting. There is still more ahead, and you are ready for it.

SUMMARY

Every man reaches moments in life where the road becomes quiet and the crowd disappears. It is in those moments that character is revealed and destiny is shaped. The lonely seasons are not wasted seasons. They are the training ground where God builds courage, discipline, faith, and endurance within a man. While others may see isolation, God sees preparation. While others see hardship, God sees transformation. The man who learns to walk faithfully through those seasons will discover that strength is not built in comfort but in perseverance. Conviction is not formed in popularity but in courage. And true leadership is not born in crowds but in quiet places where a man chooses obedience over approval.

The journey of soaring alone is not about independence from God - it is about deeper dependence upon Him. When a man walks closely with God, he gains the strength to stand when others fall, the courage to speak when others remain silent, and the faith to continue when others turn back. And eventually something remarkable happens. The man who once walked alone begins to influence others. His strength becomes an example. His faith becomes a light. His life becomes a path that others are inspired to follow.

That is the legacy of a man who refuses to quit. So keep climbing. Keep believing. Keep standing. Because the road that feels lonely today may be the very road God is using to lift you higher than you ever imagined. And when you finally rise above the noise of the world, you will discover something powerful: The man who learns to soar alone with God will never truly walk alone again.